Every Day Life in the Massachusetts Bay Colony

by Dow, George Francis

ISBN: 9781318072668

HardPress
8345 NW 66TH ST #2561
MIAMI FL 33166-2626
USA
Email: info@hardpress.net

Ordering Information:

Quantity sales. Special discounts are available on quantity purchases by corporations, associations, and others. For details, contact the publisher by email at the address above.

Printed in the United States of America, United Kingdom and Australia

EVERY DAY LIFE IN THE MASSACHUSETTS BAY COLONY

EVERY DAY LIFE
IN THE
MASSACHUSETTS BAY
COLONY

BY

GEORGE FRANCIS DOW

Massachusetts Bay Colony Seal, 1675

ꓱ

ARNO PRESS
A New York Times Company New York / 1977

First Published in Boston, 1935 Reissued in 1967, by Benjamin Blom, Inc. Reprint Edition 1977 by Arno Press Inc. LC# 77-82079 ISBN 0-405-09125-7 Manufactured in the United States of America

---

[v]

PREFACE

A picture of some phases of life in the early days of the Massachusetts Bay Colony is presented in the following pages; lightly sketched, as much of the detail has become dim or has disappeared with the passage of years, it never having been placed on record even among the traditions. For why keep an exact record of doings with which every one is familiar? It follows that many of the every day happenings, the manners and customs of daily life—much of the intimate detail of existence in the Colony, in the seventeenth century, have been lost forever.

Few realize how modern are the furnishings and comforts of our present-day houses and how different was the home life of our ancestors. Chairs were unknown in ordinary English households until a generation or so before the sailing of the *Mayflower*. Hats were worn at meals and the use of table forks did not become general until the last of the 1600s. Food was placed in the mouth with the knife or the fingers. Washing the hands and face was not considered essential on rising from bed in the morning and few of the laboring classes in any country in Europe washed their faces every day.

This is a collection of source materials, somewhat digested, rather than a comprehensive, well-balanced narrative of daily life in the Colony—an impossible task at this late day. Moreover, the exact limitations of the Colonial Period have not been observed too closely as it has seemed desirable to include some material from newspapers and other later sources.

CONTENTS

EVERY DAY LIFE IN THE MASSACHUSETTS BAY COLONY

---

[3]

Every Day Life in the Massachusetts Bay Colony

CHAPTER I

THE VOYAGE TO MASSACHUSETTS

"Before you come," wrote Rev. Francis Higginson, the first minister at Salem, "be careful to be strongly instructed what things are fittest to bring with you for your more comfortable passage at sea, as also for your husbandry occasions when you come to the land. For when you are once parted with England you shall meete neither markets nor fayres to buy what you want. Therefore be sure to furnish yourselves with things fitting to be had before you come: as meale for bread, malt for drinke, woolen and linnen cloath, and leather for shoes, and all manner of carpenters tools, and a great deale of iron and steele to make nails, and locks for houses, and furniture for ploughs and carts, and glasse for windows, and many other things which were better for you to think of there than to want them here."[1] Elsewhere the good pastor set down "A catalogue of such needfull things as every Planter doth or ought to provide to go to New England" in which he enumerated the necessary victuals per person for the first year, viz.:

"8 Bushels of meale, 2 Bushels of pease, 2 Bushels of Otemeale, 1 Gallon of Aquavitae, 1 Gallon of Oyle, 2 Gallons of Vinegar, 1 Firkin of Butter; also Cheese, Bacon, Sugar, Pepper, Cloves, Mace, Cinnamon, Nutmegs and Fruit."

The household implements listed were: "1 Iron pot, 1 Kettel, 1 Frying pan, 1 Gridiron, 2 Skellets, 1 Spit, Wooden Platters, Dishes, Spoons and Trenchers."

[4]

Mr. Higginson listed in detail the food supplies required per person for a year, including a good variety of spices; and also the clothing for a man, which included a Monmouth cap, a suit of canvas, a suit of freize, a suit of cloth, four pairs of shoes, three shirts and three falling bands, a pair of blankets, a coarse rug and seven ells of canvas with which to make a bed and bolster. The settler must also bring with him a complete armor, with a long piece, sword, bandoleer and ammunition, tools for cultivating the soil and for working wood, and also household implements—a limited equipment, comparable with the kit packed by the scout or mining prospector of more recent times.

On looking backward over the span of three centuries, Time lends an enchantment to these Puritan forefathers of present-day Massachusetts. Worshiping descendants have placed halos about their heads and the hardships of life during the early years have been magnified to the extent that these independent-minded Englishmen have become types of suffering fortitude—martyrs to the noble cause of free religion and self-government. That is a long tale, however, carrying with it many qualifications, and cannot be enlarged upon here. In what follows, it should always be borne in mind that aside from the Dutch at New Amsterdam and the small colony of Swedes on the Delaware, it was English stock that settled the American colonies and that these men and women brought with them a background of generations of English life. Their standards of living, manner of working their trades and natural aptitude for barter and commerce were all modeled upon English life and customs. It was only natural that this should be so. The ships crossed the Atlantic at comparatively frequent intervals and their holds came filled with all kinds of necessities and luxuries required by English standards of living—foodstuffs, fabrics and implements which the shops of London, Plymouth or Bristol could supply and which could not be produced by the American settlements. To obtain these refinements of life the colonists required only money or merchandise. Lumber, raw or manufactured, salted fish, beaver and peltry, plantation-built vessels and other products of the colonies,[5] could be easily converted into the comforts of English life for sale in the shops across the Atlantic.

The Rev. Francis Higginson came over in the *Talbot*, a ship of three hundred tons burden, which was armed with nineteen guns and carried a crew of thirty men. She brought over one hundred passengers. Sailing with her was the ship *George* of three hundred tons, in which came fifty-two passengers and a stock of cattle, twelve mares, thirty cows and some goats. From the original records of the Massachusetts Bay Company in New England we learn what food supplies were shipped on board the *Talbot* for the American voyage. The amount was supposed to be sufficient for one hundred and thirty-five men for three months. As a matter of fact, the voyage from Gravesend to the anchorage in Salem harbor occupied sixty-eight days.

The ship carried 22 hogsheads of salted beef, 12,000 of bread (biscuits), 40 bushels of peas, 20 barrels of oatmeal, 450 pounds of salt fish, 10 firkins of butter and 1,200 pounds of cheese. To wash down this food they took on board 6 tons of water, 45 tons of beer, 20 gallons of brandy, 20 gallons of Spanish wine (Malaga and Canary), 2 tierces of beer vinegar and 20 gallons of olive oil.[2] During the voyage two died of smallpox, including a blasphemous seaman. A child died of consumption and a dog fell overboard and could not be recovered. The rest came through and reached Salem harbor in a good state of health.

The Massachusetts Bay Company seems to have maintained a "company store," in the modern phrase, at which the colonists might obtain clothing, fabrics, foodstuffs and supplies of all sorts. When Governor Endecott came over in 1628, the Company sent extra clothing sufficient for one hundred men including three hundred suits of clothes, four hundred shirts and four hundred pairs of shoes. Two hundred of the suits of clothes consisted of doublet and hose made up of leather, lined with oiled skin leather, and fastened with hooks and eyes. The other suits were made up of Hampshire kerseys, the doublets lined with linen and the hose with skins.[6] There were a hundred waistcoats of green cotton bound about with red tape, a hundred Monmouth caps, at two shillings each, five hundred red knit caps, milled, at five pence each, and one hundred black hats, lined in the brows with leather. This store supplied the natural wear and tear of headgear among the hundred men. The stock contained four hundred pairs of knit stockings, ten dozen pairs of Norwich garters, three hundred plain falling bands, two hundred handkerchiefs and a stock of sheer linen with which to made up other handkerchiefs. Scotch ticking was supplied for beds and bolsters, with wool to put therein. The blankets were of Welsh cotton and fifty rugs were sent over to place over the blankets, while mats were supplied "to lye vnder 50 bedds aboard shippe."[3]

During the ten years that followed the settlement of the Massachusetts Bay, a continuous flow of emigration from England crossed the Atlantic in all kinds of available sailing craft.[4] The passage usually cost £5 per person and this included provisions provided by the ship such as "salt Beefe, Porke, salt Fish, Butter, Cheese, Pease, Pottage, Water-grewell, and such kinde of Victualls, with good Biskets, and six-shilling Beere; yet it will be necessary to carry some comfortable refreshing of fresh victuall. As first, for such as have ability, some Conserves, and good Clarret Wine to burne at Sea; Or you may have it by some of your Vintners or Wine-Coopers burned here, & put into Vessels, which will keepe much better than other burnt Wine, it is a very comfortable thing for the stomacke; or such as are Sea-sicke: Sallat-oyle likewise, Prunes are good to be stewed: Sugar for many things: White Biskets, and Egs, and Bacon, Rice, Poultry, and some weather-sheepe to Kill aboard the Ship: and fine flowre-baked meates, will keepe about a weeke or nine days at Sea. Iuyce of Lemons well put[7] up, is good either to prevent or curre the Scurvy.[5] Here it must not be forgotten to carry small Skillets or Pipkins, and small frying-panns, to dresse their victualls in at Sea. For bedding, so it be easie, and cleanly, and warme, it is no matter how old or coarse it be for the use of the Sea: and so likewise for Apparrell, the oldest cloathes be the fittest, with a long coarse coate to keepe better things from the pitched ropes and plankes. Whosoever shall put to Sea in a stoute and well-conditioned ship, having an honest Master, and loving Seamen, shall not neede to feare, but he shall finde as good content at Sea, as at Land.[6]

The *Mayflower* shipped 15,000 brown biscuit and 5,000 white, that is, hard bread, i.e. crackers; also smoked or half-cooked bacon, as it came from the smokehouse, which was much liked with the biscuit and when fried was considered a delicacy. Haberdyne (dried salted codfish) was also a staple article of diet; also smoked herring. Potatoes were practically unknown at that time and the store of cabbages, turnips, onions, parsnips, etc., soon ran short and gave way to boiled mush, oatmeal, pease puddings, etc. Their beer was carried in iron-bound casks.

When passengers came aboard vessels bound for New England in those early days, how did they stow themselves and their possessions? The *Mayflower* had a length of about 110 feet and measured about 244 tons. It was originally intended that she should carry ninety passengers, men, women and children, but when the *Speedwell* put back, twelve of her passengers were taken aboard, and two boys were born during the voyage. The ship also carried a crew of twenty to twenty-five men, and officers and petty officers, about sixteen in number, would bring the total of those aboard to one hundred and forty or more. Goats, pigs, and poultry occupied pens on the upper or spar deck and in the boats carried there. Small sleeping cabins were provided for the ship's officers and the more[8] important passengers; most of the company slept in narrow bunks, in hammocks, and on pallet beds of canvas filled with straw, placed on the deck beneath the hammocks. The crew bunked in the forecastle. The chests and personal possessions of the passengers were stowed below on the lower deck where the food, water and ship's stores were kept. On the *Arbella*, Governor Winthrop's ship, the male passengers lodged on the gundeck and four men were "ordered to keep that room clean."

The ship *Whale*, in 1632, brought thirty passengers, including Mr. Wilson and Mr. Dummer, all in good health, and seventy cows of which they lost but two. The ship *Regard* of Barnstaple, 200 tons, arrived in 1634, brought twenty passengers and about fifty cattle. The ship *Society* of Boston, N. E., 220 tons, with a crew of thirty-three men, arrived in 1663, with seventy-seven passengers. A notable example of fortitude is found in the voyage of the sloop *Sparrow Hawk*, that sailed from London in 1626 for Virginia and having been blown off her course was wrecked on Cape Cod.

She was only forty feet in length, had a breadth of beam of twelve feet and ten inches, and a depth of nine feet, seven and one-half inches. Bradford in his *History* records that she carried "many passengers in her and sundrie goods ... the cheefe amongst these people was one Mr. Fells and Mr. Sibsie, which had many servants belonging unto them, many of them being Irish. Some others ther were y^t had a servante or 2 a piece; but ye most were servants, and such as were ingaged to the former persons, who also had ye most goods ... they had been 6 weeks at sea, and had no water, nor beere, nor any woode left, but had burnt up all their emptie caske."[7] And this happened in the month of December!

In those days cooking on shore was done in an open fireplace. On shipboard, the larger vessels were provided with an open "hearth" made of cast iron sometimes weighing five hundred pounds and over. More commonly a hearth of bricks was laid on deck, over which stood an iron tripod from which the kettles hung. More[9] crudely still a bed of sand filled a wooden frame and on this the fire was built, commonly of charcoal. On the ship *Arbella*, in which came Governor John Winthrop and his company, in 1630, the "cookroom" was near a hatchway opening into the hold. The captain, his officers and the principal men among the passengers dined in the "round house," a cabin in the stern over the high quarter-deck. Lady Arbella Johnson and the gentlewomen aboard dined in the great cabin on the quarter-deck. The passengers ate their food wherever convenient on the main deck or in good weather, on the spar deck above. Years later, a new ship lying at anchor in Boston harbor was struck by lightning which "melted the top of the iron spindle of the vane of the mainmast" and passing through the long boat, which lay on the deck, killed two men and injured two others as "they were eating together off the Hen-Coop, near the Main Mast."

The ship supplied each passenger with a simple ration of food distributed by the quartermasters, which each family or self arranged group of passengers cooked at a common hearth as opportunity and the weather permitted. Of necessity much food was served cold and beer was the principal drink. John Josselyn, Gent., who visited New England in 1638, records "the common proportion of Victualls for the Sea to a Mess, being 4 men, is as followeth:

"Two pieces of Beef, of 3 pound and ¼ *per* piece.

"Four pound of *Bread*.

"One pint ¼ of *Pease*.

"Four Gallons of *Bear*, with *Mustard* and *Vinegar* for three flesh dayes in the week.

"For four fish dayes, to each Mess *per* day, two pieces of *Codd* or *Habberdine*, making three pieces of fish.

"One quarter of a pound of *Butter*.

"Four pound of *Bread*.

"Three quarters of a pound of *Cheese*.

"*Bear* is before.

"*Oatmeal per* day, for 50 men, Gallon 1. and so proportionable for more or fewer.

[10]

"Thus you see the ship's provision, is *Beef* or *Porke*, *Fish*, *Butter*, *Cheese*, *Pease*, *Pottage*, *Water gruel*, *Bisket*, and six-shilling *Bear*.

"For private fresh provision, you may carry with you (in case you, or any of yours should be sick at Sea) Conserves of *Roses*, *Clove-Gilliflowers*, *Wormwood*, *Green-Ginger*, *Burnt-Wine*, *English Spirits*, *Prunes* to stew, *Raisons* of the *Sun*, *Currence*, *Sugar*, *Nutmeg*, *Mace*, *Cinnamon*, *Pepper* and *Ginger*, *White Bisket*, or *Spanish Rusk*, Eggs, Rice, *Juice* of *Lemmons*, well put up to cure, or prevent the Scurvy. Small *Skillets*, *Pipkins*, *Porrengers*, and small *Frying pans*.

"To prevent or take away Sea sickness, Conserve of *Wormwood* is very proper."[8]

The settler also must take with him a supply of food to answer his needs on reaching Massachusetts, and it was advised that enough for the space of a year might be required in which case each person should be certain to have in store 8 bushels of meal, 2 bushels pease, 2 bushels oatmeal, 1 gallon brandy, 1 gallon oil and 2 gallons vinegar. Sugar could be had in New England as the Colonial vessels were bringing it from the West Indies in the way of trade, but spices, necessary to the English diet, must be brought from England.

John Josselyn, writing in 1638, listed the following articles as necessary equipment for every family coming to New England, viz.:

	£		
Bellows	0	2	0
Scoop		0	9
Great pail		0	10
Casting shovel		0	10

A sack	2	4
Lanthorn	1	3
Tobacco pipes		
5 broad howes	10	0
5 narrow howes	6	8

5 felling axes	7	6
2 hand saws	10	0
1 whip saw	10	0
1 file and wrest	10	
2 hamm	2	0

ers			
2 augers		1	0
Wheels for a cart		14	0
Wheel barrow		6	0
Canoe	3	0	0
Short oak la		0	10

dder		
Plough	3	9
Axletree	0	8
Cart	10	0
[11]3 shovels	4	6
2 spades	3	0
2 broad axes	7	4

6 chisels		3	0
3 gimblets		0	6
2 hatchets		3	6
2 frows		3	0
2 handbils		3	4
Nails of all	2	0	0

sorts		
3 locks and 3 pr. fetters	5	10
2 curry combs	0	11
Brand for beasts	0	6
Hand vise	2	6

100 wt. spikes nails and pins (120)	2	5	0
2 pick axes	0	3	0
Chain and lock for a		2	2

boat			
Coulter (10 pound)		3	4
Pitchfork		1	4
Ploughshare		2	11

Household implements for a family of six persons, viz.:

1 iron pot	0	7	0
1 gre	2	0	0

Item		
at copper kettle		
1 small kettle	10	0
1 lesser kettle	6	0
1 large frying pan	2	6
1 small frying ng	1	8

Item			
pan			
1 brass mortar	0	3	0
1 spit		2	0
1 gridiron		1	0
2 skillets		5	0
Platters, dishes and sp		4	0

oo
ns
of
wo
od

The above prices are estimated costs in England and the freight on the same would be reckoned at the rate of half a ton per person.

The vessels which carried the great emigration to New England between 1630 and 1640 were of small tonnage and the passenger accommodations on board were limited in space and barren of creature comforts. Small wonder that the health of many of the first settlers, shaken by the passage at sea, paid toll to the severity of the New England climate—the biting cold of the winter and the heat of the summer days to which they were unaccustomed.

"It was not because the Country was unhealthful, but because their bodies were corrupted with sea-diet, which was naught, their Beefe and Porke being tainted, their Butter and Cheese corrupted, their Fish rotten, and voyage long, by reason of crosse Windes, so that winter approaching before they could get warme houses, and the searching sharpnes of that purer Climate, creeping in at the crannies of their crazed bodies, caused death and sickness."[9]

The ship *Talbot*, on which Mr. Higginson sailed, brought over one hundred passengers and thirty seamen. She measured nearly[12] eighty-six feet in length and had a depth of hold of eleven feet. By present-day measurement she was about two hundred tons burden. The space between decks, where the passengers slept and spent much time during the dreary voyage, was so low that a tall man could not stand erect, and whenever a severe storm arose, so that the ports and hatches must be kept closed, the air below deck in time must have become intolerable. Such a storm arose when the *Talbot* was thirty-three days out and "ye wind blew mightily, ye sea roared and ye waves tossed us horribly; besides it was fearfull darke and ye mariners made us afraid with their running here and there and lowd crying one to another to pull at this and y^t rope."

These small emigrant ships of the seventeenth century, besides men, women and children, brought over much livestock housed in temporary pens and shelters built amidships. The long boat or pinnace was also carried on board, all of which left little room for movement about the deck. But these three hundred tons ships were traveling palaces when compared with some of the smaller craft that boldly ventured across the Atlantic. Barks, ketches, pinks and other small vessels of less than fifty tons burden were common. In 1635, a "small Norsey bark" of twenty-five tons reached Boston. She was bound for Connecticut, but a stormy voyage had forced her to seek safety in Boston harbor. This vessel, little over thirty feet in length, brought over fourteen passengers, including two women, with their household goods.

---

[13]

CHAPTER II

THEIR EARLY SHELTERS AND LATER DWELLINGS

There is a widespread misconception that the colonists on reaching Massachusetts proceeded immediately to build log houses in which to live. Historians have described these log houses as chinked with moss and clay and as having earth floors, precisely the type of house built on the frontier and in the logging camps at a much later period. A well-known picture of Leyden Street, at Plymouth, shows a double row of log houses reaching up the hillside, which the Pilgrims are supposed to have constructed. In point of fact, no contemporary evidence has been found that supports the present-day theory. The early accounts of what took place in the days following the settlement along the coast are full of interesting details relating to day-by-day happenings but nowhere do we find allusion to a log house such as modern historians assume existed at that time. This unique form of construction, however, had been used in Scandinavia since the Middle Ages and also in parts of Germany, but never did it appear in England. It also is well established that the North American Indians knew nothing of this method of construction, even the Iroquois tribe who built a "long house," so-called.

The Swedes and Finns who settled in Delaware in 1638 introduced the log house built of logs with notched ends, with which they were familiar in their homeland. What more natural? Jasper Dankers and Peter Sluyter, Dutch travelers, made a tour of the American colonies in 1679-1680, and while passing through New Jersey, describe the house of Jacob Hendricks, near the town of Burlington, as follows:

"The house, although not much larger than where we were the last night, was somewhat better and tighter, being made according to the Swedish mode, and as they usually build their houses here,[14] which are block-houses, being nothing less than entire trees, split through the middle, or squared out of the rough, and placed in the form of a square, upon each other, as high as they wish to have the house; the ends of these timbers are let into each other, about a foot from the ends, half of one into half of the other, the whole structure is thus made without a nail or a spike. The ceiling and roof do not exhibit much finer work, except amongst the most careful people, who have the ceiling planked and a glass window. The doors are wide enough, but very low, so that you have to stoop in entering. These houses are quite tight and warm: but the chimney is placed in a corner. My comrade and myself had some deer skins, spread upon the floor to lie on, and we were, therefore, quite well off and could get some rest."[10]

These travelers also spent a night at a Quaker's house near where a gristmill had been erected on a creek above the falls at what is now Trenton.

"Here we had to lodge: and although we were too tired to eat, we had to remain sitting upright the whole night, not being able to find room enough to lie upon the ground. We had a fire, however, but the dwellings are so wretchedly constructed, that if you are not close to the fire, as almost to burn yourself, you cannot keep warm, for the wind blows through them everywhere. Most of the English and many others, have their houses made of nothing but clapboards, as they call them there, in this manner: they first make a wooden frame, the same as they do in Westphalia, but not so strong, they then split the boards of clapboard, so that they are like cooper's pipe-staves, except they are not bent. These are made very thin, with a large knife, so that the thickest edge is about a little finger thick, and the other is made sharp, like the edge of a knife. They are about five or six feet long, and are nailed on the outside of the frame, with the ends lapped over each other. They are not usually laid so close together, as to prevent you from sticking a finger between them, in consequence either of their not being well joined, or the boards being crooked. When it is cold and windy, the[15] best people plaster them with clay. Such are most all the English houses in the country."[11]

The only type of log construction in use in New England in the early days existed in garrison houses built as a protection against the

Indians. In every instance the logs were carefully hewed square, to make a close fit against each other, and never notched at the ends, sometimes halved at the corners of the structure, but usually dove-tailed into each other at the ends in medieval military manner. Several of these garrison houses still exist and although afterwards used as dwellings, at first they were built as forts.

What happened at the Plymouth Colony after the *Mayflower* came to anchor? The wind blew very hard for two days and the next day, Saturday, December 23, 1620, as many as could went ashore: "felled and carried timber, to provide themselves stuff for building," and the following Monday "we went on shore, some to fell timber, some to saw, some to rive, and some to carry; so no man rested all that day."[12] Bradford writes "that they builte a forte with good timber" which Isaac de Rasieres described in 1627 as "a large square house, made of thick sawn planks, stayed with oak beams." The oldest existing houses in the Plymouth Colony are built in the same manner and some half dozen or more seventeenth-century plank houses may yet be seen north of Boston. Moreover, when the ship *Fortune* sailed from Plymouth in the summer of 1621, the larger part of her lading consisted of "clapboards and wainscott," showing clearly that the colonists soon after landing had dug saw pits and produced boards in quantity suitable for the construction of houses and for exportation.

The first settlers in the Massachusetts Bay brought with them mechanics of all kinds, well equipped with tools, and it is altogether probable that these workmen plied their trades on this side of the Atlantic exactly as they had been taught through long centuries of apprenticeship in England. The houses of that early period, still remaining, all resemble similar English structures. Upon arrival, however, the need for shelter was imperative, and all sorts of rude[16] expedients were adopted. Deacon Bartholomew Green, the printer of the *Boston News-Letter*, related that when his father arrived at Boston in 1630, "for lack of housing he was wont to find shelter at night in an empty cask," and during the following winter many of the poorer sort still continued to live in tents through lack of better housing. When Roger Clap arrived at Charlestown in 1630 he "found some Wigwams and one House ... in the meantime before they could build at Boston, they lived many of them in tents and Wigwams."

John Winthrop, in his *Journal*, writes that "the poorer sort of people (who lay long in tents) were much afflicted with scurvy and many died, especially at Boston and Charlestown." He also makes several references to English wigwams. In September, 1630, one Fitch, of Watertown, had his wigwam burned down with all his goods and two months later John Firman, also of Watertown, lost his English wigwam.

Edward Johnson, in his *Wonder-Working Providence*, mentions the rude shelters of the first settlers. "They kept off the short showers from their lodgings, but the long rains penetrated through to their disturbance in the night season, yet in those poor wigwams they sang Psalms, praise and pray their God till they can provide them homes which ordinarily was not wont to be with many till the earth by the Lord's blessing brought forth bread to feed them, their wives and little ones."

The Rev. Francis Higginson, in his *New-Englands Plantation*, printed in 1630, describes the wigwams built by the Indians living at Salem as "verie little and homely, but made with small poles prick't into the ground and so bended and fastened at the tops and on the side, they are matted with boughes and covered with sedge and old mats." It seems likely that when the English built themselves "English wigwams," they copied the small structures built by the Indians, especially as mats suitable for covering might be obtained from the Indians by barter, and old pieces of sailcloth doubtless might be obtained from the shipping stores. It seems unlikely that an Englishman living in one of these structures during[17] the winter season would be content to allow the smoke from his fire to find its way out through a hole in the roof in the Indian fashion. It is more likely that a fireplace, built of stones or bricks, would be constructed at one end of an "English wigwam." A door in hewed frame, with wooden hinges, probably was installed as a suitable substitute for the Indian mat lifted upon entering. The floors in these English wigwams undoubtedly would be covered with rushes or straw, following the custom in English cottages at that time.

Edward Johnson, the town clerk of Woburn, writing in 1652, relates of the first settlers that "after they have thus found out a place of aboad, they burrow themselves in the Earth for their first shelter under some Hill-side, casting the Earth aloft up on Timber: they make a smoaky fire against the Earth at the highest side, and thus these poore servants of Christ provide shelter for themselves, their Wives and little ones."

Alonzo Lewis, the historian of Lynn, writing a century ago, states that some of the first settlers in that town made shelters for themselves and families by digging caves into the hillsides. On the bank of the Connecticut River above Hartford, is the Loomis Institute, on the grounds of which is the site where the men from Dorchester, Mass., in 1635, constructed their first dwellings, which were dug into the river bank. The bank itself composed three walls of the shelter and the front was a framing of boards with a door and a window. The roof was thatched with river sedge. The last of these long abandoned dugouts was filled in as recently as 1926.

At Concord, Mass., the early settlers dug cellars in the earth which they spanned with wooden spars and then covered with turf. A more detailed description of such shelters is found in a report made in 1650, by the Secretary of the Province of New Netherlands:

"Those in New Netherlands and especially in New England who have no means to build farmhouses at first, according to their wishes, dig a square pit in the ground, cellar fashion, 6 or 7 feet deep, as long and as broad as they think proper, case the earth inside with wood all round the wall, and line the wood with bark of[18] trees or something else to prevent the caving in of the earth, floor this cellar with plank and wainscott it overhead for a ceiling, raise a roof of spars clear up and cover the spars with the bark or green sods, so that they can live dry and warm in these houses with their entire families for two, three or four years, it being understood that partitions are run through those cellars which are adapted to the size of the family. The wealthy and principal men of New England, in the beginning of the Colonies, commenced their first dwelling houses in this fashion."[13]

The frequent references to the English wigwam seem to indicate that some such temporary construction was usual among many of the colonists at the outset. Settlers were living at Salem as early as 1626 and Endecott, with a considerable immigration, arrived in 1628. Marblehead, just across the harbor, was settled early and yet when John Goyt came there in 1637, he "first built a wigwam and lived thar till he got a house."[14] The rude buildings also put up by planters at Salem must have been looked upon at the time as temporary structures for they had all disappeared before 1661.[15]

When Governor Winthrop arrived at Charlestown in 1630 with the first great emigration, he found a house or two and several wigwams—rude shelters patterned after the huts built by the Indians—and until houses could be erected in Boston many lived in tents and wigwams, "their meeting-place being abroad under a Tree."

In the summer of 1623, Bradford mentions the "building of great houses in pleasant situations," and when a fire broke out in November of the following year it began in "a shed yt was joyned to ye end of ye storehouse, which was wattled up with bowes." It will be seen that this shed was not crudely built of logs or slabs but that its walls were wattled and perhaps also daubed with clay, in precisely the same manner with which these colonists were familiar in their former homes across the sea. An original outer wall in the old Fairbanks house at Dedham, Massachusetts, still has its "wattle and daub" constructed in 1637.

[19]

Thomas Dudley writing to the Countess of Lincoln, in March, 1631, relates: "Wee have ordered that noe man shall build his chimney with wood nor cover his house with thatch, which was readily assented unto, for that divers houses have been burned since our arrival (the fire always beginning in the wooden chimneys) and some English wigwams which have taken fire in the roofes with thatch or boughs."[16] It was Dudley who was taken to task by the Governor in May, 1632, "for bestowing so much cost on wainscotting his house and otherwise adorning it," as it was not a good example for others in the beginning of a plantation. Dudley replied that he had done it for warmth and that it was but clapboards nailed to the walls. A few months later this house caught fire "the hearth of the Hall chimney burning all night upon the principal beam."

In 1631, John Winthrop entered in his *Journal* that the chimney of Mr. Sharp's house in Boston took fire "the splinters being not clayed at the top" and from it the thatch caught fire and the house was burnt down.

The first meetinghouse built in Salem had a "catted" chimney, that is, the chimney was built with sticks laid cobhouse fashion and the whole daubed with clay inside and out.

Thatch as a roof covering was in common use in the early days. Notwithstanding the Great and General Court forbade its use, it still persisted as necessity arose. At the outset, towns along the coastline set aside certain parts of thatch banks in the marshes, as a supply for thatching houses. Rye straw also was much used. The roofs of these thatched houses were not boarded as the thatch was fastened to slats. Dorchester built a meetinghouse in 1632 with a thatched roof.

The earliest frame houses were covered with weather-boarding and this before long was covered with clapboards. The walls inside were sheathed up with boards moulded at the edges in an ornamental manner and the intervening space was filled with clay and chopped straw, and later with imperfect bricks. This was done for[20] warmth, and was known as "nogging," following the English practice. When roofs were not thatched, they were covered with shingles split from the log by means of a "frow" and afterwards hand-shaved. The window openings were small and were closed by hinged casements, just as the houses in England were equipped at that time. Generally, the casement sash was wood, but sometimes iron was used, as was common in England.

The glass was usually diamond-shaped, set in lead "cames." Emigrants to Massachusetts were instructed by the Company to bring ample supplies of glass for windows, but the supply ran short and in the poorer cottages and wigwams, oiled paper was in common use. This was an excellent substitute and supplied a surprisingly large amount of light.

A brickyard was in operation in Salem as early as 1629, and everywhere along the coast clay was found and made up into bricks. Chimneys were built upon a huge stone foundation. The brick work began at the first floor level and the bricks were laid in puddled clay up to about the ridge line where lime was used as the chimney top became exposed to the weather.

It has been claimed and denied that bricks used in the construction of certain old houses were brought from overseas. In general the claims may be disregarded. It is certain, however, that the Massachusetts Company at the outset sent over ten thousand bricks, stowed in the ballast with five chauldrons of sea coals for the use of the blacksmiths. At the same time came iron and steel, nails, red lead, salt and sailcloth. Even fourteen hundred weight of plaster of paris, appears in the list, priced at eighteen shillings per hundred weight.

The home of the average New Englander in the late seventeenth century was a wooden dwelling of two stories built around a brick chimney containing large fireplaces. In Rhode Island and in parts of Connecticut, where shale abounded, the chimney was built of stone and not infrequently the house, in whole or at one end, was also so constructed. The roofs of these houses were covered with wooden shingles usually split from pine logs and shaved[21] smooth by hand on a shingle horse. The outside walls of the well made house were covered with clapboards, also smoothed on the shingle horse. For many years these clapboards were made from oak, but as this wood has a tendency to warp and pull itself free from fastenings, by the year 1700, its use for that purpose had very generally been replaced by pine. Outbuildings and the poorer class of dwellings were not covered with clapboards or only the part next the road, for the New Englander believes in "putting his best foot forward." Such buildings were covered with "weatherboards" or plain boarding that lapped at the lower edge.

The windows in these houses were filled by casement sash containing glass set in lead cames. The glass was usually diamond shaped, but sometimes four by six inch lights were used. This glass was imported from England and came packed in cribs, but much of it came in sheets already leaded and was cut to size by "glaziers" upon demand. Early in the eighteenth century sliding-sash windows were introduced, probably about 1710, but it was a long time before existing casements were entirely given up. One Saturday afternoon in July, 1714, lightning struck the house of Colonel Vetch in Boston. He had bought the dwelling not long before and Judge Sewall records in his diary that at the time of the storm "the Work of Transformation was not finished" to make the building fit for the occupancy of Madam Vetch. The lightning played various tricks with the house, doing considerable damage, and among other details the Judge mentions that it "lifted up the Sash Window and broke one of the squares" of glass.[17] Colonel Vetch was presumably a man of substance for he afterwards became Governor of Nova Scotia, and he is likely to have "transformed" his recently purchased house into the latest fashion of lighting.

On the other hand, Judge Sewall, the Chief Justice of the highest court in the Province, had casements in his Boston house at a time, ten years later, when his daughter Hannah died, for he records in his *Diary* that "Boston will not have her put into the Cellar [it was in August when she died]; so she is only remov'd[22] into the best Room. And because the Casements were opened for Coolness, Boston would watch all night." This entry in the ancient diary not only preserves the fact that the Judge's house had casement windows, but it also makes allusion to the old-time custom of watching with the dead body and the interest that the town of Boston had in the bereavement of the Judge.

In 1722, Benjamin Franklin in his Boston newspaper, was satirizing the extravagancies of New England housewives in "new Glazing their Houses with new fashion'd square Glass." Diamond glass had seen its day, however, and forty years later "Windows set in lead, suitable for Hot-Beds" were advertised in the newspapers, a sure sign of discarded sash. On the other hand, a hardware shop was advertising "sheet and diamond glass" as late as 1766, probably to meet the demands for repairing old casements.

The exterior of these early houses was seldom painted, in fact it was well into the nineteenth century before the outside of houses in country towns were usually painted. A diarist who rode into Boston in 1804 comments on the dingy appearance of the houses and the general lack of paint and about the same time a Salem man met with success in business, whereupon he painted his house with the result that his associates rather sneeringly remarked: "Sam is feeling his oats; he's begun to paint his house."

The paint first used on the exteriors of New England houses was usually of a dark red color called, both then and now, "Indian red." Red ochre was used and commonly was mixed with fish oil. The Indians had "paint mines" where they had found red earth and doubtless these "mines" were utilized, particularly in adjacent locations. One of these paint mines was located near what is now Augusta, Maine, and in that part of New England formerly existed, long before the coming of the European, an Indian race that used this red earth so freely that by ethnologists it has been termed the "red paint culture."

So runs the present-day tradition of Indian red in New England. In point of fact, however, red earth was brought from the East Indies long before the settlement of the American Colonies, hence[23] the name "India red," by which it was advertised in the Boston newspapers in the mid-eighteenth century. In 1766, John Gore, "at his Shop at the Sign of the Painter's Arms in Queen Street," Boston, advertised a stock of oils, paints, brushes, etc., just imported from London. He had linseed oil by the barrel or smaller quantity, boiled oil, nut oil, turpentine oil and turpentine varnish. Among his white colors, were Spanish white and French halk,—whatever that may be. Red was a color that was in demand for he carried red head, Spanish brown, India red, purple red, Venetian red, Vermillian, drop hake, carmine, umber and rose pink. Under yellows, he listed King's yellow, Princess yellow, Naples yellow, spruce yellow, stone yellow, English ochre, Orpiment-pale and deep, Dutch pink and brown pink. The blues were ultramarine, ultramarine ashes, Prussian blue of various sorts, calcined smalt, strowing ditto, verditer blue and powder blue.

Gore also sold crayons in sets and canvas for portrait painting in half-length cloths, kit-kat and three-quarters length. He carried "Colours prepared for House and Ship Painting," best London crown glass for pictures and "Water Colours ready prepared in Shells."[18]

Two years later he advertised chariot glasses, genteel looking-glasses and Wilton carpets and also announced that he did coach and carpet painting in the best and cheapest manner.

At how early a date was paint used on the exterior of a New England house? Who can solve the problem? Undoubtedly it was on a house owned by some merchant having a direct contact with England. It is an established fact that the Andrews house, built in 1707-1710, in the country town of Topsfield, Mass., was painted Indian red at the time it was built, or soon after, but only on the trim—the window frames, corner boards, etc. The clapboards and weather-boarding at the easterly end, remained unpainted until long years after.

The inside finish of town houses owned by well-to-do people, probably was painted at a comparatively early date, at least, one or[24] two rooms in a house. "A large Fashionable Dwelling-House" in Boston, "about 1¼ miles from Charlestown ferry" was advertised to be sold in 1734. It had eight "fire rooms"—that is, rooms with fireplaces. The entries and two of the rooms were "beautifully Wainscotted and laid in oil" and four were "handsomely Painted."

In 1753, George Tilley, a Boston shop keeper, advertised his house for sale. It contained "eight rooms, seven of them fire-rooms, with a Number of convenient Closets and a good Cellar, four of the said Rooms is cornish'd, and the House is handsomely painted throughout; one of the Rooms is painted Green, another Blue, one Cedar and one Marble; the other four a Lead colour, the Garrets are handsomely plaistered; the House has twenty Sash-Windows to it and is pleasantly situated on Pleasant Street, near the Hay-Market."[19]

But such glory did not exist in other parts of the same town and certainly not in the country. Rufus Choate, the lawyer, was born in a house in Essex, Mass., built in 1725 by an ancestor who was popularly called "Governor Choate." He was a man in comfortable circumstances and built for himself a house of ten rooms having good panelling in four of them. None of the finish on this house was painted until well after 1825 or a century after it was built. This paint has now been removed and the old white pine finish is revealed in all its natural beauty of varying shades of reddish brown, effectively contrasting with the whitewashed walls. Natural wood finish, laid in oil, was quite the common thing in the ordinary New England dwelling, until after the people had recovered from the financial exhaustion of the Revolution.

The plastered walls were usually whitewashed which was quite in keeping with the Puritan character that covered with limewash the beautiful mural decorations of the English churches at the time of the Commonwealth. Families of wealth covered their walls with hangings brought from England. Peter Sergeant died in 1714, possessed of a "suit of Imagery Tapestry hangings" in his cedar room. This house was one of the finest in the town of Boston and[25] afterwards became the Province House,—the residence of the Governors of the Province. Another room in this house was also furnished with hangings. Arras hangings were advertised from time to time in the Boston newspapers and in 1736, Boydell, the printer of the *Boston Gazette*, advertised a house in which one chamber in the first story was "hung with Scotch Tapestry, the other with Green cheny." The large brick house of the late Isaac Gridley, situated near

Fort Hill, in Boston, was sold in 1771. It contained thirteen rooms and three of the lower rooms were "genteelly furnished with Tapestry Hangings."

A three-story house was built in Boston about 1715 by William Clark, a wealthy merchant and member of the governor's council. His death in 1742, was attributed by some, to the loss of forty sail of vessels in the French War. In this house afterwards lived Sir Henry Frankland, Collector of the Port, who fell in love with Agnes Surriage, the beautiful sixteen-year-old maid-of-all-work at the Fountain Inn in Marblehead. Her romantic story is well-known. This house differed but little from the dozen or so of its type to be found in Boston at the time, save in its rich and elaborate decoration of the north parlor, at the right of the entrance hall. Here, the walls were divided into panels by fluted pilasters supporting an elaborate cornice, the whole heavily gilded, and each of the panels was embellished with a landscape or other decoration painted in oils. Painted arabesques and heraldic devices covered all other flat surfaces and the floor was laid in a mosaic of various colored woods. Every inch of the surface of this parlor was the product of the imagination and skill of the painter, gilder or carver. But while this magnificence actually existed in New England, by no means was it typically representative of its culture or artistic development. It merely exhibited the pride of wealth and was largely the product of European craftsmen.

The heavy strap hinges on the doors of the earlier houses and buildings were probably wrought by hand at the forge of the nearest blacksmith, but most of the hardware and iron work was imported from England. Before 1650 there was a slitting mill at the[26] Saugus Iron Works, but the principal product of this forge was cast iron manufactures, such as pots and kettles. At a later date, Parliament, at the instigation of the English manufacturers, prohibited by law the setting up of slitting mills and trip hammers, and it naturally followed that the manufactured iron and brass required by the Colonies was brought overseas from Birmingham and Sheffield.

A word or two as to the varying types of house hardware may not be amiss at this time. At the outset wooden hinges and heavy strap hinges of wrought iron were in common use. These hinges were hung on gudgeons and their points varied in design but the spear-shaped point was most common. In the best houses, at an early date and continuing until the beginning of the eighteenth century, might be found the so-called "cock's head" hinge, an ornamental survival from Roman times. The butterfly hinge was also in use at that time— usually on cupboards and furniture doors. The **H** and **HL** hinges came into use in New England in the early 1700's and lasted until after the Revolution. These hinges were cut out of heavy sheet iron and were made in factories in England. This type of hinge was superseded by the cast-iron butt, still in use, which was invented in England in 1775, and adopted very generally in the United States at the close of the Revolution.

In some old houses that have been restored and in many modern constructions done in the manner of the seventeenth and eighteenth centuries, the door hinges in painted rooms have been picked out in black making them most conspicuous. This is a modern conceit— an invention of the modern architect. It was not done in the old days, a fact easily established by carefully scraping through the various coats of paint on an old house. Our great-great-grandmothers had no itching desire for contrasts of that sort. They knew nothing of highboys, grandfather's clocks, low daddys, Lady Washington chairs, courting mirrors, fiddle back chairs or donkey-eared spindle backs. These names are inventions of collectors or antique dealers striving for the picturesque. The highboy, it is true, antedates the others, but in the early days this piece of furniture[27] was called a high chest of drawers and the lowboy was called a low chest. Recently the common **HL** hinge has been described as the "Holy Land" hinge; certainly not referring to the English colonies where there were fully as many sinners as saints.

Wooden latches were used on both outside and inside doors in early days and the wooden latch persisted in the back country until comparatively recent times. The iron thumb latch was made by the country blacksmith but more and more it came to be imported from England. The earliest type has spear-point handles. The rounded end comes in after 1700 and is common about 1750. The Norfolk latch, in brass and iron, comes in after the Revolution and was replaced by the common cast-iron thumb latch, invented by Blake in 1840. In examining old hinges and all kinds of hardware always have in mind that the machine-made pointed screw was not invented until 1846.

A feature of this hardware trade with England, which is of much interest, is the catalogues that were sent over by the manufacturers in Birmingham. About the year 1770 they began to send out drawings of different pieces of hardware, tools, etc., and this soon developed into sheets of engravings on copper which were bound into books and sent to customers at a distance who then could visualize the goods and order accordingly; size, list price and discount were indicated. Seldom was there a title-page or even a label to indicate a source, but the handmade paper bears its watermark and generally the date when it was made. These catalogues are now difficult to find and the Victoria and Albert Museum at South Kensington, esteems them so highly that a descriptive catalogue of its collection has been published. Probably the largest collection of these catalogues in America is in the library of the Essex Institute at Salem.

[28]

CHAPTER III

HOW THEY FURNISHED THEIR HOUSES

It is a lamentable fact that the present generation possesses little accurate information on the every day life and surroundings of the early settlers in Massachusetts. Some of the finer pieces of furniture have been preserved together with a few portraits and pieces of silver and here and there an article of costume of special beauty or unusual association. The newly settled country had no artists to paint pictures of household interiors in the manner of the Dutch painters and the diarists and letter writers of that time when they used a quill pen, devoted little thought to the homely happenings of the household or to the costume and furniture with which every one was familiar. Judge Samuel Sewall's diary[20] throws much light on New England life two centuries and more ago, but many are the questions we would like to ask. In August, 1702, he rode to Newbury to attend the funeral of his sister Mehitable and returned home by way of Andover where he found that the keeper of the ordinary was sick and so went to Mr. Woodman's daughters "and there din'd on Pork and Beans; afterward had Fowls rosted and dress'd very well." It would be interesting if we could know more about that dinner. Did the Judge eat in the same room in which the fowls were "rosted" and was the table furnished with woodenware or pewter, or both? Had the Woodmans begun to use two-tined forks or did the Judge hold the meat in one hand while he cut it up and conveyed it to his mouth with the knife? Was a roasting jack fastened over the fireplace? Was the dinner served on a table-board? Did all stand while "a blessing" was asked? What was served for dessert? Did the Judge wash his hands at the washbench in the kitchen and if not, where did he find the washbasin? What pictures were on the parlor walls and was there a bedstead in the corner and if so, how was it furnished[29] and how made? A bedstead known to have been used in a New England house of 1702 is almost unknown today. If the Judge had only devoted five minutes, while writing up his diary, to a close description of that bedstead and its furnishings he would have settled many existing doubts.

It seems entirely reasonable that a distinguished guest in the house would not be required in the morning to go to the washbench in the kitchen and use the family basin. The dignity of Judge Sewall and the delicacy of Madam Belcher would rebel at the thought of an exhibition of disheveled attire before the serving maid and the numerous children of the family. In the humblest home, on occasion, it would be a simple matter to place in the chamber of a guest, on a table or even on a chair, a basin and a jug of water with a towel.

In the journal of the travels of Dr. Alexander Hamilton of Annapolis, Md., who rode through New England in 1744, may be found the description of the furnishings of a chamber in an inn. Doctor Hamilton was accompanied by a negro servant and on a Sunday morning at Marblehead he asked for his portmanteau. "I was told by my man Dromo that it was in his room. I had the curiosity to go and see what kind of a room his room was, and upon a reconnoitre found it a most spacious one, furnished *a la mode de Cabaret*, with tables, chairs, a fine feather-bed with quilted counterpane, white calico canopy, or tester, and curtains, every way adapted for a gentleman of his degree and complexion."

Of course 1744 is many years after the period when oak furniture was commonly in use; yet Reid's tavern, "at the sign of the Dragon," in the fishing village of Marblehead, could not have been the resort of fashion or wealth and if a negro slave was given so well furnished a chamber what may have been the furnishings of the chamber occupied by Doctor Hamilton?

In a farmer's family, in the early days, it was undoubtedly the habit to wash faces and hands in a small tub or keeler on the washbench in the kitchen. In suitable weather it is altogether likely the men of the family may have washed out of doors, beside the back[30] door, in a bucket of water freshly drawn from the well or brought from the spring. The farm hands, on coming in from the fields, for dinner, or at night, always "washed up" at a bench out of doors and this custom persisted until well into the nineteenth century. My mother, when young, for a time lived on a farm (about 1850) and several times I have heard her describe the farm hand who came to the back door one noon, and looking at his hands remarked, "I guess they are clean enough," and so went into his dinner, without washing.

Henry W. Erving of Hartford, Conn., writes: "A couple of years ago I made a pilgrimage to my great-grandfather's former home in Westford, Conn., in company with a kinsman over eighty years old—the last of his generation. It was a very comfortable house, with four rooms and a leanto, with a stone chimney. My great-grandfather lived there as early as 1750. My cousin called my attention to the old well near the door where, by the curb, there was a large stone hollowed out like a trough. He said the 'men folks' as they came from the field, would fill that trough with a bucket or two of water from which they would 'souse' themselves thoroughly, thus not disturbing the goodwife. And of course in the rustic neighborhoods the old customs existed long after they were abandoned in the larger villages and towns.

"You will hardly believe, when I say it, but I distinctly remember as a very small boy, going to a house in this same primitive town of Westford where we were invited to dinner. The only drinking vessel on the table was one of the quart Staffordshire mugs (would that I had that mug in my collection today) which was filled with water, milk or cider, I have really forgotten which, and passed around the table at the demand of any thirsty one. The family consisted of a man and his wife, an ancient grandmother, and several children with not too clean faces. I couldn't refuse the mug when urged upon me and selecting a place on the brim at the right of the handle, I drank, when one of the children exclaimed, 'See, mar! He's got granny's place.' Of course that practice in this instance was possibly nearly a century out of period."

[31]

One of the standard examples of American humor is the picture of the *Mayflower* loaded to the cross-trees with the chairs, chests and cradles that devout New Englanders now own and claim were brought over on that memorable voyage. It is so easy to attribute age and romantic history to a treasured family relic that it has become possible for a museum in the city of New York to exhibit a punch bowl of Staffordshire ware, as a veritable relic of the *Mayflower*. The bowl could not possibly have been made before 1780-1790. There is another piece of Staffordshire treasured in the china closet of a New England family, which the owner is certain was formerly possessed by an ancestress who died years before the Revolution. Well authenticated family tradition vouches for the fact which cannot be disputed. Yet, the observer will soon discover a steamboat pictured on one side of the pitcher and what is more interesting, the stars and stripes are flying from the masthead and the canton of the flag contains fifteen stars.

It is undoubtedly true that some pieces of furniture were brought over from England by the first settlers and the tradition connected with such pieces can be authenticated by an examination of the chair or chest showing that it is made of English and not American oak. While most family possessions, for convenience in shipment, came over in bales or bundles, covered with canvas in the true European manner, a custom followed by emigrants of a later day, yet, many articles of fine clothing and the treasured belongings of the better-equipped families came over neatly stowed in chests and cupboards and some of those chests have survived.

It is all a matter of common sense reasoning which can be backed up by an examination of early records and also the furniture itself. Why pay a considerable value in money to transport, in an overcrowded ship, utilitarian pieces of furniture, that could be made in the newly settled colony, by workmen who were going over in the same ship? Timber could be had here for the cutting and until sufficient time had elapsed to permit the making of chairs, beds and other required furniture, one could sit on rudely made stools and boxes and sleep on pallet beds made up on the floor just as many of[32] them would be obliged to sleep while on board ship.

Some estimate of the culture of the New England people during the seventeenth century and of their appreciation of the refinements of life may be reached with a degree of accuracy through a study of the carefully itemized inventories of their estates made at time of death. During that period the Royal Governor from overseas, with his little court of officials and followers, had not introduced London fashions and furnishings to the extent that existed in the eighteenth century. Moreover, the wealth of the colonies had not grown to the point where the refinements of life were not only esteemed but demanded by loving spouses and by those who had taken ship for England or the Continent and there had observed how other people lived.

Among the early settlements made in the Colony of the Massachusetts Bay was one at Agawam, now the town of Ipswich. The news had reached Boston that the French were pushing their settlements westward along the coast, bringing with them "divers priests and Jesuits," which so alarmed the Governor and the Assistants that it was decided to forestall the French and hasten the planting of new towns north of Boston. The first move was to send the Governor's son John, with twelve others, to establish themselves at Agawam. There were no roads and so they sailed along the coast in a shallop and took possession of the town site in March, 1633. Their families and other settlers soon followed and the increase of population was such that in August, 1634, the Court of Assistants decreed that the place be called Ipswich, after old Ipswich in England, "in acknowledgment of the great honor and kindness done to our people, who took shipping there."

Three months later, in November, 1634, one John Dillingham arrived in Ipswich and the selectmen granted him six acres of land on which to build a house. He was from Leicestershire and with his wife and daughter had come over in the fleet with Winthrop in 1630, and remained in Boston until he removed to Ipswich. Life in the frontier settlement was too severe for him and he died during the next winter. On July 14, 1636, his widow, Sarah, made her[33] "last will and testament" being in "perfect memory though my body be weak & sick" and a few days later she too was dead, leaving her orphaned daughter to be cared for by Richard Saltonstall and John Appleton, under the direction of the Quarterly Court. And this was not at all difficult for John Dillingham had left a "goodly estate," for the times. This Dillingham home has been selected for analysis because it is one of the earliest estates in the Colony of which we have exact and detailed information, a number of documents relating to it having been preserved among the miscellaneous papers in the Massachusetts State Archives.[21] Moreover, it shows the furnishings and equipment of a settler living in a town of only two years growth from the wilderness.

The Dillingham homestead consisted of a house of two rooms and outbuildings with thirty acres of upland, sixty acres of meadow, i.e., grass land, and six acres of planting ground near the house, of which four acres were planted with corn. Apple trees and other fruits were fenced off in the garden. For livestock there was a mare, three cows, two steers, two heifers, four calves, and four pigs. There was an indentured servant, Thomas Downs, to help cultivate the land and care for the stock, and a maid, Ann Towle, who not only helped with the housework but also worked in the fields. "She hath been a faithful servant," wrote Richard Saltonstall, executor of the estate, "and though she was discharged by her mistress a little before her time was out, yet it may be borne by the estate, considering her diligence." Ann had come over in the ship *Susan and Ellen*, which arrived in April, 1635. Her passage cost £5.

The Dillinghams occupied a good social position in the youthful settlement but their two-room house did not contain any really fine furniture. The parlor was also used as a bedroom, a practice which was common everywhere in the seventeenth century. It had two bedsteads valued at £1. 6. 8.; a cupboard, 10s.; a sea chest, 10s.; two "joyned Chaires," 5s.; a round table, 7s.; a deske, 4s.; and a band box, 2s. There was also a large nest of boxes valued £2. and a small nest of boxes worth only three shillings. The feather beds,[34] boulsters, and pillows on each bed were valued at about twice as much as a bedstead and the coverlets averaged about £1. a piece. There were flaxen sheets for Mrs. Dillingham's bed and coarse sheets for the beds of the maid and the indentured servant. A warming pan bears silent testimony to the cold of the winter season. Another bedstead valued at only three shillings may have been in the garret and occupied by Ann Towle, the maid. A chest stood in the kitchen—more generally spoken of at that time as "the hall," in accordance with the English usage—and two boxes, probably used for storage and also for seats. That was all the furniture listed in the kitchen that was considered of any value. The tables, stools, benches, shelving, or other furnishings seemingly necessary to housekeeping at that time either did not exist or were so crude in construction as to have little or no value in estimating the estate. We find five cushions, however, valued at fifteen shillings.

Mrs. Dillingham died possessed of a few really fine furnishings—possibly treasured ancestral pieces—for she bequeathed a silver bowl to the wife of Richard Saltonstall, and to the wife of John Appleton she gave a silver porringer. It would be extremely interesting today to know what has become of these two pieces of Colonial silver. No other silver is mentioned but on shelving in the kitchen rested 40½ pounds of pewter valued at £2. 14. 0. As a pewter plate of the time weighs nearly two pounds and a platter much more the supply of pewter for the table was not large. Wooden plates, trenchers, and bowls are not mentioned, but there were twenty-five pewter saucers, six porringers, seven spoons, and five shillings worth of knives. As for table forks, they were practically unknown in the Colony at that time. Governor Winthrop brought over a fork in 1630, carefully preserved in a case, which is supposed to be the first and only table fork in the Colony in the earliest days of the settlements. Knives, spoons, and fingers, with plenty of napery, met the demands of table manners in the seventeenth century.

The large fireplace in the kitchen had its usual equipment of pot-hooks, fire shovel and tongs, gridiron, trivet, and bellows, and[35] beside it was an old dark lantern valued at only two shillings. There were iron pots, kettles, skillets and ladles; a brass pot and a mortar. There was a frying-pan with a hole in it and in a box were kept "bullets, hinges and other smale things." Two beer vessels were listed; a case of bottles, two jugs, three pans, a tray, and two baskets. Such was the simple equipment of the Dillingham kitchen. There were plenty of table-cloths and napkins but no curtains at any of the windows. If a broom were used it probably was made of birch twigs bound together around a long handle. Candlesticks do not appear in the inventory and the only store of food mentioned (aside from twenty-one new cheeses valued at £2. 16. 0.) was seven bushels of rye, two firkins and a half of butter, a half bushel of malt, six pounds of raisins, and some spice. Our ancestors had a highly developed appreciation of the value of condiments. In a Salem inventory at a somewhat later date appear salt, pepper, ginger, cloves, mace, cinnamon, nutmegs, and allspice.

Mrs. Dillingham's wearing apparel unfortunately is not listed item by item, but given a total value of £5. 8. 4. Her linen amounted to an almost equal sum. Some of her deceased husband's clothing is included in the inventory, such as a coat with silver buttons, a red waistcoat, a suit of serge and a black suit of serge unmade, a jacket of cloth, and an old suit and cloak. Little Sara Dillingham, the orphaned child, when sent to school to goodwife Symonds was supplied with "a stuffe petticoat & waskote" and four "shifts with shewes"; also a gown that cost £2. 10s. Perhaps after a time she may have been able to read and fully appreciate the books formerly in her loving father's chest. They were: "Perkins works in 3 volumes, Seaven Treatises bound in 2 volumes, the Spowse Royall, the bruised reade, & a little new testament."

Six years later, in 1642, there died in the same town, Richard Lumpkin, who had emigrated from Boxted, in Essex, and became an influential citizen in the new town in the new county of Essex. He was elected a representative to the Great and General Court and was deacon of the Ipswich church at the time of his death. He left an estate valued at £300. In the hall of his house stood a long[36] table, with two forms and a stool beside it, having a total value of only fifteen shillings. The hall also contained three chairs and six cushions valued at four shillings. That was all the furniture in the room that was of any value. There were books, however, valued at

£2. 10. 0., a musket and a fowling piece and other small furnishings. In the parlor was a table with six joined stools, three chairs and eight cushions, a bedstead, and a trundle bed with curtains, and a chest, the latter valued at only four shillings. In the chamber over the parlor was a bedstead with its trundle bed, a table valued at three shillings, four chests and two boxes; not a chair or stool is named in connection with the room. The kitchen was in the leanto and while it contained a good supply of brass and iron pots and kettles and also pewter dishes, the table, bench, stools and wooden plates, etc., that must have been in the room were of so little value that they do not appear in the inventory.

It is when we meet with joined and wainscot chests and court, livery, and standing cupboards that we find pieces that may have been brought from overseas. When Mr. Thomas Millard of Newbury (note the title of honor), died in 1653, he possessed a wainscot cupboard, table, chairs and stools. He also left behind him three silver spoons, a silver cup, and a silver salt seller, and among the kitchen utensils were tinned pudding pans, a brazen chaffing dish and a lanthorn and lamp made of latin ware.

The widow of the Rev. Jose Glover married, in 1641, Henry Dunster, President of Harvard College. Among the furnishings of her house were "eleven featherbeds or downe ... one of them haveing philop and Cheny curtaines in graine with a deep silke fringe on the vallance, and a smaller on the Curtaines, and a Coverlett sutable to it, made of Red Kersie, and laced with a greene lace, round the sides and 2 downe the middle, also ... an outlandish quilt, also to another a blue serdge suite very rich and costly, curtaines and valances laced, and fringe, and a blue Rug to the bed, also a greene sute in the same manner, also another red wrought suite, with a sheet and all things Compleate, also a Canopie bed, with Curtenes, a Chest of Drawers of part of this Chest was filled[37] with rich lenen a dammeske suite seuerall diepere suits a fine hollen[d] suit with a stech: with abundance of flaxen linen for Common use, in another parte of the chest of drawers tape, tafety for Chaire and Stooles ... also 29 siluer spones a very faire salt with 3 full knops on the top of it[22] 3 other siluer salts of lesser sorts a great siluer trunke with 4 knop to stand on the table and with suger: 6 porrengers, one small one: 3 bere boules 4 wine cups a siluer grate with a Couer on it: 6 siluer trencher plates: also blankets and Coverletts and Rugs euery[way] Compleat to furnish so many beds."[23]

By way of contrast let us glance at the inventory of the possessions of William Googe of Lynn, who died in 1646, ten years after Mrs. Dillingham had willed that her body be "decently buyried" and her child "religiously educated if God give it life." Googe left a house and twelve acres of land and the total value of his possessions amounted to but £28. 11. 7, with debts of £4. 9. 7. He left a widow and three small children, and though dying in very lowly circumstances he may have known better times, for John Mascoll, the servant of Mr. Googe of Lynn, was fined in 1643, for neglecting the watch. The title of honor, "Mr.," was used but sparingly in those early days and usually indicated a degree of social standing in the community.

Googe had been a soldier, for among his personal belongings at death were a sword and belt, a musket and bandoleers, and also gunpowder. One cow and four hogs comprised his entire livestock, and five bushels of wheat, ten bushels of Indian corn, and flax in the bundle lay in the garret of his house, which was frugally furnished with a chest, a chair, an old chair, a stool, and a trunk. The family probably slept on pallet beds made up on the floor, for bedding is listed but no bedsteads. They had a frying pan, a gridiron, a skillet, a posnet, an earthen pot, six spoons, and the following woodenware, viz.: "3 wood trayes & 3 wood boules & 3 wood dishes, 1s. 9d.; one runlitt, 1s.; paieles & tubs, 3s." Two bags valued at two shillings bring to a close the list of the earthly possessions[38] of William Googe of Lynn. When the inventory was brought into court it very properly gave the goods to the widow "for the bringing up of her three small children." So reads the record.

Doubtless there were many families in the Colony little better conditioned, judging from the relatively small number of estates settled through the courts when compared with the deaths and estimated population.

Googe's house and twelve acres of land were valued at only £8. This must have been a very simple, thatch-roofed house of not more than two rooms, comparable with the outlying farmhouse of Jacob Perkins that was burned in Ipswich in 1668. And thereby hangs a tale. Master Perkins and his wife had gone to town one summer afternoon leaving the house in charge of Mehitable Brabrooke, a sixteen-year-old serving maid. We will let the ancient document in the court files relate what happened.

"About 2 or 3 aclocke in the afternoone she was taking tobacco in a pipe and went out of the house with her pipe and gott upon the oven on the outside & backside of the house (to looke if there were any hogs in the corne) and she layed her right hand upon the thatch of the house (to stay herselfe) and with her left hand knocked out her pipe over her right arme upon the thatch on the eaves of the house (not thinking there had been any fire in the pipe) and imediately went downe into the corne feild to drive out the hogs she saw in it, and as she was going toward the railes of the feild ... she looked back, and saw a smoke upon her Mistress' house in the place where she had knocked out her pipe at which shee was much frighted."[24]

The wife of a neighbor came running to the assistance of Mehitable and afterwards testified that when she reached the house she looked into both fireplaces and saw no appearance of fire, only a few brands nearly dead under a great kettle hanging in the chimney. She also looked up into the chamber through the floor boards that lay very open on the side where the smoke was.

Could photographs more vividly picture the scene? The thatch-roofed[39] farmhouse had two rooms on the ground floor and a chimney with two fireplaces. An oven was built on the backside probably having an opening inside the kitchen fireplace in the usual manner. The house was of but one story judging from the low roof that the maid was able to reach when standing on the oven, and the floor of the chamber in the loft had wide cracks between the boards so that it was possible to look through from below and see the under side of the roof. In similar homes lived many a family in the early days in comparative comfort.

As for the careless Mehitable, she was brought before the Quarterly Court on suspicion of wilfully setting the house on fire; a serious offence, which as late as 1821, was the cause of the execution in Salem of a sixteen-year-old boy. Among those who deposed at her trial was a young man who said that as he and she were going into the meadow, before the fire, to make hay, she told him that her mistress was angry with her, but she had "fitted her now" for she had put a great toad into her kettle of milk. As it turned out the Court ordered Mehitable to be severely whipped and to pay £40 damages to her master Jacob Perkins. It now seems incredible that a serving maid of 1668 could ever get together so large a sum of money.

The settlers in the New England Colonies, unless persons of wealth or possessed of large families, during the early years lived generally in houses having but one room and an entry-way on the ground floor. Above would be a chamber—sometimes only a garret. As the family increased in size and became more prosperous another room would be added to the house on the other side of the entry and chimney, making the structure a so-called two-room house. Still later, with the need for more room, a leanto would be built on the back of the house, thereby supplying three additional rooms on the ground floor with a kitchen in the middle. The earlier kitchen would then become a living-room or "sitting room"—in the New England phrase. This earlier kitchen was usually called "the hall" during the seventeenth century and in it centered the life of the family. It was the room where the food was cooked and eaten.[40] There the family sat and there the indoor work was carried on. A loom sometimes occupied considerable space near a window and frequently a bed was made up in a corner, on which the father of the family slept, and there sometimes also he died.

The principal feature of this common room was its huge fireplace in which hung pots and kettles suspended by means of pot chains and trammels from the hardwood trammel-bar or lug-pole that rested on wooden cross bars and so bisected the wide flue in the chimney. These large fireplaces in the early days were sometimes called "chimneys" in the vernacular of the time. They were generally as wide as eight feet and a ten foot opening is not unknown.

This cavernous opening was spanned by a wooden lintel—a stick of timber sometimes sixteen inches or more square, and when exposed to a roaring fire, piled high with logs, this became an element of danger, the charring wood smoldering all night and setting fire to the house. The trammel-bar in the flue also caught fire not infrequently and gave way, allowing the pots and kettles to fall to the hearth, bringing disaster to the dinner or to the curdling milk and sometimes to those seated near. A trammel stick in the house of Captain Denney gave way from this cause and a large kettle filled with wort[25] fell down and spilt the boiling liquid over four of his children who were sitting or lying on the hearth, some of them asleep, "which scalded them in so terrible a manner, that one died presently after, and another's life is dispaired of" continues the record.

"Here is good living for those who love good fires," wrote Higginson in his *New-Englands Plantation*, and under the spell of the glowing flames, the bare, whitewashed walls, the brown timbers and floor boards of the ceiling, the dress of pewter, and the simple furnishings of the room, enriched by the shadows, became a place full of cheer—a place where privation and homesickness might be forgotten in the glow of the bright firelight. On cold nights the short bench inside the fireplace was a chosen place and the settle, a[41] long seat made of boards with a high back to keep off the draft, was drawn before the fire and here sat the older members of the family.

The larger kettles hanging in the fireplace, were of brass and copper and some of them were of prodigious size. Hot water was always to be had and these kettles also served for the daily cooking, the cheese-making, soap-boiling, and candle-dipping.

Much of the food of the average New Englander until comparatively recent times consisted of corn-meal, boiled meats and vegetables and stews. Every well-equipped household had its spits for roasting and many had gridirons, but the usual diet of the average family was "hasty pudding"—cornmeal mush and milk—varied by boiled meat or fish served in the center of a large pewter platter and surrounded by boiled vegetables. Baked beans and stewed beans appeared on the table several times every week in the year. Indian bannock, made by mixing corn meal with water and spreading it an inch thick on a small board placed at an incline before the fire and so baked, was a common form of bread. When mixed with rye meal it became brown bread and was baked in the brick oven with the beans and peas.

The brick oven was a feature of every chimney. Sometimes in early days it was built partly outside the house but so far as known the opening was always in the kitchen fireplace. To reach it the housewife must stoop below the oaken lintel and stand inside the fireplace, taking care that her woolen skirts did not come near the flames. To heat it for a baking, a fire was built inside, usually with specially prepared pine or birch wood that had been split and seasoned out of doors for a short time and then housed. The fire and ashes were then taken out by means of a peel—a long-handled, flat-bladed shovel made for the purpose—and when dusted out with a broom made of hemlock twigs it was ready for the brown bread, beans, peas, Indian pudding, pies, and rye drop cakes which were made with rye meal, eggs and milk and baked directly on the bricks in the bottom of the oven.

Between the years of 1635 and 1655, court records and inventories[42] of estates in the Massachusetts Bay Colony mention the following articles of food:

Bacon, beef, butter, cheese, eggs, fowls, lamb, milk, mutton, pork, suet, veal, wild game, and cod, herring, mackerel, salmon and sturgeon.

Barley, beans, Indian beans, bran, cabbages, carrots, chaff, corn, English corn, Indian corn, hops, Indian meal, rye meal, oatmeal, oats, parsnips, peas, pumpions, rye, squashes, turnips and wheat.

Apples, berries, fruit, honey, raisins, sugar and vinegar.

Biscuit, blewlman, bread, cake, malt, salad oil, porridge, rye malt, yeast, salt and many kinds of spices.

Much of this food was raised on the farm and nearly every family had its garden. Such articles of food as were imported were usually obtained at the shops in the larger towns by barter, as money was scarce. In 1651, a farmer came through the woods to Salem in his cart bringing twelve bushels of rye. He stopped at a shop owned by George Corwin and from the daybook kept at the time and still carefully preserved, we learn that among other necessaries he carried home sugar for the goodwife, and for the children a doll and a bird whistle.

In the early years domestic animals were too valuable to be killed for meat but game was plentiful and was roasted by being trussed on iron spits resting on curved brackets on the backs of the andirons. This, of course, required constant turning to expose the roast on all sides in order to cook it evenly—a task frequently delegated to a child. A skillet would be placed beneath to catch the drippings. Sometimes a bird was suspended before the fire by a twisted cord that would slowly unwind and partly wind again, requiring some one in frequent attendance to twist the cord. Families of wealth possessed a "jack" to turn the spit. This was a mechanism fastened over the fireplace and connected with the spit by means of a pulley and cord. A heavy weight suspended by a cord which slowly unwound, supplied the power that turned the spit.

In "the hall," usually upon open shelves, but sometimes upon a dresser, was displayed the pride of the housewife—the dress of[43] pewter and latten ware. "China dishes," imported by the East India Company or made in Holland, were used sparingly during the early years of the colonies. There was much earthenware and stoneware bottles and jugs, but it was wooden ware and pewter that were commonly used. When Lionel Chute died in 1645 he bequeathed his silver spoon to his son James.[26] It was the only piece of silver in the house. Of pewter he died possessed of fourteen dishes "small and great," eleven pewter salts, saucers and porringers, two pewter candlesticks and a pewter bottle. The widow Rebecca Bacon who died in Salem in 1655, left an estate of £195. 8. 6., which included a well-furnished house. She had brass pots, skillets, candlesticks, skimmers, a little brass pan, and an excellent supply of pewter including "3 large pewter platters, 3 a size lesse, 3 more a size lesse, 3 more a size lesse," having a total value of £1.16. She also had a pewter basin, six large pewter plates, and six lesser, nineteen pewter saucers, two fruit dishes, an old basin and a great plate, two candlesticks, one large salt and a small one, two porringers, a great flagon, one lesser, one quart, two pints and a half pint; and an old porringer. She also left "1 silver duble salt, 6 silver spoones, wine cup & a dram cup of silver."

Giles Badger of Newbury left to his young widow, a glass bowl, beaker, and jug valued at three shillings; three silver spoons valued at £1, and a good assortment of pewter, including "a salt seller, a tunell and a great dowruff." The household was also furnished with six wooden dishes and two wooden platters. In other inventories appear unusual items such as a pewter brim basin, pewter cullenders, pewter beer cups, pans, and mustard pots. Pewter tankards were common. There were new and old fashioned candlesticks. Pewter salts came in three sizes and the saucers were both small and large. In 1693, best London pewter plates cost the Boston shopkeepers 9½ pence per pound in quantity.

The seventeenth century "hall" must have had little spare room for its daily occupants, for in addition to its table and chairs, its settle, stools and washbench, the long ago inventories disclose such[44] chattels as powdering tubs in which the salted meats were kept, the churn, barrels containing a great variety of things, keelers and buckets, bucking tubs for washing, and the various implements used in spinning and weaving, washing and ironing, cooking and brewing, and the making of butter and cheese. In the chimney hung hams and bacon and suspended from the ceiling were strings of dried apples and hands of seed corn.

It is claimed by some that the floors were sanded. That certainly was true at a later period but there are strong elements of doubt as to the prevalence of this custom during the seventeenth century. Sand, however, was used freely with home-made soft soap, to scrub the floors which were always kept white and clean, and whenever an early house is restored or taken down sand is always found, sometimes in considerable quantity, where it has sifted down through the cracks between the floor boards. The downstairs rooms had double floors but the chamber floors were made of one thickness of boards with here and there a knothole and frequently with cracks between the boards through which the dust and dirt from above must have sifted down upon the heads of those seated at dinner or engaged in their daily tasks in the rooms below. Not only does the structural evidence show this to be true but a number of instances occur among the papers in Court files, where witnesses have deposed as to what they had seen and heard through the cracks in chamber floors. A grandson of Governor Endecott once fell a victim of two gossiping sixteen-year-old girls who had spent some time on their knees peeping through the cracks in a chamber floor. Capt. Richard More, the last survivor of the company on the *Mayflower*, late in life kept a tavern in Salem. He was spied upon in this manner and eventually brought before the justices of the Quarterly Court to answer for his evasion of the law set forth and maintained at that time.

The parlor, called "the foreroom" at a later time, was the room where guests of station were received. The best bed hung with curtains and valance and covered with a rug, stood in a corner. In those days rugs were not used on floors but as bed furnishings.[45] Even the baby's cradle had its rug. Carpets, likewise, were too fine for wooden floors and were used as table covers. Of bedsteads there were many kinds—high and low, canopy, close, corded, half-headed, joined, side, standing, inlaid, and wainscot, and slipped under the higher bedsteads during the daytime, were trundle or "truckle" beds in which the children slept at night. Lionel Chute, the schoolmaster, had an "old darnkell coverlet" on his bed while some of his neighbors possessed branched and embroidered coverlets and several had coverlets made of tapestry.

Among the better families the parlor and chamber windows had curtains hung from rods or cords. In the parlor stood chests in which were stored the family clothing and bedding, for closets did not exist in the seventeenth century house. There were great chests and small chests, long boarded and great boarded chests, chests with a drawer, carved chests, wainscot chests, trunks, and boxes. A few stools and chairs, a looking-glass, a small table, and perhaps a cupboard completed the furnishings of the well-supplied parlor. In Capt. George Corwin's best room there were chairs with leather bottoms and straw bottoms, a clock valued at £2, a screen having five leaves, a napkin press, and a "Scriture or Spice box." White calico curtains hung at his chamber windows and the maid had a "Calico Cuberd cloth" in her room. Parlor walls were whitewashed and bare of ornament. The first families owned a portrait or two in oils and here and there a map in unglazed frame decorated a wall. The Puritan character did not warm to the fine arts and austere living was the aim if not always the achievement of the time.

The chambers in the second story must have been curiously furnished rooms, containing a huddle of stores of all descriptions. Henry Short, the town clerk of Newbury, died in 1673 leaving a goodly estate valued at nearly £2,000.[27] He owned a negro slave and his house was large and well furnished. There was an old parlor and a new parlor containing beds, chests, chairs, trunks, and boxes. In the chamber over the new parlor there was a good feather-bed and bed clothing but no bedstead. Wool and yarn were stored[46] in this room together with boxes, tubs, some feathers, and miscellaneous "lumber"—the phrase of the period for odds and ends. The chamber over the kitchen, a comfortable room of course, in winter, had its bed and bedding, also "5 hogsheds, 6 barrels, 5 Iron hoopes, a pair of stockcards, meale trough & other lumber, a parcell of old Iron, a pike, a bed cord & other cordage." Small wonder in such a clutter that the rooms frequently had other tenantry than the human occupants.

When Jasper Dankers arrived in Boston in 1680, the captain of the packet took him to his sister's house where he lodged. "We were taken to a fine large chamber," he writes, "but we were hardly in bed before we were shockingly bitten. I did not know the cause, but was not able to sleep.... My comrade who was very sleepy, fell asleep at first. He tumbled about very much; but I did not sleep any the whole night. In the morning we saw how it was, and were astonished we should find such a room with such a lady."[28]

Early in the eighteenth century the walls of rooms in some Massachusetts houses began to be covered with "painted paper" hangings imported from England. These *papier paints* were first introduced into England, from France, about 1634, and probably were brought into New England by Governor Andros and his followers. Michael Perry, a Boston bookseller, who died in 1700, had in his stock "7 quires of painted paper and three reams of painted paper." His successor, Daniel Henchman, dealt in painted papers as appears from his account books commencing in 1712. In 1713 two quires of painted paper cost four shillings, and two quires of blue paper, three shillings. In 1714, Isaac Thomas of Pembroke paid £2. 10. 0 for "6 Rowls Paint'd Pap'r & 2 Q'r Paper."

When Peter Sergeant of Boston died in 1714, the inventory of his estate disclosed "one large gilt looking glass, in the cedar room, £5. One suit of Imagery Tapestry hanging, £20. One suit of red china £5." Two years later the house was purchased by the Provincial Government for a governor's residence and in 1741 we find the Provincial Treasurer paying Daniel Henchman £5. 8. 0. for[47] four rolls of painted paper and shortly another bill was presented for "New Tacking the paper hanging above in the chamber & new papering one roome below stairs."

In 1734, John Maverick, shopkeeper, bought of Henchman, four quires and five sheets of painted paper for £1. 3. 9. In 1736, Colonel Estes Hatch bought 10 rolls painted paper for £16. 5. 0. which was probably used in his mansion in Dorchester, bought after the Revolution by Colonel James Swan.

The painted paper of the eighteenth century was sold at first in sheets, 22 by 32 inches, called elephant size. Later these were pasted together to make 12 yard lengths. In the earlier stages of manufacture the designs were colored by hand. Stencils of pasteboard were used, and in the last half of the eighteenth century blocks of pear and sycamore wood were used, as in calico printing. One who painted coats of arms and other things pertaining to heraldry, as well as one who painted or stained linen cloth, was known as a "painter stainer." So, also, those who stained colored or stamped paper for hangings were known as "paper stainers."

When Thomas Hancock built his house on Beacon Hill he desired painted paper for some of his rooms. Extracts from his letter to John Rowe, stationer, London, explain his wants:

"Sir: Inclosed you have the Dimensions of a Room for a shaded Hanging to be Done after the same Pattern I have sent per Capt. Tanner. The pattern is all that was left of a Room lately come over here, and it takes much in ye Town and will be the only paper-hanging for sale here which am of opinion may Answer well.... If they can make it more beautiful by adding more Birds flying here and there, with some Landskips at the Bottom, Should like it well. Let the Ground be the same colour of the Pattern. At the top and bottom was a narrow Border of about 2 inches wide which would have to mine....

"A hanging done much handsomer sent over three or four years previous was made by Dunbar in Aldermanbury....

"In other of these Hangings are great variety of different Sorts of Birds, Peacocks, Macoys, Squirrill, Monkys, Fruit and Flowers,[48] etc.... I think they are handsomer and better than Painted hangings done in Oyle so I beg your particular Care in procuring this for me and that the patterns may be taken care off and Return'd with my Goods."—*Letter of Thomas Hancock to John Rowe, Stationer, in London*, Jan. 23, 1737/8.

In the eighteenth-century Boston newspapers may be found numerous items showing the use of wall paper and the fact that it frequently was imported from England. But while it is true that it could be purchased in the shops in Boston it does not follow that rooms in every house were papered. Nor is it likely that the rooms of houses in the country had papered walls save when the owner was a wealthy man. London fashions would first be found transplanted into the seaport towns and later would be adopted by the country. Undoubtedly the home of the Governor, or of some well-to-do sea captain, was the first house to be so decorated. On September 22, 1762, died Daniel Starr of Boston, "who has been for many years employed in Papering Rooms." This item appears in the news items of the *Boston News-Letter*. Eight years later the same newspaper prints the following advertisement:

"George Killcup, jun. Informs the Gentlemen and Ladies in Town and Country That he Paints Carpets & other Articles, and Paper Rooms in the neatest manner. He will take English or West India Goods as Pay.

"Said Killcup is ready to pay those he is indebted to, in Painting or Papering Rooms."—*Boston News-Letter*, March 17, 1768.

"Roll Paper for Rooms," with "most sorts of Stationary Ware" were advertised for sale by John Parker, over against the shop of Mr. Dolbeare, Brazier, at the Head of the Town Dock, Boston.—*Boston News-Letter*, June 3-10, 1736.

J. Boydell, the printer of the *Boston Gazette*, advertised in November, 1736, a house in Boston, to be sold, in which two chambers in the first story were "hung with Scotch Tapestry, the other Green Cheny."

John Phillips, bookseller, advertised "Stampt Paper in Rolls for to Paper Rooms," in the October 26, 1730, issue of the *New England Journal*.

[49]

"Sundry sorts of Painted Paper for Rooms" were to be sold at public vendue at the Exchange Tavern in King Street, with other importations.—*New-England Journal*, August 29, 1738.

"Flowered Paper, or Paper Hangings for Rooms, to be Sold; Inquire of the Printer."—*Boston Gazette*, February 2, 1742.

"Beautiful Arras-Hangings for a Room" to be sold at vendue.[29]— *Boston News-Letter*, August 22, 1745.

Against the earlier background of whitewashed walls hung few decorations. Between 1635 and 1681 there were 960 estates probated in Essex County, Massachusetts. The county had several seaport towns and its inhabitants were more prosperous than many other parts of the Colony. In the inventories of these 960 estates, pictures are listed but eight times and maps were found in but three homes. William Hollingsworth, the shipbuilder and merchant of Salem, possessed seven framed pictures. They are the only *framed* pictures mentioned. Hilliard Veren of Salem, who died in 1668, had three pictures in his hall chamber and Robert Gray of the same town had in his parlor a large looking-glass with some earthen dishes and a picture, the whole valued at £2. The Rev. Nathaniel Rogers of Ipswich, had two pictures in his parlor and Thomas Wells of Ipswich, bequeathed to his son Thomas, the new pictures of the King and Queen and the one of the "five sencces." He also possessed maps and paper pictures.

Fifty years later John Smibert, the portrait painter, had his shop "at his House in Queen Street, between the Town House and the Orange Tree, Boston," where he sold "all sorts of Colours, dry or ground with Oyls and Brushes, Fans of several sorts, the best Mezotints, Italian, French, Dutch and English Prints, in Frames and Glasses or without, by Wholesale or Retail, at Reasonable Rates." About the same time the "Royal Waxwork" was to be seen at the House of Mr. Thomas Brooks, shopkeeper, near the Draw Bridge, and Thomas White, the engraver, was living in a house not far away.

[50]

Here are a few advertisements from early newspapers bearing on furnishing the house:

BED HANGINGS. To be sold by Mrs. Susanna Condy, near the Old North Meeting House, a fine Fustian Suit of Curtains, with a Cornish and Base Mouldings of a beautiful Figure, drawn in London, on Frame full already worked; as also enough of the same for half a dozen Chairs. N.B. The Bed may be had by itself.—*Boston Gazette*, May 24-31, 1736.

BED-SCREWS. Mr. *John Barnard* of Boston, having some time since Lent a Pair of large Bed-screws. These are desiring the Borrower to return them again to the owner, as he desires to Borrow again, to avoid the Curse due to the Wicked, that Borrow but never Pay.— *Boston News-Letter*, Oct. 22-29, 1716.

BEDSTEAD. A Coach-head Bed and Bedstead with its Curtains and Vallents, &c., as it stands, being a blew China. To be disposed off. Inquire of the Printer.—*Boston Gazette*, June 16-23, 1735.

CANOPIE BEDS. A Couple of very good Cannopie Beds lately come from England to be Sold on reasonable terms, by Rupert Lord Upholsterer and to be seen at Mr. Ramies House in Corn-Hill the next door to the Post-office, Boston.—*Boston News-Letter*, Jan. 4-11, 1713-14.

MOHAIR BED. To be Sold reasonably for ready money, or on good Security, a yellow Mohair Bed lined with a Persian of the same Colour, and six Chairs of the same Mohair, little the worse for wear. Inquire of J. Boydell.—*Boston Gazette*, Oct. 17-24, 1737.

PRESS BED. A Very good Press-Case for a Bed, to be Sold. Enquire of the Printer.—*Boston News-Letter*, Oct. 28-Nov. 4, 1736.

CARPETS. Just imported from London, in the last ships and to be sold at Mr. Blanchard's in New Boston West End; a large assortment of fine Carpets for Rooms, very cheap for ready Cash.—*Boston Gazette*, Jan. 22, 1759.

PUBLICK VENDUE. At 5'o'Clock in the Afternoon will be sold by T. Fleet, at the Heart and Crown, in Cornhill,—Bedding, Several Suits of Curtains and Bedsteads, a fine new Silk Damask Quilt[51] and Quilted Cushions of the same, Black Walnut Chest of Drawers and Desk, Brass Candlesticks, Iron Dogs, sundry Suits of wearing apparel for men, new Castor Hats, China Ware, Rummolds, Druggets....—*Boston News-Letter*, May 18-25, 1732.

HOUSEHOLD FURNISHINGS. This Afternoon at 3 o'clock will be Sold by Publick Vendue, by Daniel Goffe, at the Dwelling House of Mr. Jonathan Barnard, over against the Town-House in Cornhill, sundry sorts of Household Goods, consisting of Beds, Bedding, a Couch, Chairs, handsome Japan'd Tea Tables, Walnut and Mahogany Tables, Chest of Drawers, Peer Glasses, Sconces, Glass Arms, China Ware, Metzotinto and other Prints, several valuable large Pieces of Paintings, one handsome large Carpet 9 Foot 6 Inches by 6 Foot 6 Inches, a fashionable yellow Camblet Bed lin'd with Satten, a great easy Chair and Window Curtains, suitable for a Room, a Field Bedstead and Bed, the covering a Blew Harrateen, Kitchen Furniture, as Pewter of the best sort, Copper, Brass and Iron, a parcel of Books and some Shop Goods.—*Boston News-Letter*, May 8-15, 1735.

FURNITURE AT AUCTION. To be sold by Auction, Household Furniture of the late Mr. Pyam Blowers, including: Fine Sconce Glasses, large Looking Glasses, Leather Bottom Chairs, sundry Mehogany and other Tables, a good Couch Squab and Pillow, a very handsome Yellow Damask Bed, an Easy Chair, a neat case of Drawers, ... two Silver watches, sundry sorts of good China Ware, etc.—*Boston News-Letter*, May 17-24, 1739.

FURNITURE AT AUCTION. To be Sold by Publick Vendue on Monday next at 3 o'Clock, Afternoon, at the House of Charles Paxton, Esq., the following Goods, viz.: A fashionable crimson Damask Furniture with Counterpain and two Sets of Window Curtains, and Vallans of the same Damask. Eight Walnut Tree Chairs, stuft Back and Seats covered with the same Damask, Eight crimson China Cases for ditto, one easy Chair and Cushion, same Damask, and Case for ditto. Twelve Walnut Tree chairs, India Backs, finest Cane, and sundry other valuable Household Furniture.—*Boston News-Letter*, Jan. 9, 1746.

[52]

FURNITURE. To be Sold, a crimson Harrateen Coach-Bed, Bedstead, and Feather-bed, six small chairs, and one two-arm Chair, with crimson Harrateen Seats, a Table, and two small Pictures, Enquire of the Printer.—*Boston News-Letter*, June 25, 1747.

HAND BOARDS. Lately arrived from London, & are to be Sold by Giles Dulake Tidmarsh at his Warehouse No. 4 on the Long Wharfe, Five Dutch Tea Tables, as Hand Boards and Looking Glasses, new Fashion.—*Boston Gazette*, Nov. 19-26, 1722.

LEONARD HOUSE, RAYNHAM, MASS.

This shows typical front-gabled roof and two-story porch

Tradition relates that King Philip's head was deposited in this house in 1676

Printed from the original wood block engraved in 1838

[53]

CHAPTER IV

COUNTERPANES AND COVERLETS

In the early days our forefathers were dependent upon the open fireplace and during the winter season everyone must wear thick clothing and provide an ample supply of warm coverings for the beds. Those were the days of warming pans and heated bricks taken to bed by both children and grown-ups, and of feather beds, comforters and patchwork quilts.

Bed coverings in the olden times, and even in our day, have a variety of names with distinctions sometimes difficult to classify. Sometimes they are counterpanes, and again coverlets. A *comforter* suggests warmth and comfort not only for the bed but for the neck. The *bed cover* is universal as is the *quilt*.

The patchwork quilt was formerly one of the most familiar and necessary articles of household furnishing and its origin reaches backward into the dim and unknown past. It was brought to the Massachusetts Bay by the first settlers. In cottage and castle it was known in the days of King John, and down through the generations its making supplied occupation and amusement to countless women whose life interests centered in their homes and household furnishings. Its manufacture may well be styled one of the household arts, for artistic indeed are the bold conceptions of many of the designs; while the piecing and the patching provide ample opportunity for needlework of the finest character.

In the early days the English spelled quilt with a final *e*—quilte—as did the French. It is a cover or coverlet made by stitching together two thicknesses of a fabric with some soft substance between them. This applies to bed covers and also to quilted petticoats so commonly worn in the old days.

What is a coverlet? Originally, any covering for a bed; now, specifically, the outer covering. The word comes from the French *couvre-lit*—a bed covering. The handwoven coverlets of many[54] beautiful designs, in blue and white and red and brown, are well known and formerly were woven everywhere.

The *counter-pane*, formerly a bed cover, now describes a light coverlet woven of cotton with raised figures. The word is a corruption of *counterpoint*, in allusion to the panes or squares of which bed covers are often composed. The counterpane was never quilted.

The *bedspread* and the *bed cover* may be considered as one and the same—the uppermost covering of a bed and accordingly of an ornamental character in general. The *comforter* was a thickly quilted bed cover made of several thicknesses of sheet cotton or wool prepared for the purpose. This was too thick to be quilted so it was knotted at regular intervals to prevent the interlining from slipping out of place. Frequently it was called a "comfort."

There is one other name that was applied to a bed covering in the Colonial times but which is never heard today in that connection. In the days immediately following the settlement many a New England bed was covered with a *rug*. When William Clarke of Salem died in 1647, in the parlor of his house was a bed with a green rug covering it which was valued by the appraisers at fourteen shillings. The term was commonly in use at the time, in fact, as commonly as the word coverlet. In the probate of Essex County, Massachusetts, estates between the years 1635 and 1674, coverlets are mentioned one hundred and forty-two times and rugs one hundred and fifty-seven times while quilts are listed only four times. These early bed rugs were usually thick woolen coverings with a shaggy nap.

A never-failing source of accurate information as to the furnishings and equipment of the New England household in the olden time is the probate records—specifically, the inventory of the property taken in connection with the settlement of the estate. For many years it was the well-nigh universal custom to list, room by room, the contents of a house and from these painstaking inventories it now becomes possible to reconstruct in mental picture the interiors of those homes where lived and died our Puritan ancestors. In connection with the present subject we learn from these inventories[55] that it was quite the usual habit to set up a bed in the parlor and we also learn of the existence of different kinds of rugs used in the bed furnishings—cotton rugs, English rugs, Irish rugs, cradle rugs, etc. There were worsted coverlets, tapestry coverlets and embroidered coverlets. A darnacle coverlet is listed in 1665; but as darnacle curtains appear in the same inventory it is safe to assume that darnacle is the name of some long-forgotten fabric. But what is a "branched coverlet?" Mrs. Thomas Newhall of Lynn possessed in 1674 a green rug and a branched coverlet.

Capt. George Corwin of Salem who died in 1684, had a calico counterpane in the red chamber in his house. In the corner chamber was a green counterpane and in the kitchen chamber was a sad colored counterpane, two coverlets, and a quilt of colored and flowered calico.

Let us have a look at a few of these wills and inventories. In 1640, the widow Bethia Cartwright of Salem, bequeathed to her sister, then living in England, her bed, bolster, blanket and coverlet. It is an open question if the value of the property equalled the probable cost of transporting it to that loving sister in distant England.

Mrs. Joanna Cummings of Salem, at her death in 1644, among many other items possessed a feather bed, flock bolster and a green rug, jointly valued at £2. 5. 0.

In the "hall" of John Goffe's house, in Newbury, in 1641, were found "3 bedsteeds, £1; 1 pr. curtains with 3 rods, 18s.; 1 green rugg, £1. 6.; 2 blankets, 15 s.; 1 bed, bolster and 4 pillows, £4. 10.; 1 coverlet, 10s.; and 1 bed matt, 2s."

The next year William Howard, afterwards the first town clerk of Topsfield, was one of the appraisers of the estate of Samuel Smith of Enon, the name by which Wenham was then known. In one of the chambers he found a "bed, blancits & coverlet" which he valued at £7. 8. Rather a valuable bed, or, may it have been the coverlet? In connection with "cobbard clothes" at £1. he lists a "carpitt" at 15s; and this carpet, curiously enough, he did not find on the floor but on a table. Joanna Cummings owned a "carpet & table" that were[56] valued at 7s. 8d. Joseph Metcalf of Ipswich had "a table & old carpett" worth £1. In the parlor of Governor Endecott's house in Boston were found a "Table, Carpet & 3 stools," valued at 50s. William Bacon's "carpets & qushens" were worth £1. 10s. and in the inventory of the estate of Rev. Ezekiel Rogers of Rowley, appears the following: "a presse and a litle Table with ther Carpets, £1. 10s."

John Whittingham lived in Ipswich and died in 1648. In the parlor of his house was found a "Joyne Table with Five chairs & one ould Carpet, 10s.; one cupboard and Cloth, 10s.; 2 paire Cobirons, 15s.; two window Curtains and curtaine rods, 6s.; one case of Bottles, 5s.; Books, £6. 5s.; Eleven Cushions, £1. 10s.; one Still, 5s.;" and perhaps most important of all—"one fetherbed, one flockbed, two boulsters, one pillow, one p. blankets, one Rugge, Curtains & valients and bedsted, £12." In the chamber over the parlor was another bedstead well supplied with furnishings, including two quilts, a blue coverlet and a trundle bed. This upstairs chamber had wall hangings which were valued at £2. 10s. and in the room were six trunks, a chest and a box, containing stores of bed linen, table cloths, napkins, hose yarn, silver plate and eleven spoons. Two chairs, four stools, a screen, two pairs of cobirons and a pair of tongs completed the furnishings of the room. It almost stands open before us. And those wall hangings valued at £2. 10s.!

Another parlor chamber in a house in Newbury, in which had lived the minister, the Rev. James Noyes, was more meagerly furnished. Here the appraisers found "2 boxes, 4 hogsheads, a musket and a gun and two swords, £2.; a bolster and a quilt & two blankets and a parsell of Cotton wooll, £3. 10s."

Just one more inventory—the estate of William Clarke who died in 1647 in Salem. The parlor contained a half-headed bedstead with curtains and vallance which was furnished with a feather bed and bolster, a straw bed and flock bolster, white blankets, sheets, and a green rug. In a corner of this parlor stood another bedstead having a mat, canvas flock bed, sheets, old blankets and a red rug, and in the chamber over the kitchen was a low bedstead[57] with a flock bed and bolster, a blanket, a rug and an old quilt.

Here are two kinds of bedsteads mentioned in this house, but there were other kinds in frequent use at the time: high beds and side beds, canopy bedsteads, half-headed, joined, cabin, corded, close, press, standing, truckle and trundle bedsteads and what is strange indeed, not a single example of these early bedsteads has been preserved. All have been worn out or destroyed—supplanted by a newer fashion—and we today can only imagine their various forms and decorations.

In the New England vernacular, materials for quilts were "skurse" in the olden times. The settlers, of course, brought all their furnishings from England and a few years elapsed before wool and flax were produced here in any quantity. Meanwhile all fabrics were imported and paid for by shipments of salt fish, furs, lumber, corn, etc. A brisk trade soon sprang up with the West Indies and Spain and cotton was brought into the New England ports. Some of the fabrics in common use before 1650 have names that sound strangely in our ears. Darnacle has been mentioned. There were baize for jackets, calico for dresses, linsey woolsey for heavy skirts, serge for various articles of clothing, coifing stuff for caps, linen for forehead bands and many other uses, dimity for bed hangings and petticoats, and a fabric known as "barber's stuff." In time some of these materials became available for quilt making and at a still later time the handwoven, home-dyed fabrics were used and some of these were rudely decorated with tied and dipped patterns or stamped and stencilled designs.

It should always be kept in mind, however, that geographical location largely enters into the production and character of the quilt, and the family that was "well-off" of course would be supplied more abundantly with furnishings and be less dependent upon homely makeshifts and the daily practice of household economy. Those living in the seaport towns, where most of the shops were found, would be likely to follow the simplest course of fashion and buy from the stock just imported from England or Holland. The hand loom was found everywhere but more generally[58] in the country. Weaving was a trade for men and so practiced, but many a farmhouse had its loom and every country home its spinning wheel. In the larger towns the dame of social position or comfortable means would devote her spare moments to needlework and embroidery, while in the country the housewives would make pieced quilts or patch the clothing of their numerous children.

It naturally follows, that the handwoven coverlet, should be a product of the country rather than the town and usually of the countryside farthest removed from the influences of the shop and of English goods. Even today it is still woven in the remote settlements of Eastern Kentucky and Tennessee, and judging from existing examples the vogue of the handwoven coverlet was greater in New York, Pennsylvania, Kentucky and the Middle West than in New England although many fine examples were produced here. The manufacture of the patchwork quilt as a domestic art also seems to have reached its highest development in the Middle West during the first half of the nineteenth century.

The patchwork quilt of New England is known as the "pieced quilt" when made in the Middle West and more correctly so, for *to piece* means to join together separate pieces of like material into sections or blocks that in turn are united to form the top of the quilt. The pieces usually are of uniform shape and size and contrasting colors are blended to form the design—usually a geometric pattern. These pieces are sewed "over and over" on the wrong side. To *patch* means to mend or adorn by adding a patch or by laying over a separate piece of cloth. The French word *applique* well describes the patched or laid-on work where the design is cut out and applied or sewed on, in fact, "sewed-on quilts" and "laid quilts" are old terms. This type of quilt is found in New England but infrequently as compared with the "pieced quilt," here commonly known as the "patchwork quilt."

In early times the pieces were nearly always of a woolen fabric, the brighter colored cloth being saved for the more central portions of the design. Every scrap and remnant of material left from the[59] making of garments was saved and the best pieces of worn-out garments were carefully cut out and made into quilt pieces. The historian of the Saco Valley, Maine, relates that a scarlet broadcloth cloak formerly worn by a Lord Mayor of London and brought to Massachusetts by a member of the Merritt family of Salisbury, Mass., after many adventures ended its days as small bits of vivid color in a patchwork quilt made in Maine. Portions of discarded military uniforms, of flannel shirts and well-worn petticoats were utilized and frequently an old blanket would be used for lining.

---

[60]

CHAPTER V

CONCERNING THEIR APPAREL

In 1630 there were differences in dress even more so than at the present time. The simple, coarse clothing of the yeoman and the worker in the various trades was far removed from the dress of the merchant and the magistrate. Leather clothing was very generally worn by laborers and servants as deerskins were cheap and leather had been in common use for jerkins and breeches in Old England, so naturally it was worn here. Stockings were made of a variety of materials and most shoes had wooden heels.

Higher in the social scale men wore doublets and full breeches and clothed themselves as well as their estates permitted—sometimes even better than they could well afford. Sleeves were slashed. Falling bands at the neck were common and a deep linen collar appears in portraits of the period. A beaver or felt hat with steeple crown was worn, and gloves, sometimes elegantly embroidered, were essential. The accepted idea of Puritan dress should be revised and the Victorian standard of sentimental simplicity be discarded. There was great variety of fabrics available in the shops of London and Bristol as will be noted in the list at the end of this chapter, and as wealth permitted probably much of this material eventually found its way to the shelves of the shopkeepers in Boston and other of the larger seaport towns.

The following list of clothing each man should provide himself with on sailing for New England in 1629, when the Rev. Francis Higginson came over, is so specific that we can easily visualize the male company that arrived at Salem that year.

> NOTE. As several excellent books are available that treat exclusively of costume in the colonies, it has not seemed necessary to elaborate on the subject in these pages. The following notes however, are thought to be of interest.

[61]

4 peares of shoes.

4 peares of stockings.

1 peare Norwich gaiters.

4 shirts

2 suits dublet and hose of leather lyn'd with oy'd skin leather, ye hose & dublett with hooks & eyes.

1 suit of Nordon dussens or hampshire kersies lyn'd the hose with skins, dublets with lynen of gilford or gedlyman kerseys.

4 bands

2 handkerchiefs

1 wastecoat of greene cotton bound about with red tape

1 leather girdle

1 Monmouth cap

1 black hatt lyned in the brows with lether

5 Red Knitt capps mill'd about 5d. apiece

2 peares of gloves

1 Mandillion [mantle or great coat] lyned with cotton

1 peare of breeches and waistcoat

1 leather sute of Dublett & breeches of oyled leather

1 peare of leather breeches and drawers to weare with both there other sutes.

Fine clothing surrounded itself with fine furnishings, according to the standards of the period, and as the wealth of the Colony increased with the successful exportation of fish, lumber, beaver, and peltry, it supplied them with all kinds of luxuries and refinements. The ships were crossing frequently and the Colony kept pace with the mother country much as the country follows the city at the present time.

In the town of Ipswich, lived Madam Rebecka Symonds, writing in her sixtieth year to her son in London to send her a fashionable "lawn whiske," for her neckwear. In due time he replied that the "fashionable Lawn whiske is not now worn, either by Gentil or simple, young or old. Instead where of I have bought a shape and ruffles, which is now the ware of the gravest as well as the young ones. Such as goe not with naked necks ware a black wifle over it. Therefore, I have not only Bought a plaine one y't you sent for, but also a Luster one, such as are most in fashion."

The dutiful son also purchased for his mother's wear a feather fan; but he writes to her "I should also have found in my heart, to have let it alone, because none but very grave persons (and of them very few) use it. Now 'tis grown almost as obsolete as Russets, and more rare to be seen than a yellow Hood." When the feather fan reached Ipswich it was found to have a silver handle and with it[62] came "two tortois fans, 200 needles, 5 yds. sky calico, silver gimp, a black sarindin cloak, damson leather skin, two women's Ivorie Knives, etc."[30]

Human nature and human frailities were much the same in the seventeenth century as at the present time, and before long, the magistrates considered it desirable to curb the extravagancies of dress that followed the London mode; and to induce a spirit of economy more fitting to the poverty of a new settlement. The ministers controlled the lawmaking body and sumptuary laws were enacted which are enlightening. Because of "newe and immodest fashions" the wearing of silver, gold and silk laces, girdles and hat bands was prohibited. It was the fashion at that time to slash the sleeves so that a fabric of another color worn beneath would show in an ornamental manner through the slash. The ministers decreed that neither man nor woman should wear clothing with more than one slash on each sleeve and another on the back. "Cutt-works, inbroidered or needle worke capps, bands & rayles," were forbidden.[31] Ruffs and beaver hats were prohibited, as was long hair.

Binding or small edging laces might be used, but the making or selling of bone lace was penalized at the rate of five shillings per yard.

But this didn't change human nature and although from time to time offenders were taken into court and punished, the wearing of fine clothing fashioned after the London mode continued and a few years later the ministers tried their hand again. Any kind of lace was anathema and "no garment shalbee made with short sleeves, whereby the nakedness of the arme may bee discovered." On the other hand, large sleeves were forbidden, so the maids and goodwives of the time must have been somewhat at a loss to know how lawfully to fashion their clothes.

The minister at Ipswich grew so ill-tempered over the ungodly state of the women in his town that he vented his spleen as follows: "When I hear a nugiperous Gentledame inquire what dress the Queen is in this week, what the nudius tertian of the Court, I[63] look at her as the very gizzard of a trifle, the product of a quarter of a cypher, the epitome of nothing, fitter to be kickt, if she were of a kickable substance than either honoured or humoured."[32]

The minister in the adjoining town, Rowley, actually cut off his nephew from his inheritance because he wore his hair long in the prevailing fashion. Later in the century the offense of wearing long hair was forgotten in the unspeakable sin of wearing wigs. The Great and General Court again took a hand and in 1675 condemned "the practise of men's wearing their own or other's hair made into periwigs." Judge Sewall in his *Diary* alludes to the custom. In 1685 three persons were admitted to the Old South Church in Boston. "Two wore periwigs," comments the Judge.

"1708, Aug. 20, Mr. Chievar died. The Wellfare of the Province was much upon his Spirit. He abominated Periwigs."[33]

The Great and General Court at one time ordered that no person should smoke tobacco in public under a penalty of two shillings and six pence, nor in his own house with a relative or friend. But everybody smoked who wanted to, even the maids, and the repressive legislation in time met the usual fate of similar efforts to restrain individual liberty and manners.

It is sweet to fancy Priscilla at her spinning wheel wearing the coif and nun-like garb of the Puritan maiden of the poet and the artist. But the inventories of estate in the early years of the Colony, as well as at a later time, furnish evidence of a different character. The variety of fabrics listed is amazing and holds its own with the modern department store. There are most of the well-known fabrics of today, such as calico, cambric, challis, flannel, lawn, linen, plush, serge, silk, velvet, and many others; and there are also names that sound strangely in modern ears, viz.: cheney, darnex, dowlas, genting, inckle, lockrum, ossembrike, pennistone, perpetuana, sempiternum, stammell, and water paragon.

As for dress—the women wore bonnets, caps, silk hoods, coifs, forehead cloths, ruffs, and whisks. Gowns, cloaks, mantles, and muffs are mentioned frequently; as are many kinds of lace and[64] even fans and veils. Shawls and scarfs were not unknown and there were gold, silver, and enamelled rings. Women possessed masks, and stomachers were not uncommon. Tortoise shell combs appear; all well-to-do persons wore gloves, and as for shoes—there were shoes with French heels, fall shoes, and those with silver buckles. Even shoe strings appear in the inventories. There were silver, pewter, and steel buttons and those of gympe, thread, and silk.

Laboring men wore leather and coarse fabrics and for others there were suits, doublets, waistcoats and breeches. Trousers are mentioned; also a cane and periwigs. Of caps and hats there were a number of kinds—felt, castor, demi-castor, and even straw. Capt. George Corwin, a Salem merchant, owned a cloth coat trimmed with silver lace, a velvet coat, a tabby doublet, an old-fashioned Dutch satin doublet, four cloaks of various kinds, two pairs of golden topped gloves, one embroidered pair, and a pair with black fringe. He also took his walks abroad wearing silk stockings, with a hat encircled by a silver band and carrying a silver-headed cane or a plate hilt rapier, according to fashion. He possessed two silver watches. Who shall say that the men and women of the New England colonies did not dress well and live well in the early days according to their means?[34]

In the late 1600's, and until comparatively recent times, working men very generally wore frocks, a custom in dress that dates back into the centuries. It was an almost universal custom for farmers and those employed in the mechanic trades to wear a frock. The farmer generally looked upon the frock as an outer garment—something to put on in colder weather or to slip on to protect underclothing or to conceal an untidy appearance. It was a garment to take off on coming into the house or to put on when going to the village or to market.

[65]

Carters or truckmen also habitually wore frocks. Drake, in his "Landmarks of Boston," describes the old-time trucks, not to exceed eighteen feet in length, with their loads of hogsheads of molasses and other heavy merchandise balanced on the one axle and the two horses harnessed tandem, the head horse led by the truckman. With the disappearance of these ponderous vehicles also went "that distinctive body of men, the 'Boston Truckmen,' who once formed a leading and attractive feature of our public processions, with their white frocks and black hats, mounted with their magnificent truck-horses. Hardy and athletic, it would be hard to find their equals on either side of the water. The long jiggers now used are scarcely less objectionable than the old trucks." Drake wrote this only seventy-five years ago but the "jiggers" of his time have now almost entirely disappeared.

The frock was a loose garment slipped on over the head and in length usually reached halfway between the knees and the feet. The opening in front reached from the neckband nearly to the waist and was closed by buttons, though sometimes a gathering string was used. The bottom was cut up eight or ten inches, on the sides, to permit greater freedom in walking. There were long frocks and short frocks, the latter being generally worn indoors. The frocks worn in workshops by mechanics were short.

One early source of information exists in the advertisements of runaway servants to be found in the eighteenth-century Boston newspapers. During the quarter-century following 1725, the *Boston News-Letter* printed thirty-seven advertisements asking for the detention of white male servants, twenty-one of whom ran away during the cold-weather months. Of the latter, six wore frocks or carried frocks in their bundle of clothing. It is fair to assume that some of these men may have taken with them only their best clothing and left working garments behind, hence the small number of frocks specifically mentioned. This possibly may have been the fact in the instance of an Irish servant, aged twenty-six, who ran away in December, 1741, from his master, James Hunt of York, Maine. He wore a broadcloth coat and jacket of a cinnamon[66] color, a pair of orange colored plush breeches and a good beaver hat. The reward for his detention was £3.

John Davis, a servant of Mr. Okenden of Boston, absented himself from service in March, 1728, and among other clothing he took with him a brown fustian frock, and a pair of striped ticking breeches.

Frocks and "trouzers" were part of the personal effects of William Davison, a tailor, in King Street, Boston, that were advertised for sale at public vendue in November, 1729.

Charles Daly, an Irish boy, who ran away from his master in Boston, in December, 1732, wore a fustian frock and another Irish servant who ran away from a brigantine at Boston four years later, wore a new frock and trowsers.

An Irish servant of Captain Luce of Boston, a cooper by trade, took with him when he disappeared in December, 1737, a frock and a pair of "trowsers." Ten years later a negro servant who ran away from the North End of Boston, took with him a new ozen-brig frock.

The settlers came provided with English-made shoes it is likely of a quality similar to those provided by John Hewsen in 1629, the contract reading: "To make eight pair of welt-neat's leather shoes, crossed on the outside with a seam, to be substantial, good over leather of the best, and two soles, the inner sole of good neat's leather, and the outer of tallowed backs."[35] In 1651, the stock of Robert Turner of Boston, shoemaker, was inventoried as follows: 23 pairs of children's shoes at 9d. per pair; 29 pairs of No. 11, at 4/4; of No. 12, at 4/8; of No. 13, at 4/10 per pair; 20 dozen wooden heels at 8d. per dozen; 14 pairs boots at 14/ per pair.

In 1672, a committee of the town of Boston, considering that people in low circumstances "will wear no other shoes or boots generally but of the newest fashion and highest price" proposed that a law should be enacted that no shoemaker shall sell to any inhabitant, shoes of 11 or 12 sizes above five shillings a pair and so in proportion as to other sizes.[36]

[67]

During the first half century following the arrival of the settlers, red colored stockings were much worn in New England and russet and green colored stockings were also in fashion. Stockings made of wash leather were worn. In 1675 cloth stockings sold at 14/ to 18/ a dozen pairs. In 1675 John Usher of Boston wrote to his principal in London: "Your stirrups and turn-down stockings are not salable here."

The Massachusetts Bay Company sent over in its stock, in 1629, a hundred black hats made of wool and lined in the brim with leather and at the same time came one hundred Monmouth caps, so-called from the place where they were manufactured, and valued at two shillings each. With them came five hundred red knit caps, milled, at five pence each. Beaver hats were also worn at that time and in 1634 prohibited by order of the General Court. In 1651, a shopkeeper in Boston, sold black hats at 14s. 16s. and 5s.; colored hats brought 10s. and others, 8s.; children's were 3/6; black castors, 14s. and coarse felt hats, 3s. each.

In 1675 a Bostonian wrote to a friend in London, that the local market for sugar-loaf or high-crowned hats was dull.

The Monmouth or military cocked hat, for men, began to come into fashion about 1670, with an average width of brim of six inches. Their inconvenient width led to the practice of having one flap fastened to the side of the crown, either before or behind, and then to having two flaps alike secured. During the reign of Queen Anne, the brim was caught up in three flaps, and so the triangularly cocked hat became the fashion.[37]

Doublets were made of leather, usually red in color, and fastened with hooks and eyes. They were large on the shoulders, having much cutwork showing the linen shirt beneath. Toward the end of the century their popularity waned and they were succeeded by the waistcoat. The jerkin was made of leather and also various kinds of cloth and sometimes is mentioned in inventories. It was worn by laboring men.

[68]

SNOW SHOES were used after a great storm; "which our People do much use now, that never did before."—*Boston News-Letter*, Jan. 29-Feb. 5, 1704/5.

STOLEN or carried privately away out of the house of Capt. John Bonner in Cow Lane, near Fort Hill, Boston, sometime before the late Sickness of his late Wife, or about the time of her decease, which was the Month of January last: the following Particulars, viz.: Of his Wife's Wearing apparel three Silk Gowns, one changable colour, a second flowr'd and the third stript; Three other Gowns, one where of a double gown, one side silk stuff the other russel, a second double Gown of silk-stuff and Petticoat of the same, the third a black Crape Gown and Petticoat of the same; Four other Petticoats, one changable colour'd silk, a second black flowr'd silk, a third plain black silk, the fourth a flowr'd Sarge, one Lutstring Hood and Scarff, three laced Headdresses and one plain, three laced Caps, two laced Handkerchiefs, three under Caps laced, three white Aprons, three pair of laced Sleves, two white Muslin Hoods, one Amber Necklace, one Muff...."—*Boston News-Letter*, Mar. 5-12, 1710/11.

GLOVES. Mens Topt fine Kid Gloves, and womans at 3s. 6d. per Pair, fine Glaz'd Lamb and Mittens at 2s. 6d. per Pair, and Rough Lamb for Men and Women at 2s. 6d. per Pair, and further Incouragement to any that buys in Quantity: To be Sold by Mr

Daniel Stevens lately come from England, At his House in Pudding-Lane, Boston.—*Boston News-Letter*, Sept. 3-10, 1711.

MAN'S MUFF. Any Person that took up a Man's Muffe, dropt on the Lord's Day between the Old Meeting House & the South, are desired to bring it to the Post Office in Boston, and they shall be Rewarded.—*Boston News-Letter*, Jan. 9-16, 1715/16.

VENETIAN SILKS. Imported from London in the Last Ship, and to be Sold by Mr. A. Faneuil, Merchant, at his Warehouse in King-Street, Boston, flowered Venetian Silks of the newest Fashion, in Pieces that contain enough for a suit for a woman.—*Boston Gazette*, Feb. 8-15, 1719/20.

WIGG. Taken from the Shop of Powers Marriot, Barber, in[69] Boston, either on the 2d or 3d of August Instant, a light Flaxen Natural Wigg; parted from the Forehead to the Crown, the narrow Ribband is of a Red Pink Colour, the Caul is in Rows of Green, Red and White. Whoever will give Information of the said Wigg, so as it be restor'd again, they shall have Twenty Shillings Reward.— *Boston News-Letter*, July 31-Aug. 7, 1729.

PUBLIC VENDUE. To be Sold, at Publick Vendue, by William Nichols at the Royal Exchange Tavern, in King Street, Boston, on This Day, beginning (if the Company attend) precisely at 4 o'clock Afternoon, a Variety of Merchandize; which may be seen till the Sale begins, viz:

A curious and compleat double Sett of Burnt China, Broad Cloths, Druggets, Shalloons, Cottons and long Ells, Buckrams, Scots Cloths, Dowlas, Garlixs, Hollands, Chints, Patches, Qualities, FINE NUNS THREADS, Garterings, Mens and Womens fine Hose, Mens superfine Silk Hose, fine Shirt Buttons, Womens superfine Mittens, yellow, blue and Tabby, a sattin Coverlid, curiously embroidered with Gold Lincey for Curtains, &c., some Household Goods, such as Case of Draws, Tables, Paints, Maps, Alabaster Effigies, China, &c. Sundry suits of Mens Apparel, new and second hand; sundry very good Watches, Shoes, Boots, Green Tea, Chocolate, and many other Things.—*Boston News-Letter*, May 18-25, 1738.

WOMEN'S SHOES. To be Sold, at the House of Joseph Henderson in Winter-Street, Boston. Women's flower'd Silk, Russell & Mourning Shoes, Cloggs and Pattoons, Lace & Eagins.—*Boston News-Letter*, Oct. 15-22, 1741.

FABRICS, ETC. To be Sold At Robert Jenkins's on the North-Side of the Town House in King-Street, Boston,—India Damasks, China Taffeties, fine India Patches, Chinces and Callicoes, fine Cambricks, Bag and Sheeting Hollands, Huckabuck and Damask Table Cloths, with other Linnens of all Sorts, fine Plushes of divers Colours, Scarlet and other Broad Cloths, Shalloons, figured Fustians, Ratteens, Whitneys, Duffles, Camblets, Callamancoes, Floretta's, with a Variety of Haberdashery and Millinary Wares;[70] Gold and Silver Lace, Crapes, and Sundrys for Mourning; Caps, Stockings and Gloves of all Sorts, Ozenbrigs, English Sole Leather, Hogsheads of Earthen Ware, Casks of Red Herrings, Cloaths Flaskets, China Baskets and Voiders, white Lead & Sieve Bottoms, and Sundry other Goods.—*Boston News-Letter*, Oct. 29-Nov. 5, 1741.

LEATHER BREECHES. Philip Freeman, lately from London, makes and sells super-fine black Leather Breeches and Jackets, not to be discerned from the best super-fine Cloth; likewise makes Buff and Cloth Colour after the neetest Manner, also makes all sorts of Gloves by wholesale and retale. The said Freeman lives in Prison Lane, near the Town House in Boston.—*Boston Gazette*, June 21, 1743.

EMBROIDERED PETTICOAT. On the 11th of Nov. last, was stolen out of the yard of Mr. Joseph Coit, Joiner in Boston, living in Cross street, a Woman's Fustian Petticoat, with a large work'd Embroder'd Border, being Deer, Sheep, Houses, Forrest, &c., so worked. Whoever has taken the said Petticoat, and will return it to the owner thereof, or to the Printer, shall have 40s. old Tenor Reward and no Question ask'd.—*Boston Gazette*, Dec. 19, 1749.

LEATHER STOCKINGS. Made and Sold by Philip Freeman, at the Blew Glove next the Cornfields in Union Street; Leather Stockings of different Colours, viz. Black, Cloth colour'd, and Yellow made after the neatest manner.—*Boston Gazette*, June 25, 1754.

FABRICS USED IN THE EARLY DAYS

The fabrics included in the following list all appear in probate inventories, court records, or in newspaper advertisements.

Alamode. A thin, light, glossy black silk. Used for hoods (1676); for hat bands and covered with black crape (1702).

Alepine, Alapeen, Allapine. A mixed stuff either of wool and silk or mohair and cotton.

Algiers Cloth. Essex Co. (Mass.), Court Records (1680).

Attabanies, Silk. Boston Gazette, June 29, 1729.

[71]

Baize, Bays. A coarse woolen stuff, having a long nap, formerly, when made of finer and lighter texture, used as material for clothing. Used for a waistcoat (1634). Pepys owned a cloak of Colchester bayze (1667). Red bays was used for underpetticoats (1732). First introduced into England about 1561.

Barber's Stuff. 1¾ yards, 5/. Essex Co. (Mass.) Probate (1654).

Barley Corns, Dresden. Boston Gazette, Aug. 22, 1757; Boston News-Letter, July 16, 1761.

BARRATINE. A woven fabric. A black barratine mantua and petticoat (1689). Barratees (sic) from Frankfort (1745).

Barronet, Silk, query, Barrantine.

BEARSKIN. A shaggy kind of woolen cloth used for overcoats.

Belgrades, Silk. Boston News-Letter, Mar. 28, 1723.

Bendoarines, Striped. Boston Gazette, Aug. 22, 1757.

BENGAL. Piece goods (apparently of different kinds) exported from Bengal in the seventeenth century. Bengal stripes, striped ginghams, originally from Bengal were afterwards manufactured at Paisley, Scotland. "Bengalls and Painted Callicoes used for Hanging of

Rooms" (1680). There are two sorts, fine striped and plain (1696). Thin slight stuff, made of silk and hair, for women's apparel (1755).

Berlins, Double. Boston Gazette, Aug. 22, 1757.

Bezoarines, Tobine. Boston Gazette, Aug. 22, 1757.

Birds' Eyes. A fabric marked as with birds' eyes. A yellow birds-eye hood (1665). Olive colored birds' eye silk (1689).

Bombasine, Bombazeen, Bombase. A twilled or corded dress material, composed of silk and worsted; sometimes of cotton and worsted or worsted alone. In black, much used for mourning. A doublet of white bombasyne (1572). Pepys owned a black bombazin suit (1666).

Bream. 4 yards 4/. Essex Co. (Mass.) Probate (1674).

Bredaws, Silk. Boston Gazette, Aug. 22, 1757.

Broglios, Changeable. Boston Gazette, Aug. 22, 1757.

Buckrum. At first a fine linen or cotton fabric; later stiffened with gum or paste. A cross of blue buckrum for the rood (1475).[72] Vestments of blue buckam (1552). Our gallants wear fine laces upon buckram (1665).

Burdett. A cotton fabric. A blue burdit mantua and petticoat (1710).

Cabbis. A coarse cheap serge. A carpet of cadys for the table (1536). A blue saddlecloth bound with green and white caddis (1691). The varigated cloaths of the Highlanders (1755).

Calamanco, Callimancoe. A woolen stuff of Flanders, glossy on the surface, and woven with a satin twill and checkered in the warp, so that the checks are seen on one side only; much used in the eighteenth century. Calamanco breeches (1605), diamond buttoned callamanco hose (1639). His waistcoat of striped calamanco (1693). A gay calamanco waistcoat (1710). A tawny yellow jerkin turned up with red calamanco (1760).

Calico. Originally a general name for all kinds of cotton cloth imported from Callicut, India, and from the East. Painted calicuts they call calmendar (1678). Pepys bought calico for naval flags (1666). Dressed in white cotton or calico (1740).

Cambletteens. Boston News-Letter, Dec. 18, 1760.

Camlet. Originally made of silk and camel's hair, hence the name, but later of silk and wool. Red chamlett (1413). His camlet breeches (1625). Rich gold or silver chamlets (1634). Watering the grograms and chambletts (1644). Pepy owned a camelott riding coat (1662). Camlet was also made with a wavy or watered surface. Water Chamolet of an azure color (1624). A watered camlet gown (1719).

Camleteen. An imitation camlet. Made of fine worsted (1730).

Cantaloon. A woolen stuff manufactured in the eighteenth century in the west of England. Trusses of cantaloons or serges (1711). Cantaloons from Bristol (1748).

Canvas. (1) Strong or coarse unbleached cotton cloth made of hemp or flax, formerly used for clothing. A coverlet lined with canvas (1537). (2) The thin canvas that serves women for a ground unto their cushions or purse work (1611). Working canvas for cushions (1753). St. Peter's Canvas.

[73]

Carpet. Originally a thick fabric, commonly of wool, used to cover tables, beds, etc. Lay carpets about the bed (1513). A carpet of green cloth for a little folding table (1527). A table wanting a carpet (1642). A green carpet for the communion table (1702).

Carsey, see *Kersey.*

Castor. Generally a hat, either of beaver fur or resembling it.

Challis. A fine silk and worsted fabric, very pliable and without gloss, used for dresses, introduced at Norwich, England, about 1632.

Checks. A fabric woven or printed in a pattern forming small squares, i.e., check Kersey. Hungarian checks.

Cheercoones. Boston Gazette, June 23, 1729.

Cheese Cloth.

Chello. A fabric imported from India in the eighteenth century.

Cheney, Cheyney. A worsted or woolen stuff. My red bed of Phillipp and Cheyney (1650). Colchester cheanyes (1668).

Cherry derries. Boston News-Letter, Dec. 18, 1760.

Coifing Stuff. 3 yards, ¾. Essex Co. (Mass.) Probate (1661).

Copper plate. A closely woven cotton fabric on which patterns, landscapes, pictorial representations have been printed from engraved copper plates; much in fashion during the eighteenth and early nineteenth centuries.

Dakaple, see *Dornick.*

Darnacle, see *Dornick.*

Darnex, see *Dornick.*

Dianetts. Boston Gazette, Aug. 22, 1757.

Diaper. Since the fifteenth century a linen fabric (sometimes with cotton) woven with lines crossing diamond-wise with the spaces variously filled with lines, a dot or a leaf. A boad cloth of dyaper (1502), a vestment of linen dyoper (1553), a suit of diaper for his table (1624).

Dimity. A stout cotton fabric, woven with raised stripes or fancy figures, for bed hangings, etc. A vestment of white demyt (1440), a hundred camels loaden with silks, dimmeties, etc. (1632). A book wrapt up in sea green Dimmity (1636). A half bedstead with[74] dimity and fine shade of worstead works (1710). His waistcoat was white dimity (1743).

Dimothy, see *Dimity.*

Dornick, Darnix, Darnacle. A silk, worsted, woolen or partly woolen fabric, used for hangings, carpets, vestments, etc. Two old cushions of white and red dornix and a hanging of dornix (1527), dornicks for the master's bed chamber (1626), a darnock carpet (1672).

Dowlas. A coarse linen much used in the sixteenth and seventeenth centuries, originally made in Brittany. Where the said linen cloth called dowlas and lockrum is made (1536). Dowlas for saffron bags (1640). Dowlas from Hamborough (1696).

Draft. Silk and worsted. 1 piece orange colored worsted draft, £2. 5. 0. Essex Co. (Mass.) Probate (1678). 24 yards flowered silk draft at 2/. per yard. Essex Co. (Mass.) Probate (1678).

Drugget. Formerly a fabric of all wool or mixed with silk or linen, used for wearing apparel. A pair of druggett courtings (1580). A drugget suit lined with green (1675). In drugget dressed, of thirteen pence a yard (1721).

Ducape. A plain-wove stout silk fabric of soft texture sometime woven with a stripe. Its manufacture was introduced into England by French refugees in 1685. Women's hoods made of ducape (1688).

Duffel, Duffle. A coarse woolen cloth having a thick nap or frieze, originally made at Duffel near Antwerp. This fabric is also called "shag," and by the early traders "trucking cloth." Indian goods such as duffels, shirts, etc. (1695). A duffel blanket (1699). A light duffel cloak with silver frogs (1759). Duffel great coats (1791).

Durant, Durance. A woolen stuff sometimes called "everlasting," a variety of tammy. Both tammy and durant were hot pressed and glazed.

Duroy. A coarse woolen fabric formerly manufactured in the west of England, similar to tammy. Wearing a grey duroy coat and waistcoat (1722). Curley duroy.

[75]

Erminettas. Boston Gazette, May 26, 1755.

Everlasting. Another name for durant, a material used in the sixteenth and seventeenth centuries for the dress of sergeants and catchpoles. In later times a strong twilled woolen stuff, also called "lasting," and much used for women's shoes.

Farandine. A cloth of silk and wool or hair, invented about 1630 by one Ferrand. Pepys mentions her new ferrandine waistcoat (1663). I must wear black farandine the whole year (1668). Peach colored farandine (1685).

Frieze. A coarse woolen cloth, with a nap, usually on one side only. A gown of green frieze (1418). A home-spun frieze cloth (1611). His waistcoat of red frieze (1627). An old calash lined with green frieze (1765).

Fugere. Red satin fuger (1465). Cover of a field bed of fuger satin yellow and red (1596). A petticoat of fuger satin laid with silver and gold lace and spangled (1638).

Fustian. A coarse cloth made of cotton and flax. His clothing was black fustian with bends in the sleeves (1450). White fustian for socks for the Queen (1502). Blankets of fustian (1558). Then shall the yeoman take fustian and cast it upon the bed and the sheet likewise ... then lay on the other sheet ... then lay on the over fustian above (1494).

Galloway. Essex Co. (Mass.) Court Records (1681).

Garlits, Garliz, Garlix. Linens made in Gorlitz, Prussian Silesia. There are several kinds in shades of blue-white and brown.

Ghenting. A kind of linen, originally made in Ghent, Flanders. Used for handkerchiefs, etc.

Grisette, Grizet. An inferior dress fabric, formerly the common garb of working girls in France. His doublet was a griset-coat (1700).

Grogam, Grosgrane. A coarse fabric of silk, of mohair and wool, or these mixed with silk; often stiffened with gum. Used for aprons, cloaks, coats, doublets, gowns and petticoats. My watered grogram gown (1649). Grograms from Lille (1672).

Haircloth. Cloth made of hair and used for tents, towels, and[76] in drying malt, hops, etc. Every piece of haircloth (1500). Coal sacks made of hair-cloth (1764).

Hamald, Hamel, Hammells. Homemade fabrics. Narrow hammells. Boston Gazette, June 30, 1735.

Harrateen. A linen fabric used for curtains, bed hangings, etc. Field bedsteads with crimson harrateen furniture (1711). Harrateen, Cheney, flowered cotton and checks (1748). For curtains, the best are linen check harrateen (1825).

Holland. A linen fabric, originally made in Holland. When unbleached called brown holland. A shift of fine holland (1450). Women cover their head with a coyfe of fine holland linen cloth (1617). Fine holland handkerchiefs (1660).

Humanes at 18 d. per yard. Essex Co. (Mass.) Court Records (1661).

Huswives, Housewife's Cloth. A middle grade of linen cloth, between coarse and fine, for family uses. Howsewife's cloth (1571). Neither carded wool, flax, or huswives cloth (1625).

Inkle, Incle, Incle Manchester. A narrow linen tape, used for shoe ties, apron strings, etc. A parcel of paper bound about with red incle (1686).

Jeans. A twilled cotton cloth, a kind of fustian. Jean for my Lady's stockings (1621). White jean (1766).

Kenting. A kind of fine linen cloth originally made in Kent. Canvas and Kentings (1657). Neckcloths, a sort that come from Hamborough, made of Kenting thread (1696).

Kersey. A coarse, narrow cloth, woven from long wool and usually ribbed. His stockings were Kersie to the calf and t'other knit (1607). Trowsers made of Kersey (1664), black Kersie stockings (1602). Thy Kersie doublet (1714). Kerseys were originally made in England. Her stockings were of Kersey green as tight as any silk (1724). Kerseys were used for petticoats and men's clothing.

Lawn, Lane. A kind of fine linen, resembling cambric. Used for handkerchiefs, aprons, etc. A coyfe made of a plyte of lawne (1483). A thin vail of calico lawne (1634), a lawn called Nacar (1578).

[77]

Lemanees. Boston Gazette, May 26, 1755.

Linds. A linen cloth. Kinds of linne or huswife-cloth brought about by peddlers (1641).

Linsey, Lincey. In early use a coarse linen fabric. In later use—Linsey-woolsey. Clothes of linsey (1436). Blue linsey (1583).

Linsey-woodsey, Lindsey-woolsey. A fabric woven from a mixture of wool and flax, later a dress material of coarse inferior wool, woven on a cotton warp. Everyone makes Linsey-woolsey for their own wearing (New York, 1670). A lindsey-woolsey coat (1749). A linsey-woolsey petticoat (1777).

Lockram, Lockrum. A linen fabric of various qualities, for wearing apparel and household use. Lockram for sheets and smocks and shirts (1520). Linings of ten penny lockram (1592). His lockram band sewed to his Linnen shirt (1616). A lockram coife and a blue gown (1632).

Lutestring. A glossy silk fabric. Good black narrow Luto-Strings and Alamode silks (1686). A flowing Negligee of white Lutestring (1767). A pale blue lutestring domino (1768).

Lungee, Lungi. A cotton fabric from India. Later a richly colored fabric of silk and cotton. Wrapped a lunge about his middle (1698). A Bengal lungy or Buggess cloth (1779). Silk lungees. Boston Gazette, June 23, 1729.

Manchester. Cotton fabrics made in Manchester, England. Manchester cottons and Manchester rugges otherwise named Frices (1552). Linen, woolen and other goods called Manchester wares (1704). A very showy striped pink and white Manchester (1777).

Mantua. A silk fabric made in Italy. Best broad Italian colored Mantuas at 6/9 per yard (1709). A scarlet-flowered damask Mantua petticoat (1760).

Medrinacks, Medrinix. A coarse canvas used by tailors to stiffen doublets and collars. A sail cloth, i.e., pole-davie.

Missenets. Boston News-Letter, Dec. 18, 1760.

Mockado. A kind of cloth much used for clothing in the sixteenth and seventeenth centuries. Tuft mockado was decorated[78] with small tufts of wool. It was first made in Flanders and at Norwich, England, by Flemish refugees. A farmer with his russet frock and mockado sleeves (1596). Crimson mochadoes to make sleeves (1617). A rich mockado doublet (1638).

Molecy. 2 yards, 12 s. Essex Co. (Mass.) Probate (1672).

Nankeen. A cotton cloth originally made at Nankin, China, from a yellow variety of cotton and afterwards made at Manchester and elsewhere of ordinary cotton and dyed yellow. Make his breeches of nankeen (1755). His nankeen small clothes were tied with 16 strings at each knee (1774).

Niccanee. A cotton fabric formerly imported from India. Mentioned in the London Gazette in 1712.

Nilla. A cotton fabric from India. There are two sorts, striped and plain, by the buyers called Bengals ... used for Gowns and Pettycoats (1696).

Noyals, Noyles, Nowells. A canvas fabric made at Noyal, France. Noyals canvas (1662). Vitry and noyals canvas (1721).

Osnaburg Oznabrig, Ossembrike. A coarse linen cloth formerly made at Osnabruck, Germany. Ossenbrudge for a towell to the Lye tabyll (1555). A pair of Oznabrigs trowsers (1732).

Pack Cloth. A stout, coarse cloth used for packing. Packed up in a bundle of pack cloth (1698).

Padusoy, Padaway. A strong corded or gross-grain silk fabric, much worn by both sexes in the eighteenth century. *Padusay* was a kind of serge made in Padua and imported into England since 1633 or earlier. A pink plain poudesoy (1734). A laced paduasoy suit (1672). A petticoat lined with muddy-colored pattissway (1704). A glossy paduasoy (1730). A fine laced silk waistcoat of blue paduasoy (1741).

Palmeretts. Boston Gazette, Aug. 22, 1757.

Pantolanes. Essex Co. (Mass.) Court Records (1661).

Pantossam. Essex Co. (Mass.) Court Records (1661).

Paragon. A kind of double camlet used for dress and upholstery in the seventeenth and eighteenth centuries. 12 yards of water paragon at ⅝ and 5 yards of French green paragon at 25/10[79] (1618). Hangings for a room of green paragon (1678). Black paragon for a gown (1678).

Parisnet, Black and White. Boston News-Letter, Dec. 18, 1760.

Patch. A kind of highly glazed printed cotton, usually in bright-colored floral designs, used for window draperies and bed hangings. Advertised in Boston News-Letter, June 24, 1742. English and India patches. Boston News-Letter, Dec. 18, 1760.

Pealong, White English. Boston Gazette, Mar. 30, 1734.

Pellony. Essex Co. (Mass.) Court Records (1680).

Penistone, Penniston. A coarse woolen cloth made at Penistone, Co. Yorkshire, England, used for garments, linings, etc. Clothes called pennystone or forest whites (1552). Red peniston for petticoats (1616).

Pentado. Essex Co. (Mass.) Court Records (1680).

Perpetuana. A durable woolen fabric manufactured in England from the sixteenth century, similar to *everlasting, durance*, etc. The sober perpetuana-suited Puritan (1606). A counterpane for the yellow perpetuana bed (1648).

Philip. A kind of worsted or woolen stuff of common quality. 12 yards of philip and cheney for a coat for Mrs. Howard (1633). My red bed of Phillip and China (1650).

Pocking Cloth. Essex Co. (Mass.) Court Records (1674).

Poldavy, Poledavis. A coarse canvas or sacking, originally woven in Brittany, and formerly much used for sailcloth. A canvas of the best poldavie (1613). Pole-Davies for sails (1642).

Pompeydones. Boston Gazette, Aug. 22, 1757.

Poplin. A fabric with a silk warp and worsted weft, having a corded surface. Lined with light colored silk poplin (1737).

Porstotana. Essex Co. (Mass.) Court Records (1680).

Prunella, Prenella. A strong stuff, originally silk, afterwards worsted, used for clergymen's gowns, and later for the uppers of women's shoes. Plain black skirts of prunella (1670).

Rash. A smooth-surfaced fabric made of silk (*silk rash*) or worsted (*cloth rash*). A cloak of cloth rash (1592). My silk rash gown (1597). He had a cloak of rash or else fine cloth (1622).

[80]

Ratteen, Rating. A thick twilled woolen cloth, usually friezed or with a curled nap, but sometimes dressed; a friezed or drugget. A cloak lined with a scarlet Ratteen (1685). A ratteen coat I brought from Dublin (1755). A brown ratteen much worn (1785).

Romal. A silk or cotton square or handkerchief sometimes with a pattern. 12 pieces of Romals or Sea Handkerchiefs (1683). There are three sorts, silk Romals, Romals Garrub and cotton Romals (1696).

Russel. A woolen fabric formerly used for clothing, especially in the sixteenth century, in various colors; black, green, red, grey, etc. A woman's kertyl of Russell worsted (1552). A black russel petticoat (1703).

Sagathy, Sagatheco. A slight woolen stuff, a kind of serge or ratteen, sometimes mixed with a little silk. A brown colored sagathea waistcoat and breeches (1711).

Sarsenet, Sarcenet. (Saracen cloth). A very fine and soft silk material made both plain and twilled, in various colors. Curtains of russet sarsenet fringed with silk (1497). A doublet lined with sarcenet (1542). Some new fashion petticoats of sarcenett (1662). A scarlet coat lined with green sarcenet (1687).

Satinette, Satinet. An imitation of satin woven in silk or silk and cotton. A cloth-colored silk sattinet gown and petticoat (1703). A thin satin chiefly used by the ladies for summer nightgowns, &c. and usually striped (1728).

Satinisco. An inferior quality of satin. His means afford him mock-velvet or satinisco (1615). Also there were stuffs called perpetuano, satinisco, bombicino, Italicino, etc. (1661).

Say. Cloth of a fine texture resembling serge; in the sixteenth century sometimes partly of silk and subsequently entirely of wool. A kirtle of silky say (1519). A long worn short cloak lined with say (1659). Say is a very light crossed stuff, all wool, much used for linings, and by the Quakers for aprons, for which purpose it usually is dyed green (1728). It was also used for curtains and petticoats.

Scotch Cloth. A texture resembling lawn, but cheaper, said to[81] have been made of nettle fibre. A sort of sleasey soft cloth ... much used for linens for beds and for window curtains (1696).

Sempiternum. A woolen cloth made in the seventeenth century and similar to perpetuana. See *Everlasting.*

Shag. A cloth having a velvet nap on one side, usually of worsted, but sometimes of silk. Crimson shag for winter clothes (1623). A cushion of red shag (1725).

Shalloon. A closely woven woolen material used for linings. Instead of shalloon for lining men's coats, sometimes use a glazed calico (1678).

Sleazy. An abbreviated form of silesia. A linen that took its name from Silesia in Hamborough, and not because it wore sleasy (1696). A piece of Slesey (1706).

Soosey. A mixed, striped fabric of silk and cotton made in India. Pelongs, ginghams and sooseys (1725).

Stammel. A coarse woolen cloth, or linsey-woolsey, usually dyed red. In summer, a scarlet petticoat made of stammel or linsey-woolsey (1542). His table with stammel, or some other carpet was neatly covered (1665). The shade of red with which this cloth was usually dyed was called stammel color.

Swanskin, Swanikins. A fine, thick flannel, so called on account of its extraordinary whiteness. The swan-skin coverlet and cambrick sheets (1610).

Tabby. Named for a quarter of Bagdad where the stuff was woven. A general term for a silk taffeta, applied originally to the striped patterns, but afterwards applied also to silks of uniform color waved or watered. The bride and bridegroom were both clothed in white tabby (1654). A child's mantle of a sky-colored tabby (1696). A pale blue watered tabby (1760). Rich Morrello Tabbies. (Boston Gazette, March 25, 1734).

Tabling. Material for table cloths; table linen, Diaper for tabling (1640). 12 yards tabling at 2/6 per yard. Essex Co. (Mass.) Probate (1678).

Tamarine. A kind of woolen cloth. A piece of ash-colored wooley Tamarine striped with black (1691).

[82]

Tammy. A fine worsted cloth of good quality, often with a glazed finish. All other kersies, bayes, tammies, sayes, rashes, etc. (1665). A sort of worsted-stuff which lies cockled (1730). Her dress a light drab lined with blue tammy (1758). A red tammy petticoat (1678). Strain it off through a tammy (1769).

Tandem. A kind of linen, classed among Silesia linens. Yard wide tandems for sale (1755). Quadruple tandems (1783).

Thick Sets. A stout, twilled cotton cloth with a short very close nap: a kind of fustian. A Manchester thickset on his back (1756).

Ticklenburg. Named for a town in Westphalia. A kind of coarse linen, generally very uneven, almost twice as strong as osnaburgs, much sold in England. About 1800 the name was always stamped on the cloth.

Tiffany. A kind of thin transparent silk; also a transparent gauze muslin, cobweb lawn. Shewed their naked arms through false sleeves of tiffany (1645). Black tiffany for mourning (1685).

Tow Cloth. A coarse cloth made from tow, i.e., the short fibres of flax combed out by the hetchell, and made into bags or very coarse clothing. Ropes also were made of tow.

Tobine. Probably a variant of tabby. With lustre shine in simple lutestring or tobine (1755). Lutestring tobines which commonly are striped with flowers in the warp and sometimes between the tobine stripes, with brocaded sprigs (1799). A stout twilled silk (1858).

Trading Cloth, see *Duffell.*

Turynetts. Boston Gazette, Aug. 22, 1757.

Venetians. A closely woven cloth having a fine twilled surface, used as a suiting or dress material.

Villaranes. Essex Co. (Mass.) Court Records (1661).

Vitry, Vittery. A kind of light durable canvas. Vandolose [vandelas] or vitrie canvas the ell, 10s. (1612). Narrow vandales or vittry canvas (1640).

Water Paragon, see *Paragon.*

Witney, Whitney. A heavy, loose woolen cloth with a nap made up into blankets at Witney, Co. Oxford, England. Also, formerly,[83] a cloth or coating made there. True Witney broadcloth, with its shag unshorn (1716). Fine Whitneys at 53 s. a yard, coarse Whitneys at 28 s. (1737).

In the Inventory of the Estate of Henry Landis of Boston, shopkeeper, taken Dec. 17, 1651, the following fabrics are listed, viz.:

Black Turky tamet,	Green Italiano
Turkie mohaire	Say
Green English Tamett	Red Calico
Cotton cloth	Red Serge
Kersey	Cheny
Yellow cotton	Double Cheny
Linsie woolsey	Red satinesco
English mohaire	Olive serge
Mixed Italiano	Holland
Grey ditto	Tufted Holland
Broadcloth	Fine Holland
Green cotton cloth	Nuns Holland

Course Yorkshire Kersey	Broad dowlas
Tamy Cheny	Dowlas
Padway serge	Broad lining
Adretto	Lockrum
Hair Camelion	White Calico
Castelano	1 pr dimity drawers
Herico Italiano	1 pr girls bodys
White serge	Addevetto
Perpetuano	2 childs waistcoats at 9 d.
Best ditto	9 tawney bonnets at 16 d.
Mixed serge	46 pr ear wiers at 4 d.
Cloth	17 calico neck cloths at 12 d.
Kersey	2 gro tin buttons at 2/6.
Italiano	9 yds silk galoon at 2½ d.

Sad hair coloured Italiano	Breeches bottons
Taunton serge	Silk breast buttons
Mixed stuff	Hair buttons
Green mixed serge	Great silk buttons
Herico Kersey	A great variety of silk and bone lace
Green Tamy	1 black satin cap, 3/.

—*Suffolk Co. Probate Records*, Vol. II, p. 127.

[84]

CHAPTER VI

PEWTER IN THE EARLY DAYS

In the spring of 1629, when the Secretary of the Company of the Massachusetts Bay in New England was preparing a memorandum of materials to be obtained "to send for Newe England" in the ships that sailed on April 25th of that year, among the fabrics and food stuffs, the seed grain, potatoes, tame turkeys, and copper kettles of French making without bars of iron about them, were listed brass ladles and spoons and "pewter botles of pyntes & qrts." The little fleet reached Naumkeck (now Salem) on June 30th, and on its return voyage, a month later, Master Thomas Graves, the "Engynere," expert in mines, fortifications, and surveys, who had come over with Governor Endecott the previous year, sent home a report to the Company in which he listed "such needefull things as every Planter doth or ought to provide to go to New-England," including victuals for a whole year, apparel, arms, tools, spices, and various household implements, among which appear "wooden platters, dishes, spoons and trenchers," with no mention of pewter. The records of the Company make mention of carpenters, shoemakers, plasterers, vine planters, and men skillful in making pitch, salt, etc., but nowhere does the trade of the pewterer appear.

Pewter did not come into general use among the more prosperous farmers in England until about the middle of the sixteenth century and then only as a salt—a dish of honor, or three or four pieces for use on more formal occasions. It was the wooden trencher that was commonest in use in all middle-class families until well after the year 1700, and this was true both in New England and Old England. In homes where the shilling was made to go as far as possible, the wooden trencher, like the homespun coat, lingered in use for a century later. At least one family in Essex County, Massachusetts, was still using its wooden plates of an earlier[85] period as late as 1876, when the menfolk left home to work for two or three days in the early fall on the thatch banks beside Plum Island river. And this happened in a comfortably situated, but thrifty, family. The rough usage given the common tableware in the crude camp by the marshes had taught the housewife the desirability of bringing down from the chest in the attic, at least once a year, the discarded wooden plates used in her childhood.

Pewter appears early in the Massachusetts Colony in connection with the settlement of estates of deceased persons. By means of the detailed inventories taken at such times, it is possible to reconstruct with unquestioned accuracy the manner in which the homes of the early settlers were furnished, and by means of this evidence it is possible to show that the hardships and crudities of the first years were soon replaced by the usual comforts of the English home of similar station at the same time. The ships were crossing the Atlantic frequently and bringing from London, Plymouth or Bristol, to the new settlements, all manner of goods required for sale in the shops that had been set up in Boston, Salem and elsewhere.

In 1635 the widow Sarah Dillingham died at Ipswich, leaving a considerable estate. Among the bequests were a silver bowl and a silver porringer, and the inventory shows 40½ pounds of pewter valued at £2.14.0.

In 1640, Bethia Cartwright of Salem bequeathed to her sister, Mary Norton, three pewter platters and a double saltcellar and to a nephew she gave six spoons and a porringer.

In 1643, Joseph, the eldest son of Robert Massey of Ipswich, was bequeathed by his father, four pewter platters and one silver spoon. Benjamin, another son, was to receive four pewter platters and two silver spoons, and Mary, a daughter, received the same number as did Joseph.

In 1645, Lionell Chute died in Ipswich. His silver spoon he bequeathed to his son James. It was the only piece of silver in the house. Of pewter, he had possessed fourteen dishes, "small and great," eleven pewter salts, saucers and porringers, two pewter candlesticks and a pewter bottle.

[86]

The widow, Mary Hersome of Wenham, possessed in 1646 one pewter platter and two spoons. The same year Michael Carthrick of Ipswich possessed ten pewter dishes, two quart pots, one pint pot, one beaker, a little pewter cup, one chamber pot and a salt. In 1647, William Clarke, a prosperous Salem merchant, died possessed of an interesting list of furniture; six silver spoons and two small pieces of plate; and the following pewter which was kept in the kitchen—twenty platters, two great plates and ten little ones, one great pewter pot, one flagon, one pottle, one quart, three pints, four ale quarts, one pint, six beer cups, four wine cups, four candlesticks, five chamber pots, two lamps, one tunnel, six saucers and miscellaneous old pewter, the whole valued at £7. The household also was supplied with "China dishes" valued at twelve shillings. John Lowell of Newbury, in 1647, possessed three pewter butter dishes. John Fairfield of Wenham, the same year, had two pewter fruit dishes and two saucers; also four porringers, a double salt, one candlestick and six spoons, all of pewter. His fellow-townsman, Christopher Yongs, a weaver, who died the same year, possessed one bason, a drinking pot, three platters, three old saucers, a salt and an old porringer, all of pewter and valued at only ten shillings. There were also alchemy spoons, trenchers and dishes and a pipkin valued at one shilling and sixpence.

When Giles Badger of Newbury died in 1647 he left to his young widow a glass bowl, beaker and jug, valued at three shillings; three silver spoons valued at £1, and a good assortment of pewter, including "a salt seller, a tunnell, a great dowruff" and valued at one shilling. The household was also furnished with six wooden dishes and two wooden platters. The inventory of the estate of Matthew Whipple of Ipswich totalled £287.2.1, and included eighty-five pieces of pewter, weighing 147 pounds and valued at £16.9.16. In addition, there were four pewter candlesticks valued at ten shillings; two pewter salts, five shillings; two pewter potts, one cup and a bottle, four shillings and sixpence; one pewter flagon, seven shillings; twenty-one "brass alchimic spoones" at four shillings and four pence each; and nine pewter spoons at[87] eighteen pence per dozen. The inventory also discloses one silver bowl and two silver spoons valued at £3.3.0; six dozen wooden trenchers, valued at three shillings; also trays, a platter, two bowles, four dishes, and "one earthen salt."

The widow Rebecca Bacon died in Salem in 1655, leaving an estate of £195.8.6 and a well-furnished house. She had brass pots, skillets, candlesticks, skimmers, a little brass pan, and an excellent supply of pewter, including "3 large pewter platters, 3 a size lesse, 3 more a size lesse, 3 more a size lesse, £1.16; 1 pewter bason, 5s; 6 large pewter plates & 6 lesser, 9s; 19 Pewter saucers & 2 fruite dishes, 11s, 6d; 1 old Pewter bason & great plate, 3s; 2 pewter candlesticks, 4s; 1 large pewter salt & a smal one; 2 pewter porringers, 3s.6d; 1 great pewter flagon; 1 lesser, 1 quart, 2 pints & a halfe pint, 13s; 2 old chamber pots & an old porringer, 3s." She also died possessed of "1 duble salt silver, 6 silver spones, 1 wine cup & a dram cup of silver, both £6."

The Rev. James Noyes of Newbury, when he died in 1656, was possessed of an unusually well-equipped kitchen, supplied with much brass and ironware and the following pewter, viz.: "on one shelfe, one charger, 5 pewter platters and a bason and a salt seller, £1.10.0; on another shelfe, 9 pewter platters, small & great, 13 shillings; one old flagon and 4 pewter drinking pots, 10 shillings." No pewter plates or wooden trenchers are listed.

In other estates appear some unusual items, such as: a pewter brim basin, pewter cullenders, pewter beer cups, pewter pans, pewter bed pans, and a mustard pot.

The trade of the pewterer does not seem to have been followed by many men in New England during the seventeenth century. The vessels were bringing shipments from London and moreover, the bronze moulds used in making the ware were costly. Pewter melted easily and frequently required repairing, and it was here that the itinerant tinker or second-rate pewterer found employment. The handles of pewter spoons broke easily, and a spoon mould was a part of the equipment of every tinker. The earliest mention we have noted of the pewterer practising his trade in New[88] England is one

Richard Graves of Salem. He was presented at a Quarterly Court on February 28, 1642-43 for "opression in his trade of pewtering" and acquitted of the charge. Then he was accused of neglecting to tend the ferry carefully, so it would seem that pewtering occupied only part of his time. This he acknowledged, but said that he had not been put to it by the Court and also that it was necessary to leave the ferry when he went to mill, a quite apparent fact. He seems to have been a somewhat reckless fellow in his dealings with neighbors, for he was accused of taking fence rails from Christopher Young's lot and admonished by the Court. At the same session he was fined for stealing wood from Thomas Edwards and for evil speeches to him, calling him "a base fellow, & yt one might Runn a half pike in his bellie & never touch his hart."

Graves came to Massachusetts in the "Abigail," arriving in July, 1635. He settled at Salem and was a proprietor there in 1637. Sometimes he is styled "husbandman." He got into trouble with the authorities very soon, and in December, 1638, was sentenced to sit in the stocks for beating Peter Busgutt in his own house. Peter made sport of the Court at the time of the trial, and in consequence was ordered to be whipped, this time by the constable. In 1641 Graves was brought into court again and William Allen testified that "he herd Rich Graves kissed Goody Gent twice." Richard confessed that it was true, and for this unseemly conduct he was sentenced to be fined or whipped. The records do not disclose his individual preference as to the penalty eventually inflicted. In 1645 he was in Boston in connection with some brazen moulds that were in dispute. A Mr. Hill and Mr. Knott were concerned in the affair, and very likely the moulds were for pewterers' use. On another occasion a few years later, when Graves went to Boston, he got drunk at Charlestown, and in consequence was mulct by the Quarterly court. Only a month later he was complained of for playing at shuffleboard, a wicked game of chance, at the tavern kept by Mr. Gedney in Salem, but this time he escaped the vengeance of the law, for the case against him was not proved. He was still pursuing[89] his trade of pewterer in 1655 when he so styled himself in a deed to John Putnam, and sometime between that date and 1669 he passed out of reach of the courts to that bourne from which no pewterers ever return.

Mention has been made of the fact that London-made pewter was brought into New England at frequent intervals to supply the natural demand. An invoice of pewter shipped from London in 1693 has recently come to light in the Massachusetts Archives, and is here printed as being of interest not only as showing the market prices for pewter, but also the kind of utensils in demand at that time. This particular shipment of pewter was a part of a consignment made by John Caxy of London to Joseph Mallenson, his agent in Boston. It consisted of a great variety of clothing, fabrics, hardware, implements, kitchen utensils and pewter. The part of the invoice that comprised the shipment of pewter follows, viz.:

One Drume
Fatt No. 2
Containing

12	Pottle Tankards at 3s 10d ps	£2. 6.0
12	Quart ditto at 3s	1.16. 0
24	Midle ditto at 2/6	3. 0.0
24	Small ditto at 2/	2. 8.0
12	doz: Large Poringers	5.14. 0

	at 9s 6d p doz	
12	doz: Small ditto at 8/	4.16.0
3	pr New-fashon'd Candlesticks at 4s	12.0
3	pr ditto at 3s	9.0
2	pr Round ditto at 2s 10d	5.8
	a Fatt Cost	7.0
	One Drume Fatt No. 3 quantity	
18	Large Chamber Potts at 2/10s ps	2.11.0
30	Middle ditto at 2s 8d	3.10.0

40	small ditto at 2s	3.10.0
12	doz Alcamy Spoons at 2/9	4. 0.0
24	doz Powder ditto at 2/3d p doz	2.14.0
12	Large Salts at 2s 2 ps	1. 6.0
24	Middle ditto at 20d ps	2. 0.0
48	Small ditto at 12d ps	2. 8.0
18	Basons qt 32 at 12d	1.12.6
2	doz: Sawcers at 9s p doz	18.0
4	doz Small ditto at 7s p doz	1. 8.0

2	Pottle Wine Measure Potts at 5/6	11.0
[90] 6	Quart ditto Potts at 2/8	16.0
6	Pint ditto Potts at 22d ps	11.0
6	halfe Pint ditto at 14d	7.0
6	Quartern ditto Potts at 9d p ps	4.6
	a Fatt Cost 7s	7.0
	One halfe Barell Fatt No 4 cont more pewter	
78	dishes qt 265 at 9d½	10. 9.9½

A Fatt Cost
3s 6

3. 6

——

——

—

£76.
2.5½

[91]

CHAPTER VII

THE FARMHOUSE AND THE FARMER

The farmers in the early days had few conveniences and comforts and were largely dependent for the supply of their wants upon the products of their farms. But little food was purchased. At the outset domestic animals were too valuable to be killed for food but deer and other wild game were plentiful. When this no longer became necessary and an animal was killed by a farmer, it was the custom to lend pieces of the meat to the neighbors, to be repaid in kind when animals were killed by them. In this way the fresh meat supply was kept up for a long time by the killing of one animal. Other parts of the meat were salted and kept for a number of months before all was eaten. Nearly every family had a beef and a pork barrel (called a "powdering tub"), from which most of the meat used in summer was taken. Meat was not found upon the table every day.

The chimney in the farmhouse was of great size, occupying relatively a large amount of the space inside the house. The kitchen fireplace usually was large enough to accommodate logs four feet in length, oftentimes even larger. In making a fire a backlog, a foot or more in diameter, was placed against the back of the fireplace; a forestick was then placed across the andirons in front, and wood piled between, producing a hot fire, and giving the kitchen a very cheerful appearance. Large stones were sometimes used instead of a backlog, and an iron bar was laid on the andirons in front of the forestick. Ample ventilation was had by the constant current of air that passed up the chimney.

In sitting before an open fire it was often complained that while one was roasted in front he was frozen in the back and this led to the use in nearly every family of a long seat made of boards called a "settle," with a high back to keep off the wind from behind,[92] which, when placed before the fire, was usually occupied by the older members of the family.

At night, any fire that remained was carefully covered with ashes and was expected to keep until morning to kindle for the next day. This was called "raking up the fire," and calculation was made to have enough fire to cover up every night, so it need not be lost. If the fire didn't keep over, some one would go with a fire pan to a neighbor, if one lived near, and borrow some fire. But if this was inconvenient, resort was then had to the tinder box. Tinder was made by charring cotton or linen rags. The box containing this was usually kept in a niche made in the side of the fireplace, by leaving out a couple of bricks. By striking fire with flint and steel, the tinder was ignited. Homemade matches, which had been dipped in melted brimstone, were set on fire by touching the burning tinder and in this way a fire was obtained. Sometimes fire was kindled by flashing powder in the pan of a flint-lock musket, thereby setting paper on fire. Friction matches did not come into use until about 1832.

The cooking was done over and before the open fire. Boiling was done by suspending kettles from pot hooks which were upon the crane and of different lengths to accommodate the height of the fire. An adjustable hook which was called a "trammel" was not infrequently used. Meat was roasted by passing through it an iron rod called a spit and this was rested on brackets on the back of the andirons in front of the fire and by repeated turning and exposing on all sides, the meat was evenly cooked. Another method was to suspend the meat or poultry by a line before the fire. By twisting the line hard it would slowly unwind. Of course some one had to be in frequent attendance to twist the cords and usually it was a child. A dish placed underneath caught the drippings from the roast. Sometimes the line would burn off, and have to be replaced before the cooking could be completed.

Potatoes and eggs were roasted in the ashes by wrapping them in wet leaves or paper, and then covering with hot coals. In half an hour or so the potatoes would be well cooked.

[93]

At first bread and other things were baked in a Dutch oven. It was a shallow cast-iron kettle with long legs and a cover of the same material, having a raised edge. The cover was filled with live coals, and then the oven was suspended from a pot hook or stood in the hot coals. It was used for both baking and frying. Indian bannock, made from corn meal mixed with water and spread about an inch thick on a board or wooden trencher, was baked before the fire by setting it on an incline against a sad-iron or skillet, the top a couple of inches back from the bottom, and when baked and made into milk toast it was considered a dish fit to be "set before a king"!

The brick oven was in the chimney of nearly every well-built house. The opening was inside the fireplace and was closed by a wooden door. In heating the oven dry pine wood, which had been spilt and seasoned out of doors for a short time and then housed, was a necessity for the best results. The oven was considered hot enough for a baking when the black was burned off the roof and the whole inside had assumed a uniform light color. The coals and ashes inside the oven were then removed with a "peel," a long-handled iron shovel made for the purpose. The bottom of the oven was then swept clean with a broom made of hemlock or other boughs. The process of removing the fire and getting it ready for use was called "clearing the oven."

The food to be cooked was then put in the oven: brown bread made from rye and Indian meal, drop cakes made with milk and eggs and wheat flour, which were placed directly upon the bricks and when baked and eaten hot with butter, were considered a great luxury. Beans, meats, potatoes, pies, and many other things were cooked in the brick oven at the same time.

Families in good circumstances, made it a rule to heat the oven daily, but Saturday was generally reserved for the week's baking.

The skins of animals killed on the farm were tanned by some local tanner and a year or more was required by the old process, but it produced an excellent quality of leather.

The utmost economy was practiced. Nearly all the young people and some of the older ones went barefoot during the summer. In[94] going to meeting on Sunday the girls and young women often walked a number of miles. They wore heavy shoes or went barefooted, carrying their light shoes in their hands to save wear until near the meeting house.

In the early years following the settlement, all clothing or materials were brought from overseas but in time, flax and wool were produced on many farms, and the women of the family were capable of taking the wool as it came from the sheep, cleansing, carding and spinning it into yarn, and then weaving it into cloth, from which they cut and made the clothes for the family. The carding was done with hand cards similar to those used for carding cattle, only a little larger and of finer mesh. The carded rolls were spun into yarn upon the hand wheel. Five skeins was considered a good day's work.

The yarn was woven into cloth on the hand loom, which was a ponderous affair and occupied a great deal of room. Not every family possessed a loom, but there were weavers in every locality. The yarn which went lengthwise of the cloth had to be drawn into the harness by hand; that which went the other way came from the shuttle. The yarn which was in the shuttle was wound upon short quills, which were pieces of elder three inches in length with the pitch punched out, and these quills were wound on a wheel called a "quill wheel" which made a great deal of noise. This work was usually done by children or some helper, while the woman of the house was weaving.

Weaving was hard work and five or six yards was considered a good day's work. Cotton was sometimes bought and worked in about the same manner as wool. When the yarn was to be knitted, it was generally colored before using. The dye pot was of earthenware and had its place in the chimney corner just inside the fireplace. It was covered with a piece of board or plank on which the children often sat. The dye was made of indigo dissolved in urine. Into this the yarn was put and remained until it was colored. When the yarn was wrung out, or the contents disturbed, the odor that arose had no resemblance to the balmy breezes from "Araby the blest."

[95]

The cloth for men's wear was called "fulled cloth." After it was woven it was taken to the clothier, where it was fulled, dyed, sheared, and pressed. That worn by women was simply dyed and pressed, and was called pressed cloth. Baize without any filling or napping was woven for women's use.

Flax was grown on the farm. It was pulled in the fall and placed upon the ground, where it remained a number of months until the woody portion was rotted and the fiber became pliable. When at the right stage it was broken by a clumsy implement called a "flax brake," which rid the fiber of the woody parts. It was then "swingled," which was done by beating it with a wooden paddle called a "swingling knife," which prepared it for the comb or "hatchel" made of nail rods. Its teeth were pointed and about six inches longer, seven rows with twelve in each row. The combing took out the short and broken pieces which was called tow and spun into wrapping twine, small ropes and bagging. When the flax had been combed sufficiently it was put upon the distaff and spun.

The linen wheel was about twenty inches in diameter and was operated by the foot resting upon a treadle. The wheel had two grooves in the circumference, one to receive a band to drive "the fliers," the other to drive the spool with a quicker motion to take up the threads. The thread when spun and woven into cloth, was made up into shirts, sheets, table covers, dresses, handkerchiefs, strainer cloths, etc. Ropes used about the farm were often home-made of linen and tow. In the summer men wore tow and linen clothes. A cloth made of cotton and linen was called fustian.

Cider mills were found on a great many farms where the apples, which were mostly natural fruit, were made into cider. This was a common drink and found a place upon the table three times a day with each meal, and was carried into the fields to quench thirst forenoon and afternoon. The men of those days assumed to be unable to labor without a liberal supply of cider, as water seldom agreed with them. The drawing and putting the cider upon the table usually fell to the younger members of the family and was generally considered an irksome task. In some cases it was[96] made the rule that the one who got up the latest in the morning should draw the cider for the day. Cider which had been drawn for a little time and had become warm was not considered fit to drink. Any that remained in the mug was emptied into a barrel kept for the purpose in the cellar and was soon converted into vinegar. In this way the family supply was made and kept up, and it generally was of the best quality.

When David Cummings of Topsfield died in 1761, he provided by will that his wife Sarah should be supplied annually with five barrels of cider, in fact, it was common among farmers to so provide for their widows, together with a horse to ride to meeting, and a certain number of bushels of vegetables, corn, rye, etc., etc.

The tallow candle was used for light in the evening. When this was supplemented by a blazing fire in the fireplace it gave the room a cheerful appearance. Most of the candles were "dips," although a few were run in moulds made for the purpose. All the tallow that came from the animals killed on the farm was carefully saved and tried out and rendered by heating. The liquid thus obtained was put in pans to cool and when enough had been accumulated it was placed in a large kettle and melted. The candle wicking was made of cotton, and was bought at the shops in town. It came in balls. The wicking was cut twice the length of the candle and doubled over a stick made for the purpose and then twisted together. These sticks were two feet in length and half an inch in diameter. Six wicks were placed upon each stick, and as many used as would hold all the candles to be made at one time. Two sticks six or eight feet in length, often old rake handles, were used for supports. These were placed upon two chairs and about eighteen inches apart. On these the sticks were placed with the wicks hanging down. By taking a couple of the sticks in the hands the wicks were placed in the hot tallow until they were soaked. When all had been thus treated dipping began. Each time a little tallow adhered, which was allowed to cool, care being taken not to allow the dips to remain in the hot tallow long enough to melt off what had already cooled. While the dipping was going on the candles were[97] suspended where a draft of air would pass over and cause them to cool quickly. Care was also taken not to have the candles touch each other.

The dipping continued until the candles were large enough for use. If the tallow in the kettle became too cool to work well, some boiling water was put in which went to the bottom and kept the tallow above warm enough to work. The tallow candle made a dim, disagreeable light, as it smoked considerably and required constant snuffing or cutting off of the burnt portions of the wick. Snuffers were used for this purpose, in which the portions of the wick cut off were retained, and this was emptied from time to time as the receptacle became filled.

Nearly every family made the soft soap used in washing clothes and floors. Ashes were carefully saved and stored in a dry place. In the spring the mash tub, holding sixty or seventy gallons, was set up, and on the bottom a row of bricks were set on edge. On them a framework was placed which was covered with hemlock boughs or straw, over which a porous cloth was placed. The tub was then filled with ashes. If any doubt existed as to the strength of the lye, thus produced, a little lime was put in. Boiling water was then poured on in small quantities, at frequent intervals and this was allowed to settle. When no more water would be taken it was left to stand an hour or more, when the first lye was drawn off. If an egg dropped into the lye floated, all was well and good luck with the soap was certain.

Ashes from any wood except pine and beech were considered good and used with confidence. Grease that had accumulated during the year and been saved for this purpose was then placed in a kettle with some of the lye, and when boiled, if it did not separate when cooled, soft soap was the result. Most farmers' wives dreaded soap making. It was one of the hardest day's work of the year. Usually it was made a point to have the soap making precede the spring cleaning.

Men generally rode horseback to meeting and elsewhere, and when a woman went along she rode behind on a pillion, which was[98] a small cushion attached to the rear of the saddle with a narrow board suspended from the cushion—a support for the women's feet. To assist in mounting and dismounting horse blocks were used at the meetinghouse and in other public places. Small articles were carried in saddle-bags, balanced one on each side of the horse. Grain was carried to mill laid across the horse's back, half in each end of the sack.

In the early days baked pumpkin and milk was a favorite dish. A hard-shelled pumpkin had a hole cut in the stem end large enough to admit the hand. The seeds and inside tissue were carefully removed, the piece cut out was replaced, and the pumpkin was then put in a hot oven. When cooked it was filled with new milk and the contents eaten with a spoon. When emptied the shells were often used as receptacles for balls of yarn, remnants of cloth and other small articles.

Bean porridge was another dish that was popular. In cold weather it was often made in large quantities and considered to grow better with age. Hence the old saying:

"Bean porridge hot;Bean porridge cold;Bean porridge in the pot,Nine days old."

While iron shovels were brought in from England and in a limited way were made by local blacksmiths, most shovels used by farmers were made of oak, the edges shod with iron. Hay and manure forks were made of iron by the blacksmith. They were heavy, had large tines that bent easily, and were almost always loose in the handle. It took a great deal of strength to use them. Hoes were made by the blacksmiths, who also made axes, scythes, knives, etc.

When help was wanted on the farm, the son of some neighbor who was not as well off, or who had not enough work to profitably employ all his sons, could be hired. He became one of the family, took an active interest in his employer's business, and in not a few[99] instances married his daughter, and later with his wife succeeded to the ownership of the farm. If help was wanted in the house, some girl in the neighborhood was willing to accept the place. She was strong and ready, capable and honest, and in the absence of her mistress was able to take the lead. She was not looked upon as a servant, and often established herself permanently by becoming the life partner of the son.

Clocks were seldom found in the farmhouse. Noon marks and sundials answered the needs of the family and when the day was cloudy, one must "guess." Because so many had no means of telling the time, it was customary to make appointments for "early candlelight."

It was usual with most families to gather roots and herbs to be used for medicinal purposes. Catnip, pennyroyal, sage, thoroughwort, spearmint, tansy, elderblows, wormwood, and other plants were saved to be used in case of sickness. Gold thread or yellow root was saved and was a remedy for canker in the mouth. Many of the old women who had reared families of children were skilful in the use of these remedies, and were sent for in case of sickness, and would prescribe teas made from some of these herbs, which were cut when in bloom and tied in small bundles and suspended from the rafters on the garret to dry, causing a pleasant aromatic smell in the upper part of the house.

The well was usually at some distance from the farmhouse and often located in an exposed and wind-swept position requiring much daily travel over a snowy and slippery path in winter and through mud and wet at other times. Convenience in the location of the well was in too many cases overlooked. From the well all the water used for domestic purposes was brought into the house in buckets. The water in the well was usually drawn by means of a well-sweep.

In some towns the selectmen were chosen by "pricking." A number of names were written upon a sheet of paper. This was passed around and each man pricked a hole against the names of his choice. The one having the most pin holes was chosen first[100] selectman, the next highest the second, and the next the third.

When a couple concluded to marry they made known their intention to the town clerk, who posted a notice of their intended marriage in the meetinghouse. This was called "being published." By law this notice must be published three Sabbaths before the ceremony was performed, so that any one who knew of any reason why such marriage should not take place might appear and make objection. In addition to the posting, the town clerk would rise in the meeting and read the intention to marry.

Each landowner not only maintained his own fences around cultivated fields, but also gave of his labor in building long ranges of fencing about the common pasture lands in proportion to his interest in the land. A law was enacted as early as 1633 requiring the fencing of corn fields.

The earliest fences were usually made of five rails and must be up by early in April when the cattle and hogs were turned out to roam at large. The New England farmer, clearing his land for cultivation, soon devised another form of fence where stones were plentiful and by piling up these stones into walls divided off his fields and gave them substantial protection. The well-built stone wall must have a foundation of small stones laid in a trench to prevent its being thrown by the frost and when carefully built it would last for generations. Meanwhile the adjoining field had been cleared of stones and made useful for cultivation. Hedge fences were also in frequent use as in parts of England whence the settlers had emigrated.

The roads outside the villages were seldom fenced. In fact, the early roads were little more than ill-defined paths winding their way across pastures and cultivated fields and whenever a dividing farm was reached, there would be a gate or bars to be opened and closed by the traveler.

[101]

CHAPTER VIII

MANNERS AND CUSTOMS

When the first considerable emigration ceased about the year 1640, of the 25,000 settlers then living in the Colony, probably ninety-five per cent were small farmers or workmen engaged in the manual trades, together with many indentured servants who had come over under the terms of a contract whereby they were bonded to serve their masters for a term of years—usually five or seven. The remaining five per cent of the population was composed of those governing the colony—the stockholders in the Company, so to speak; ministers enough to supply the spiritual needs of each town and settlement, however small; a few of social position and comparative wealth; one lawyer; and a sprinkling of shopkeepers and small merchants living in the seaport towns. Here and there a physician or chirurgeon might be found, but the physical welfare of the smaller towns was usually cared for by some ancient housewife with a knowledge of herbs and simples. Sometimes it was the minister who practiced two professions and cared for the bodies as well as the souls of his congregation.

The founders of the colony in the Massachusetts Bay, and most of those who immediately followed them, were men who did not conform to the ritual and government of the Established Church in England. They were followers of John Calvin whose Geneva Bible was widely read in England and whose teachings had profoundly influenced English thought and manners. Calvin taught a great simplicity of life and a personal application of the teachings found in the Bible. In the Commonwealth that he set up in Geneva, the daily life and actions of its citizens were as closely guarded as if in a nursery for children. All frivolous amusements were forbidden; a curfew was established; and all were constrained to save souls and to labor for material development. There was a minute[102] supervision of dress and personal conduct, and a literal construction of Bible mandates was carried so far that children were actually put to death for striking their parents.

Calvin's theology was based on the belief that all men were born sinners and since Adam's fall, by the will of God, predestined from birth to hell and everlasting torment, unless, happily, one of the elect and so foreordained to be saved. In this belief the Puritans found life endurable because they considered themselves of the elect; and in cases of doubt, the individual found comfortable assurance in the belief that although certain of his neighbors were going to hell *he* was one of the elect. It naturally followed that the imagination of the Puritans was concentrated on questions of religion.

The teachings of Calvin spread rapidly in England and among his followers there came about an austerity of religious life and a great simplicity in dress and manners.

It is true that most of the settlers of Massachusetts were poor in purse and with many of them mere existence was a struggle for a long time. But the growth of wealth in the Colony, although it brought with it more luxury in living and better dwellings, did not add much to the refinement of the people. It was the influence and example of the royal governors and a more frequent commercial intercourse with England and the Continental peoples that brought about a desire for a richer dress and an introduction of some of the refinements of life. This by no means met the approval of the Puritan ministers who frequently inveighed against "Professors of Religion who fashion themselves according to the World." The Rev. Cotton Mather, the leading minister in Boston and the industrious author of over four hundred published sermons and similar works, again and again exhorted against stage plays and infamous games of cards and dice. "It is a matter of Lamentation that even such things as these should be heard of in New England," he exclaimed. "And others spend their time in reading vain Romances," he continued. "It is meer loss of time."

With such a background and burdened with such a far-reaching[103] antagonism toward the finer things of life, that help to lighten the burden of existence and beautify the way, it is small wonder that the esthetics found little fertile soil in New England; and much of this prejudice and state of mind lingered among the old families in the more remote and orthodox communities, until recent times.

The New England Puritans only allowed themselves one full holiday in the course of the year and that was Thanksgiving Day, a time for feasting. To be sure, there was Fast Day, in the spring, which gave freedom from work; but that was a day for a sermon at the meetinghouse, for long faces and a supposed bit of self denial— somewhere. The celebration of Christmas was not observed by the true New England Puritan until the middle of the nineteenth century.

A number of sermons preached by Rev. Samuel Moodey, an eccentric minister at York, Maine, for nearly half a century, were printed and among them: "The Doleful State of the Damned, especially such as go to hell from under the Gospel." This sermon was followed by its antidote, entitled: "The Gospel Way of Escaping the Doleful State of the Damned." Another of his sermons was upon "Judas the Traitor, Hung up in Chains." Parson Moodey's son, Joseph, followed him in the pulpit at York. He was known as "Handkerchief Moodey," as he fell into a melancholy; thought he had sinned greatly; and after a time wore a handkerchief over his face whenever he appeared in public. In the pulpit he would turn his back to the congregation and read the sermon, but whenever he faced his people it would be with handkerchief-covered features. Think what must have been the influence of two such men on the life and opinions of a town covering a period of two generations!

During the late seventeenth century and well into the eighteenth, the books usually found in the average New England family were the Bible, the Psalm Book, an almanac, the New England Primer, a sermon or two and perhaps a copy of Michael Wigglesworth's terrific poem—"The Day of Doom." The latter was first[104] printed in 1662 in an edition of 1800 copies not one of which has survived. Every copy was read and re-read until nothing remained but fragments of leaves. Seven editions of this poem were printed between 1662 and 1715 and few copies of any edition now exist.

The book expressed the quintesscence of Calvinism. Here is stanza 205, expressing the terror of those doomed to hell:

"They wring their hands, their caitiff-hands,and gnash their teeth for terrour:They cry, they roar, for anguish soreand gnaw their tongues for horrour.

But get away without delay,Christ pities not your cry:Depart to Hell, there may you yell,and roar Eternally."

Pastor Higginson of Salem wrote enthusiastically of the natural abundance of the grass that "groweth verie wildly with a great stalke" as high as a man's face and as for Indian corn—the planting of thirteen gallons of seed had produced an increase of fifty-two hogsheads or three hundred and fifty bushels, London measure, to be sold or trusted to the Indians in exchange for beaver worth above £300. Who would not share the hardships and dangers of the frontier colony for opportunity of such rich gain?

But the housewives in the far-away English homes were more interested in the growth of the vegetable gardens in the virgin soil, and of these he wrote: "Our turnips, parsnips and carrots are here both bigger and sweeter than is ordinary to be found in England. Here are stores of pumpions, cucumbers, and other things of that nature I know not. Plentie of strawberries in their time, and pennyroyall, winter saverie, carvell and water-cresses, also leeks and onions are ordinary." Great lobsters abounded weighing from sixteen to twenty-five pounds and much store of bass, herring, sturgeon, haddock, eels, and oysters. In the forests were several kinds of deer; also partridges, turkeys, and great flocks of pigeons, with[105] wild geese, ducks, and other sea fowl in such abundance "that a great part of the Planters have eaten nothing but roast-meate of divers Fowles which they have killed."

These were some of the attractive natural features of the new colony in the Massachusetts Bay, as recounted by the Salem minister. Of the hardships he makes small mention, for his aim was to induce emigration. There was much sickness, however, and many deaths. Higginson himself lived only a year after reaching Salem. The breaking up of virgin soil always brings on malaria and fever. Dudley wrote "that there is not an house where there is not one dead, and in some houses many. The naturall causes seem to bee in the want of warm lodgings, and good dyet to which Englishmen are habittuated, at home; and in the suddain increase of heate which they endure that are landed here in somer ... those of Plymouth who landed in winter dyed of the Scirvy, as did our poorer sort whose howses and bedding kept them not sufficiently warm, nor their dyet sufficient in heart." Thomas Dudley wrote this in March, 1631. He explained that he was writing upon his knee by the fireside in the living-room, having as yet no table nor other room in which to write during the sharp winter. In this room his family must resort "though they break good manners, and make mee many times forget what I would say, and say what I would not."

But these hardships and inconveniences of living which the New England colonists met and overcame differ but little from those experienced in every new settlement. They have been paralleled again and again wherever Englishmen or Americans have wandered. In a few years after the coming of the ships much of the rawness and discomfort must have disappeared, certainly in the early settlements, and comparative comfort must have existed in most homes. If we could now lift the roof of the average seventeenth-century house in New England it is certain that we should find disclosed not only comfortable conditions of living but in many instances a degree of luxury with fine furnishings that is appreciated by few at the present time.

[106]

Of the early days following the settlement Roger Clap, who lived at Dorchester, afterwards wrote as follows:

"It was not accounted a strange thing in those days to drink water, and to eat Samp or Homine without Butter or Milk. Indeed it would have been a strang thing to see a piece of Roast Beef, Mutton or

Veal; though it was not long before there was Roast Goat. After the first Winter, we were very Healthy: though some of us had no great Store of Corn. The Indians did sometimes bring Corn, and Trade with us for Clothing and Knives; and once I had a Peck of Corn, or there abouts, for a little Puppy-Dog. Frostfish, Muscles and Clams were a Relief to Many."

When Governor Winthrop landed at Salem in June, 1630, he supped on a good venison pasty and good beer, while most of those who came with him went ashore on Cape Anne side (now Beverly) and gathered strawberries. That was a fine beginning, but when winter set in many of them were "forced to cut their bread thin for a long season" and then it was that they fully realized that "the Ditch betweene England and their now place of abode was so wide.... Those that were sent over servants, having itching desires for novelties, found a reddier way to make an end of their Master's provision, then they could finde means to get more; They that came over their own men had but little left to feed on, and most began to repent when their strong Beere and full cups ran as small as water in a large Land.... They made shift [however] to rub out the Winter's cold by the Fireside, having fuell enough growing at their very doores, turning down many a drop from the Bottell, and burning Tobacco with all the ease they could."[38]

Lacking bread they lived on fish, mussels and clams. The rivers supplied bass, shad, alewives, frost fish and smelts in their season, also salmon, and corn meal could be bartered for with the Indians and shortly raised from seed.

"Let no man make a jest at Pumpkins, for with this fruit the Lord was pleased to feed his people to their good content, till Corne and Cattell were increased," wrote Johnson. Later (by[107] 1650) the goodwives served "apples, pears and quince tarts instead of their former Pumpkin Pies," and by that time wheat bread was no dainty.

Society in the Massachusetts Bay in the seventeenth century was divided into several groups. First came the merchant class which also included the ministers and those possessed of wealth. Edward

Randolph reported to the Lords of Trade in 1676, that in Massachusetts there were about thirty merchants worth from £10,000. to £20,000. "Most have considerable estates and a very great trade." Next came the freemen and the skilled mechanics. This class furnished the town officials and constituted the backbone of the colony. Then came the unskilled laborer and a step lower was the indentured servant. The merchant lived well and wore fine clothing forbidden to his more humble neighbors. The status of the servant may well be shown by the deposition presented in Court at Salem in 1657 by an apprentice to a stone-mason in the town of Newbury, Massachusetts, who testified that it was a long while before "he could eate his master's food, viz. meate and milk, or drink beer, saying that he did not know that it was good, because he was not used to eat such victualls, but to eate bread and water porridge and to drink water."[39]

It has been stated frequently that in the olden times in New England every one was obliged to go to church. The size of the meetinghouses, the isolated locations of many of the houses, the necessary care of the numerous young children, and the interesting side-lights on the manners of the time which may be found in the court papers, all go to show that the statement must not be taken literally. Absence from meeting, breaking the Sabbath, carrying a burden on the Lord's Day, condemning the church, condemning the ministry, scandalous falling out on the Lord's Day, slandering the church, and other misdemeanors of a similar character were frequent.

Drunkenness was very common in the old days. "We observed it a common fault in our young people that they gave themselves[108] to drink hot waters immoderately," wrote Edward Johnson. Every family kept on hand a supply of liquor and wine, and cider was considered a necessity of daily living in the country, where it was served with each meal and also carried into the fields by the workers. It was stored in barrels in the cellar and the task of drawing the cider and putting on the table usually fell to the younger members of the family. A man would often provide in his will for the comfort of his loving wife by setting aside for occupancy during her life, one half of his house, with a carefully specified number of bushels of rye, potatoes, turnips and other vegetables; the use of a horse with which to ride to meeting or elsewhere; and lastly, the direction that annually she be provided with a certain number of barrels of cider— sometimes as many as eight.

Rev. Edward Holyoke, the President of Harvard College, was in the habit of laying in each year thirty or more barrels of cider as he had to provide for much entertaining. Late in the winter he would draw off part of his stock and into each barrel he would pour a bottle of spirit and a month later some of this blend would be bottled for use on special occasions.

What was their conduct not only in their homes but in their relations with their neighbors? Did they live peaceably and work together in building up the settlements? Did they set up in the wilderness domestic relations exactly like those they had abandoned overseas? It was a raw frontier country to which they came and it is apparent that at the outset they felt themselves to be transplanted Englishmen. So far as possible they lived the lives to which they had been accustomed and they engrafted in their new homes the manners and customs of the generations behind them. Most of them fully recognized, however, that they were not to return; that they had cut loose from the old home ties and it was not long before the necessities and limitations of frontier life brought about changed conditions in every direction. Politically, religiously and socially, they were in a different relation than formerly in the English parish life. Many of them, especially those somewhat removed from the immediate supervision of magistrate and minister, before[109] long seem to have shown a tendency to follow the natural bent of the frontiersman toward independent thought and action. Their political leaders made laws restricting daily life and action and their religious leaders laid down rules for belief and conduct, that soon were repellent to many. Civil and clerical records are filled with instances showing an evasion of and even contempt for the laws and rules laid down by the leaders of their own choosing. Some of it doubtless was in the blood of the men who had come in search of a certain individual freedom of action, but much of it may be attributed to frontier conditions and primitive living. There were many indentured servants, and rough fishermen and sailors have always been unruly. Simple houses of but few rooms accommodating large families are not conducive to gentle speech or modesty of manner nor to a strict morality. The craving for landholding and the poorly defined and easily removed bounds naturally led to ill feeling, assault, defamation, and slander.

---

[110]

CHAPTER IX

SPORTS AND GAMES

This is a subject on which there is little recorded information to be found. Undoubtedly the background of English life, restrained by Calvinistic severity, was continued by the children and youth among the settlers. This must have been among the commonplaces of daily life and of so little importance to the future that no one considered it worthy of recording. It is impossible to think of child life without its natural outlet of sports and games—throw ball, football, running, swimming, etc., and we know that dolls and toys for children were for sale in the shops of Boston and Salem as early as 1651.

The Indians indulged in similar sports and played "hubbub," a game resembling dice, with much shouting of "hub, hub, hub," accompanied by slapping of breasts and thighs.

The innocent games of childhood may be taken for granted and their English origins may be studied in Strutt's *Sports and Pastimes of the People of England*. It was gambling, and tavern amusements that the magistrates endeavored to control.

In 1646 complaints having been made to the General Court of disorders occasioned "by the use of Games of Shuffle-board and Bowling, in and about Houses of Common entertainment, whereby much precious time is spent unprofitably, and much waste of Wine and Beer occasioned"; the Court prohibited shuffle-board and bowling, "or any other Play or Game, in or about any such House" under penalty of twenty shillings for the Keeper of the house and five shillings for every person who "played at the said Game." As we now read this ancient law the waste of precious time and the undue amount of wine and beer consumed would seem to be the principal occasion for the anxiety of the Court, for the game of bowls is excellent exercise and innocent enough; shuffle-board, however, may well be looked upon with sour eyes. It required[111] a highly polished board, or table, sometimes a floor thirty feet in length, marked with transverse lines, on which a coin or weight was driven by a blow with the hand. It bore some resemblance to tenpins, the object being to score points attained by sliding the coin to rest on or over a line at the farther end of the board. The game induced wagers and thereby a waste of substance and even in Old England was unlawful at various times, but difficult to suppress.

Massachusetts magistrates also enacted a law at the 1640 session, prohibiting any play or game for money or anything of value and forbade dancing in taverns upon any occasion, under penalty of five shillings for each offence. The observance of Christmas or any like day, "either by forbearing labor, feasting, or any other way" was also prohibited under penalty of five shillings for each person so offending. This action was occasioned by "disorders arising in several places within this jurisdiction by reason of some still observing such Festivals, as were superstitiously kept in other Countries, to the great dishonour of God and offence of others."

Strange as it may now seem, the non-observance of Christmas existed in orthodox communities, especially in the country towns, until well up to the time of the Civil War.

The magistrates having learned that it was a "custome too frequent in many places, to expend time in unlawful Games, as Cards, Dice, &c." at the same court decreed a fine of five shillings imposed on all so offending. Twenty-four years later the penalty was mightily increased to five pounds, one half to go to the Treasurer of the Colony and the other half to the informer. This was because of the increase of "the great sin of Gaming within this Jurisdiction, to the great dishonour of God, the corrupting of youth, and expending of much precious time and estate."[40]

All this legislation seems to have been directed against indulgence in gaiety and human weakness in and about a public tavern. What took place within the home was another matter although the orthodox Puritan continued to frown upon card playing and dancing[112] until very recently. But cards and gambling were common at all times among the merchants and governing class as well as among the laborers and this was especially true in the seaport towns where sailors congregated and where there was more or less contact with the Southern colonies and with foreign lands. In 1720 playing cards cost a shilling a pack at James Lyndell's shop in Boston and a few years later David Gardiner was advertising Bibles, Prayer Books, account books, playing cards, and a great variety of other goods. Card tables appeared in inventories of estates, and were offered for sale by the cabinet makers.

At an early date horses became a prime article of trade with the West Indies, where they were used in the sugar cane crushing mills, and wherever horses are bred, questions of speed must naturally arise and therefore trials of speed and racing in the public eye.

This was a corrupting influence in the opinion of the Magistrates— "that variety of Horse racing, for money, or moneys worth, thereby occasing much misspence of precious time, and the drawing of many persons from the duty of their particular Callings, with the hazard of their Limbs and Lives." It therefore became unlawful "to practice in that Kind, within four miles of any Town, or in any Highway, the offenders, if caught, to pay twenty shillings each, the informer to receive one half."

But public opinion at a later date changed somewhat and here are a few items gleaned from Boston newspapers that demonstrate the fact that human nature two centuries ago was much the same as at the present time.

HORSE RACE. This is to give Notice that at Cambridge on Wednesday the 21st day of September next, will be Run for, a Twenty Pound Plate, by any Horse, Mare or Gelding not exceeding Fourteen and a half hands high, carrying 11 Stone Weight, and any Person or Persons shall be welcome to Run his Horse &c. entering the same with Mr. *Pattoun* at the Green Dragon in Boston, any of the six Days preceding the Day of Running, & paying Twenty Shillings Entrance.—*Boston News-Letter*, Aug. 22-29, 1715.

A horse race was advertised to take place at Rumley Marsh[113] (Chelsea), on a £10 wager.—*Boston News-Letter*, Nov. 11-18, 1717.

HORSE RACE. On the 2d of June next at 4 in the afternoon, A Silver Punch Bowl Value Ten Pounds will be run for on Cambridge Heath, Three Miles by any Horse, Mare or Gelding 13 hands 3 inches High, none to exceed 14, carrying Nine Stone Weight, if any Horse is 14 hands high to carry Ten stone weight; The Horses that put in for the Plate are to Enter at the Post-Office in Boston on the 1st of June between the Hours of 8 & 12 in the morning, and pay down Twenty Shillings. The winning Horse to pay the charge of this Advertisement.—*Boston News-Letter*, May 15-22, 1721.

PIG RUN. On the same day that the silver Punch Bowl is run for on Cambridge Common by horses, "There will be a Pig Run for by Boys, at 9 in the morning. The Boy who takes the Pig and fairly holds it by the Tail, wins the Prize."—*Boston Gazette*, May 22-29, 1721.

HORSE RACE. This is to give Notice to all Gentlemen and others, that there is to be Thirty Pounds in money Run for on Thursday the 13th of May next at 9 o'clock, by Six Horses, Mares, or Geldings, Two miles between Menotomy & Cambridge, to carry 9 Stone weight, the Standard to be 14 hands high, all exceeding to carry weight for inches. Each one that Runs to have their Number from 1 to 6, to be drawn, and to run by 2 together only as the Lots are drawn, the 3 first Horses to run a second heat, and the first of them to have the Money, allowing the 2d, 5£. if he saves his Distance, which shall be 100 yards from coming in.

Each Person to enter & pay 5£. to Mr. Philip Musgrave, Postmaster of Boston, 15 days before they Run.—*Boston Gazette*, Apr. 19-26, 1725.

HOG RACE. On Monday, the 27th Instant between 2 & 3 a Clock in the afternoon, a Race will be run (for a considerable Wager) on the Plains at Portsmouth, New Hampshire, between a Hog and a Horse.—*Boston Gazette*, Aug. 30-Sept. 6, 1725.

We hear from New-Hampshire, that on Monday the 27th of[114] Sept. last, there was a Race Run, for a considerable sum of money, between a Hog and a Horse, the former of which had the advantage most part of the way, which the party that were for the Horse, it is thought, caused the Hog to be frighten'd, so that with much ado the Horse got the advantage.—*Boston Gazette*, Sept. 27-Oct. 4, 1725.

BEAR BAITING. On Thursday next the 2d of June, at 3 o'clock P.M., in Staniford's Street, near the Bowling Green, will be Baited a Bear, by John Coleson; where all Gentlemen and others that would divert themselves may repair.—*Boston Gazette*, May 23-30, 1726.

HORSE FAIR. This is to give Notice of a Horse Fair which is to be at Mr. John Brown's, Innholder at Hampton Falls, about seven miles to the Eastward of Newbury Ferry, upon the 20th and 21st days of April next; at which time 'tis expected that there will be brought thither some Hundreds of Horses, to be sold or otherwise traded for.—*Boston News-Letter*, Mar. 23-30, 1732.

For many years it was necessary for Massachusetts men to defend their families from marauding Indians and the French, and military trainings were held at regular intervals. In May, 1639, a thousand men took part at a training in Boston and in the fall of that year there were twelve hundred. Such occasions provided opportunity for feasting and drinking—perhaps we should say drunkenness—but as the years went by the prayers and singing of psalms gave way to days of public enjoyment and not infrequently to boisterous license. Governor Bradford wrote that the water of Plymouth was wholesome though not, of course, as wholesome as good beer and wine. Even so!

New England Puritans hated Christmas, a day for Popish revelry. On Christmas Day in 1621, those who had recently arrived at Plymouth in the ship *Fortune* entertained themselves with pitching the bar and playing stoolball, but at noon Governor Bradford appeared and ordered them to stop "gameing or revelling in the street."[41] On Christmas Day, 1685, Judge Sewall wrote in his[115] Diary, "Carts come to town and shops open as usual. Some somehow observe the day, but are vexed I believe that the Body of the People Prophane it, and blessed be God no authority yet to compel them to keep it."

Commencement Day at Harvard was also a day for diversion and vied in importance in the public eye with election day and training days.

By the year 1700 billiard tables might be found in many of the larger taverns and sometimes a ninepin alley. In 1721, Thomas Amory of Boston was shipping billiard tables to his correspondents in the Southern ports.

There was a bowling green in Boston as early as 1700. It was located at what is now Bowdoin Square and a bronze tablet now marks the spot. Here are advertisements from Boston newspapers.

BOWLING GREEN. This is to give Notice, that the Bowling Green, formerly belonging to *Mr. James Ivers* in Cambridge Street, Boston, does now belong to *Mr. Daniel Stevens* at the British Coffee House in Queen Street, Boston, which Green will be open'd, on Monday next the Third Day of this Instant May, where all Gentlemen, Merchants, and others, that have a mind to Recreate themselves, shall be accommodated by the said *Stevens.—Boston News-Letter*, Apr. 26-May 3, 1714.

BOWLING GREEN. Hanover Bowling Green, at the Western Part of the Town of Boston, is now open and in good order for the Reception of all Gentlemen who are disposed to Recreate themselves with that Healthful Exercise.—*Boston Gazette*, June 10-17, 1734.

CHARLESTOWN FROLICK. The Set Company that went upon a Frolick to Mrs. Whyers at Charlestown, on Tuesday Night being the 12th of September, is desired to meet at the aforesaid House of Mrs. Whyers, on the 19th of this Instant, then and there to pay the Just Reckoning that was then due to the House. And likewise to pay the honest Fidler for his trouble and wearing out of his strings, for he gathered but 12 d. among the whole Company that night.—*Boston Gazette*, Sept. 11-18, 1727.

[116]

CONCERT OF MUSIC. On Thursday the 30th of this instant December, there will be performed a Concert of Musick on sundry Instruments at Mr. Pelham's great Room being the House of the late Doctor Noyes near the Sun Tavern. Tickets to be delivered at the place of performance at Five Shillings each, the Concert to begin exactly at six a Clock, and no Tickets will be delivered after Five the Day of performance. N.B. There will be no admittance after Six.—*Boston News-Letter*, Dec. 16-23, 1731.

POPE'S NIGHT, THE 5TH OF NOVEMBER. There being many complaints made by divers of his Majesty's good subjects in the town of Boston, that in the night between the 5th and 6th days of November, from year to year, for some years past, sundry persons with sticks, clubs and other weapons have assembled themselves together and disfigured themselves by blacking their faces, dressing themselves in a very unusual manner, and otherwise disfiguring themselves as well as insulting the Inhabitants in their houses, by demanding money of them, and threatening them in Case of Refusal: which Doings being very disorderly, and contrary to the good and wholesome laws, the Justices of the Peace in said town have concluded to take effectual methods to prevent or punish such irregularities for the future, and would particularly caution and warn all Persons to forbear such Proceedings hereafter.—*Boston Gazette*, Oct. 28, 1746.

POPE'S NIGHT CELEBRATION. Friday last was carried about town the Devil, Pope and Pretender; as also the Effigies of a certain English Admiral, hung upon a gibbet, with a wooden sword on the right side, and one of steel run through the body; upon the front of the stage was written in capitals,

Come hither brave Boys, be jolly and sing,Here's Death and Confusion to Admiral B—g.

—*Boston Gazette*, Nov. 8, 1756.

FIRE WORKS. On the evening of the day when the Royal Commission appointing William Shirley, Governor of the Province of Massachusetts Bay, was published in the Council Chamber, "there[117] was several fine Fire-Works displayed from the Top of the Town-House and other Places; but unluckily one of the Serpents fell into the Town House Lanthorn where all the Fire-Works lay, and set them all off at once, which made a pretty Diversion; several Gentlemen were in the Lanthorn, and some of them were a little scorcht, but no other Damage done, except breaking a few of the Lanthorn Windows."—*Boston Gazette*, Aug. 10-17, 1741.

FLYING MAN. This is to give Notice to all Gentlemen and Ladies, that *John Childs* has flewn off of most of the highest steeples in Old England, and off of the monument by the Duke of Cumberlands' Desire, and does intend this Day, and two Days following, to fly off of Dr. Cutler's Church, where he hopes to give full Satisfaction to all spectators.—*Boston Gazette*, Sept. 12, 1757.

The next issue of the newspaper states that he performed the feat "to the satisfaction of a great Number of Spectators. It is supposed from the steeple to the place where the Rope was fix'd was about 700 Feet upon a slope, and that he was about 16 or 18 seconds performing each Time. As These Performances led many People from their Business, he is forbid flying any more in the Town."

CURRANTS. Any Person that has a mind to take a walk in the Garden at the Bottom of the Common, to eat Currants, shall be Kindly Welcome for Six Pence a piece.—*Boston News-Letter*, July 10-17, 1735.

Jacob Bailey, a country boy born in 1731 of humble parentage in Rowley, Mass., was inspired by the local minister to obtain a college education, and after graduating at Harvard, he taught school, eventually obtained a license to preach, and finally went to England where he took orders in the Anglican Church. Bailey had a gift for versification and while teaching school in the country town of Kingston, N.H., his muse led him to describe a corn husking, a favorite frolic in country towns until very recent times, an occasion when the finding of an ear of red corn entitled the finder to kiss the girls. He begins:

[118]

"The season was cheerful, the weather was bright,When a number assembled to frolic all night."

At Aunt Nabby's, "where kisses and drams set the virgins on flame," horseplay soon developed. Ears of corn were thrown, especially at loving couples, the girls were tumbled about on the husks and practical jokes found their victims. When supper was ready

"Like crows round a carcass each one took his place

"The girls in a huddle stand snickering byTill Jenny and Kate have fingered the pie."

And after supper the "scenes of vile lewdness" abashed the country schoolmaster:

"The chairs in wild order flew quite round the room:Some threatened with fire brands, some branished a broom,While others, resolved to increase the uproar,Lay tussling the girls in wide heaps on the floor."

"Quite sick of confusion, dear Dolly and IRetired from the hubbub new pleasures to try."

Bailey's closing comment is illuminating; "from many of these indecent frolics which I have seen in these parts, I must conclude that rustics are not more innocent than citizens,"[42] and we may rest assured that country manners and customs south of the Merrimack River were no different from those north of it.

In country towns much of the population was thinly distributed and it was impossible for the housewife to run in next door for a few moments' idle chat. Frequently the nearest house was a half-mile or more distant and the feminine desire for social diversion was sadly curbed by the constant demands of farm labor for horses that otherwise might have been used in the chaise or wagon. The[119] weekly gathering at the meetinghouse was always looked forward to with some anticipation by both old and young and the sacredness of the day did not prevent discreet conversation on purely secular topics. But the day when farmer Perkins raised the frame of his barn was made a social event in the full meaning of the word and when the "raising" of the meetinghouse took place, it certainly was a gala day, for in town meeting it was voted to buy a barrel of rum and twelve barrels of cider, with sugar, beef, pork, and brown and white bread in proportion with which to refresh the gathering. Eighty-seven pounds of cheese were eaten and the town paid one shilling and six pence for the mugs that were broken—let us hope purely by accident. But "raisings" occurred at infrequent intervals. Each fall, however, there were corn huskings in various parts of the town and afterwards always plenty to eat for the jolly workers. The women were invited to apple bees and sometimes there were spinning parties. Every winter brought its singing school in the district schoolhouse and spelling matches sometimes brought together the fathers and mothers of the district as well as their sons and daughters. But the quilting party was always welcomed by the women with the keenest relish. It was their personal affair. They were free for a time from the noisy interruptions of the children and the men were not in the way although sometimes invited to a supper. As the quilted pattern advanced over the surface "the women gossiped of neighborhood affairs, the minister, the storekeeper's latest purchases, of their dairies, and webs and linens and wools, keeping time with busy fingers to the tales they told."

---

[120]

CHAPTER X

TRADES AND MANUFACTURES

In the new settlements on the Massachusetts Bay, one of the prime necessities was men skilled in the various trades, "an ingenious Carpenter, a cunning Joyner, a handie Cooper, such a one as can make strong ware for the use of the countrie, and a good brickmaker, a Tyler, and a Smith, a Leather dresser, a Gardner, and a Taylor; one that hath good skill in the trade of fishing, is of special use, and so is a good Fowler."[43] The Company had sent over men to govern and ministers to care for spiritual affairs and many of those who came were skilled husbandmen.

Many of the smaller towns found themselves without men skilled in the mechanic trades and this was particularly the case with blacksmiths, a very essential trade in every community. This led to grants by towns of land and buildings as inducement for smiths to settle and work their trade. Carpenters were found everywhere, and brickmakers naturally gravitated to deposits of clay while the other craftsmen became distributed in accordance with the law of supply and demand, each taking on apprentices as had been customary in their old homes in England.

The principal productions available for commerce were fish, lumber, furs and foodstuffs, but the building of shipping and the importance of the carrying trade must not be overlooked. In the way of domestic manufactures the sawmill came first. The earliest were built on or near the Piscataqua River, but wherever water power was available they soon were set up replacing the laborious saw pits. As the woodlands were cut off the sawmills moved farther up the stream or logs were brought to the mill-sites by floating down with the current. The best of the tall trees were marked with the King's broad arrow and reserved for masts for the royal navy and mast ships sailed for England from Portsmouth, N.H., at frequent intervals.

[121]

The shipbuilding industry required iron and shortly an iron works was set up at Saugus, where bog iron from the neighboring swamps and meadows was smelted. The enterprise was financed in London and largely worked by Scotch prisoners sent over after the defeat at Dunbar, but the quality of the product proved unsatisfactory, save in the way of casting pots and kettles, and before long the enterprise got into financial difficulties and was abandoned.

The high cost of imported iron forced the colonists to fashion wood to serve their needs not only for agricultural implements but for nearly all the utensils used in the household. Massachusetts staves and hoops were important articles of export to the sugar islands in the West Indies.

The raising of flax and the manufacture of linen were attempted early to supply domestic needs in country households. Families in seaport towns very generally bought their fabrics in the local shops which imported their stocks from London or Bristol.

In 1642 it was estimated there were a thousand sheep in Massachusetts and it was not long before the colony was sending wool to France and Spain in exchange for wines, fruits and other luxuries.

The history of early American manufactures has been told in Edward H. Knight's *American Mechanical Dictionary*, 3 volumes, Boston, 1876, and William B. Weeden's *Economic and Social History of New England* (1620-1789), 2 volumes, Boston, 1894, makes easily available an immense amount of research. In the following pages are printed gleanings from Boston newspapers and court records that supplement these works and have the readable flavor of their period.

ANVILS. Samuel Bissel, anvil smith, lately come from England, living at New-Port on Rhode Island, makes all sorts of Blacksmiths and Gold-smiths' anvils, Brick-irons and stakes and new Faces old ones, at reasonable Rates, and may be spoke with or wrote to, at his House or Shop near the Topsaile Street in said Town.—*Boston News-Letter*, Mar. 4-11, 1716-17.

APOTHECARY. William Woodcocke of Salem, apothecary, was[122] licensed to still strong water and sell at retail.—*Essex Co. Court Records*, Mar. 25, 1662.

AQUÆDUCTS. For the Public Good, aquæducts made & sold by Rowland Houghton which Instrument being properly applyed to the outside of a Pump Tree, prevents said Pump from freezing tho' scituate in the most bleak Place & sharpest Season.

Said Houghton has lately improv'd on his New Theodolate, by which the Art of Surveying is rendered more plain & easy than heretofore.—*Boston Gazette*, Jan. 17-24, 1737.

ASSAYER. If any Persons desire to know the true value of ores, minerals or metals, of what kind soever, may have them justly essay'd on reasonable terms, by Robert Baden, at Mrs. Jackson's, Founder, at the Brazen Head in Cornhill, Boston.—*Boston Gazette*, Sept. 27-Oct. 4, 1736.

BAKER. "John Webster the Baker was admonished for brewing and tipleinge."—*Essex Co. Court Records*, June 30, 1640. James Underwood, a baker, was living in Salem in 1655 and Obadiah Wood, baker, was in Ipswich, before 1649.

BAKER. Any Persons wanting good brown Bisket fit either for the Fishery or for Shipping Off, may be supplyed by *Lately Gee* at the Sign of the Bakers Arms in Hannover Street, at the following Rates, *viz.* If Wheat be at 6 *s*, per Bushel, then Bread at 22 *s* per Hundred, if at 7 *s*, then 25 *s*, and if at 8 *s*, then Bread at 28 *s*, and so proportionable either for money or Good Wheat at the Prices above said.—*New England Courant*, Sept. 10-17, 1722.

Whereas in the Courant of the 17th Instant, an Advertisement was publish'd by *Lately Gee* of Boston, Baker, offering brown Bisket at lower Prices than usual. These are to give Notice, That Bread of the same Courseness with the said *Gee's*, and with the same Quantity of Bran remaining in it, may be had for the same Prices at other Bakers in Town; but they being willing to avoid the Curse of the Common Sailors, those employ'd in the Fishery, etc., generally make their

Bread better, and sell it for a better Price.—*New England Courant*, Sept. 17-24, 1722.

BARBER'S UNION IN 1724. Boston, Dec. 7, on Tuesday the first[123] of this Instant in the Evening, Thirty-two Principal Barbers of this Place, assembled at the Golden Ball, with a Trumpeter attending them, to debate some important Articles relating to their occupations; where it was propos'd, that they should raise their Shaving from 8 to 10 *s.* per Quarter, and that they should advance 5 *s*, on the Price of making common Wiggs and 10 *s.* on their Tye ones. It was also propos'd, that no one of their Faculty should shave or dress Wiggs, on Sunday Mornings for the future, on Penalty of forfeiting 10 Pounds for every such Offence: From whence it may fairly be concluded, that in times past such a Practice has been too common among them.—*New England Courant*, Nov. 3O-Dec. 7, 1724.

BARBER'S SHOP. To be Sold by Publick Vendue at the Sun Tavern in Boston, on Tuesday next the 30th Instant at 4 of the Clock, P.M. Sundry Goods belonging to the Estate of James Wright, Barber, deceased, viz: Wiggs, Hair on the Pipes, Sash Lights and Shutters fitting for a Barber's Shop, and also sundry other Goods.—*Boston Gazette*, Oct. 20-27, 1729.

BARBER'S SHOP. To be Let in a pleasant Country Town on the Post Road to Portsmouth, a Barber's Shop with proper Implements or Utensils for that Business, where there is enough to keep two Hands employ'd. Inquire of the Publisher.—*Boston Gazette*, May 7-14, 1739.

BELLOWS MAKER. Joseph Clough near the Charlestown Ferry in Boston, makes and mends all sorts of Bellows for Furnaces, Refiners, Blacksmiths, Braziers and Goldsmiths; and also Makes and Mends all sorts of House Bellows after the best Manner; where all Gentlemen, and others, in Town and Country may be served at very reasonable Rates.—*Boston Gazette*, Dec. 15, 1741.

BELLS. This is to give notice to all Persons that have occasion for a Bell or Bells in Churches or Meeting-houses, that in New York they may be supplyed with New Bells, or if they have any old Bell broke they may have it new cast at a reasonable Price, and warranted good for Twelve Months, that if it Crack or Break it shall be new Cast for nothing: And all New Bells shall be made of[124] better mettal than any other that comes out of Europe for Churches or Meeting-houses. All Persons that have Occasion may apply themselves to Joseph Phillips who is now building a Furnace for that purpose, and hath already agreed with some Persons, and is ready to do the same with any that are disposed.—*Boston News-Letter*, June 10-17, 1717.

BELL FOUNDER. John Whitear, of Fairfield [Conn.], Bell-Founder, makes and sells all sorts of Bells from the lowest size to Two Thousand Weight.—*Boston Gazette*, May 29-June 5, 1738.

BLACKSMITH'S WORK. This is to give Notice, that there is one William Bryant, Blacksmith, that now keeps a shop adjoining to the Presbyterian Meeting House in Long Lane, Boston, who makes and mends Glaziers' Vises, Cloathers' Screws, and worsted Combs, and makes, grinds and setts Cloathers' Shears; he also makes and mends Smiths' Vises, Ship Carpenters', Blockmakers', Tanners', Glovers' and Coopers' Tools, Braziers' and Tinsmens' Shears, and makes House work, with many other things too tedious to mention here. He will make and engage his work to any of his Employers according to the value of them.—*Boston News-Letter*, July 6-13, 1732.

BLACKSMITH AND LOCKSMITH. Made and Sold by Robert Hendrey, on Scarlet's Wharff in Boston, Horse Shoeer, Spinning Wheel Irons after the best Manner, at *Ten Shillings*, old Tenor per sett: Also all sorts of Locks are made and mended by the said Hendrey, who keeps a Man that served his Time to the Lock Smith's Business.—*Boston Gazette*, Dec. 10, 1751.

Four months later he also advertised "fine White-Smiths Work; Also Spades and the best sort of Steel Shod Shovels made very reasonably."—*Boston Gazette*, Apr. 21, 1752.

BOARDING SCHOOL. Any Gentlemen (Members of the Church of England) that are desirous of having their Sons Educated after the Method of Westminster School, may be further inform'd by applying to J. Boydell. Conditions, To find their own Bed, Bedding, etc. and to bring as Entrance, one pair of Sheets, six Towels,[125] six Napkins, one Silver Spoon value 10 s. Sterling, one Knife, Fork, and Pewter Porringer; which Entrance on their leaving the School is not to be returned. None to be admitted but such as can read well and write; nor the Number of six to be exceeded.—*Boston Gazette*, Oct. 24-31, 1737.

BOOKKEEPER. Mr. *Brown Tymms* Living at Mr. *Edward Oakes* Shopkeeper in Newbury Street, at the South End in Boston, keeps Merchants & Shopkeepers Books, also writes Bills, Bonds, Leases, Licenses, Charter-parties, &c., for any Person that may have Occasion, at reasonable Rates. And likewise teacheth Young Men Arithmetick and Merchants Accounts.—*Boston News-Letter*, Feb. 17-24, 1717-18.

BRAZIER AND IRONMONGER. The late Mr. *Edward Jackson's* Stock in Trade, consisting of a great variety of Articles in the Braziery and Ironmongery Way, in larger or smaller Lots as will best accommodate Customers.—Lead, Shot, bloomery, brittle, refined and Guinea Iron, Hollow Ware, best heart and clubb German Steel, best London Steel in half Faggots, Blowers' best Wool Combs, Iron Hearths for Ships, a Copper Furnace for ditto, Cannon shot, Iron Backs, Deck, Sheathing and Drawing Nails, Newcastle Coals, &c. &c. Enquire at the House where the Deceased's Family dwells, or at his Shop.—*Boston Gazette*, Sept. 12, 1757.

BRAZIERS AND PEWTERERS. A Good Set of Sundry Sorts of Braziers and Pewterers' Molds, and other Tools, as good as New, belonging to the Estate of Mr. Thomas Thacher, deceased, To be sold by Oxenbridge Thacher at his Shop near the Town Pump, Boston. And also almost all sorts of Brass, Pewter and Iron Ware, viz. Nails, Locks, Hinges, Pots, Kettles, &c....—*Boston News-Letter*, Sept. 17-24, 1724.

BRAZIERS' WARES. William Coffin, at the Ostrich, near the Draw-Bridge, makes and sells Mill Brasses, Chambers for Pumps, Brass Cocks of all Sizes, Knockers for Doors, Brasses for Chaises and

Sadlers, Brass Doggs of all Sorts, Candlesticks, Shovels and Tongs, small Bells, and all sorts of Founders ware. Also, all sorts of Braziers and Pewterers ware, small Stills and worms, and all[126] Sorts of Plumbers work; likewise Buys old copper, Brass, Pewter, and Lead.—*Boston News-Letter*, Feb. 17-24, 1736-7.

BRAZIERS' SHOP. Thomas Russell, Brazier, near the Draw-Bridge in Boston, Makes, Mends, and New-Tins, all sorts of Braziery ware, viz. Kettles, Skillets, Frying-Pans, Kettle-Pots, Sauce Pans, Tea Kettles, Warming Pans, Wash Basins, Skimmers, Ladles, Copper Pots, Copper Funnels, Brass Scales, Gun Ladles, &c. makes all sorts of Lead Work for Ships, Tobacco Cannisters, Ink Stands, &c. and buys old Brass, Copper, Pewter, Lead and Iron.—*Boston News-Letter*, Oct. 30-Nov. 6, 1740.

BRAZIERS' WARES. To be sold by Publick Vendue this Afternoon, at 3 o'Clock, at the House of the late Mr. Stephen Apthorpe, Brazier, deceas'd, Codlines, Match, Warming-Pans, Frying-Pans, Kettle-Potts, Brass-Kettles, Pewter Plates, Dishes, Spoons, &c. Locks of several Sorts, Jacks, Knives of several sorts, Hinges of several sorts, Snuff Boxes, Buttons, Trowells, Shod Shovels, Fire Shovel and Tongs, Lanthorn Leaves, Brass Candlesticks, Chaffin-Dishes, Horn-Combs and Wire with a great Variety of other Articles.—*Boston News-Letter*, May 31, 1750.

Mary Jackson, at the Brazen-Head, Cornhill, Boston, advertised by Wholesale and Retail, Brass Kettles and Skillets, etc. "N. B., Said Mary makes and sells Tea-Kettles, and Coffee-Pots, Copper Drinking Pots, Brass and Copper Sauce-Pans, Stew-Pans, and Baking-Pans, Kettle-Pots and Fish-Kettles."—*Boston News-Letter*, June 21, 1750.

BUCKRAM. Any Person that has occasion to have any Linnen Cloth made into Buckram, or to buy Buckram ready made, or Callendring any Silk, Watering, Dying or Scouring: they may apply themselves to Samuel Hall, lately from London, and Thomas Webber near the New North Brick Meeting House, or at their Work-house near the

Bowling-Green, Boston.—*Boston News-Letter*, June 25-July 2, 1722.

BUTCHER. Humphrey Griffin, a butcher by trade, was living at Ipswich as early as 1641.—*Essex Co. Court Records*, Sept., 1658.

CABINET MAKER. Edward Browne, cabinet maker, was living[127] in Ipswich as early as 1637 and at his death in 1659 left in his shop unfinished chairs, spinning wheels, etc.—*Essex Co. Court Records*, Nov., 1659.

CABINET MAKER. Mr. John Davis, Cabinet-Maker in Summer-Street, has for sale extraordinary good English Glew, by Wholesale or Retail, at the cheapest Rate, for ready Cash.—*Boston News-Letter*, Apr. 8-15, 1736.

CALICO PRINTER. Francis Gray, Callicoe Printer, from Holland; Prints all sorts of Callicoes of several Colours to hold Washing, at his House in Roxbury near the Meeting-House.—*Boston Gazette*, June 16-23, 1735.

CARD MAKER. Francis Smith of Boston, cardmaker, probably came with Winthrop in 1630.

CARD MAKER. Imported in the *Wilmington*, and to be sold in School street, by Joseph Palmer, cardmaker from London, at his House next above the French Meeting House viz. Broad cloths, the best steel Wire, Exeter Fish Hooks, Buckles, Mettal & Horse Hair Buttons, Tinplate Ware of several sorts, and other Goods; also the best Wool and Cotton Cards are there made (as good as any brought from England) by the said Palmer, and sold by Wholesale or Retail. N. S. The said Palmer wants a servant Maid, and a Negro boy.—*Boston Gazette*, Nov. 25, 1746.

CHANDLER AND SOAPBOILER. To be sold by *Edward Langdon*, in Fleet Street, near the Old North Meeting House, A Quantity of Hard Soap by the Box, soft Soap by the Barrel, and good old Candles both Mould and Dipt, fit for Shipping or Families, also Mould Candles of Bayberry Wax, all by the Box or by Retail.—*Boston Gazette*, July 24, 1750.

SPERMA-CETI CANDLES. To be sold on Minot's T. by James Clemens, Sperma Ceti Candles, exceeding all others for Beauty, Sweetness of Scent when extinguished; Duration, being more than double Tallow Candles of equal size; Dimensions of Flame, nearly four Times more, emitting a soft easy expanding Light, bringing the Object close to the Sight, rather than causing the Eye to trace after them, as all Tallow-Candles do, from a constant Dimness[128] which they produce.—One of these Candles serves the Use and Purpose of three Tallow Ones, and upon the whole are much pleasanter and cheaper.—*Boston News-Letter*, Mar. 30, 1748.

CHAPMAN OR PEDDLER. "On Thursday last Dyed at Boston, James Gray, That used to go up and down the Country selling of Books, who left a considerable Estate behind him."—*Boston News-Letter*, Apr. 9-16, 1705.

CHOCOLATE MILL. Salem, Sept. 3. By a Gentleman of this Town is this Day bro't to perfection, an Engine to Grind Cocoa; it is a Contrivance that cost much less than any commonly used; and will effect all that which the Chocolate Grinders do with their Mills and Stones without any or with very Inconsiderable Labour; and it may be depended on for Truth, that it will in less than six Hours bring one Hundred weight of Nuts to a consistance fit for the Mold. And the Chocolate made by it, is finer and better, the Oyly Spirit of the Nut being almost altogether preserved, and there is little or no need of Fire in the making.—*Boston Gazette*, Sept. 5-12, 1737.

COFFIN FURNITURE. To be sold by Arthur Savage Tomorrow Evening at his Vendue Room, about 50 Sett of neat Polished Coffin Furniture, consisting of Breast-plates, Angels, Flowers, Posts, etc.—*Boston Gazette*, May 29, 1758.

COOPER. John Henry Dyer, Cooper, lately arriv'd from London, living on Mr. Henshaw's Wharffe, near the South Market House in Boston; makes all sorts of Cooper's Ware, after the best manner, as Rum Hogsheads, Barrels, Caggs, little Tubs and Trays, as cheap and good as any in the Town.—*Boston Gazette*, July 30, 1751.

CURRIER. The Trade of a Currier is very much wanted in *Middletown* the Metropolis of Connecticut: any Prudent person that is Master of that Trade may get a pretty Estate in a few Years.— *Boston Gazette*, Nov. 6, 1758.

DYER. Alexander Fleming, Dyer, lately from Great Britain, has set up said Business in Boston, in a House of Mr. Arthen's near Dr. Gardner's in Marlborough Street, on the same side of the[129] Way, who can dye all sorts of Colours, after the best Manner and Cheapest Rate, viz. Scarletts, Crimsons, Pinks, Purples, Straws, Wine Colours, Sea-Greens, Saxon ditto, common Blues, shearing, dressing and watering of clothes: Also he can dye linnen Yarn either red, blue, green, yellow or cloth colours, and all Colours on silks, and cleaning of Cloths.—*Boston Gazette*, May 14, 1754.

DUTCH TILES. Several sorts of Neat Dutch Tiles, to be set in chimneys, to be sold by Mr. Richard Draper; at the lower end of Cornhill, Boston.—*Boston News-Letter*, May 6-13, 1725.

DUTCH TILES. To be sold at Capt. Stephen Richard's in Queen Street, Boston. All sorts of Dutch Tyles, viz. Scripture (round and square), Landskips of divers sorts, sea monsters, horsemen, soldiers, diamonds, etc., and sets of brushes; London quart bottles; and a chest of Delph ware.—*Boston Gazette*, Feb. 6-13, 1738.

EARTHEN WARE. To be sold by Capt. Arthur Savage at the White House near Mr. Coleman's Church, Boston, Earthen Ware and Glasses per the Hogshead, fine Holland Tiles, Earthen and Stone Ware in Parcels, likewise the long London Tobacco Pipes, all very Reasonable.—*Boston News-Letter*, Apr. 23-30, 1716.

FELLMONGER. Edmond Farrington of Lynn, fellmonger [dealer in hides] arrived in Massachusetts in 1635.

FIRE ENGINE. To be sold, a Large and extraordinary good Copper Fire-Engine, newly fixed, that works well, and will be of excellent Use in Time of Fire, in any populous Place. Enquire of Mr. James Read, Blockmaker, near Oliver's Bridge in Boston.—*Boston News-Letter*, Feb. 19-26, 1735-6.

GLAZIERS' DIAMONDS. To be sold by Gershom Flagg, in Hanover Street near the Orange Tree, viz. Spanish Whiten, and choice Diamonds fit for Glazier's use, English Sole Pieces for Shoes and Boots, fine Jelly Glasses and Crewits of double Flint, all sorts of Coffin Gear, silvered, plain and lackered, and sundry other Articles.—*Boston Gazette*, Aug. 6, 1745.

GLASS was being manufactured in Salem as early as 1639, the main product being bottles and beads used in barter with the Indians. The glass made was a dark-colored brownish-black.

[130]

CROWN GLASS. To be sold by Alexander Middleton at Warehouse Number 3, in Butlers' Row, Crown Glass in Cases uncut, Ditto in Chests cut in Squares, ordinary ditto cut in squares per the Chest, Bar & Sheet Lead, white & brown Earthen ware, Glass Bottles, Quarts & Pints, bottled Ale in Hampers, ... Pipes, glaz'd and ordinary ditto. And best Sunderland Coal on board the ship *Betty*, William Foster, Commander, lying at the North side of the Long Wharff.—*Boston Gazette*, June 4-11, 1739.

GLASS MAKING. Tuesday last a ship arrived here from Holland, with about 300 Germans, Men, Women & Children, some of whom are going to settle at Germantown, (a Part of Braintree) and the others in the Eastern Parts of this Province.—Among the Artificers come over in this ship, there are Numbers of Men skilled in making of Glass, of various sorts, and a House proper for carrying on that useful manufacture, will be erected at Germantown as soon as possible.—*Boston Gazette*, Sept. 26, 1752.

GLASS MANUFACTORY AT GERMANTOWN. Notice is hereby given, That for the future none will be admitted to see the new manufactory at Germantown [Braintree], unless they pay at least one shilling lawfull money; and they are desired not to ask above three or four Questions, and not to be offended if they have not a satisfactory answer to all or any of them.

Note.—The manufactory has received considerable Damage, and been very much retarded by the great Number of People which are constantly resorting to the House.—*Boston Gazette*, Sept. 4, 1753.

KNOT GLASS. To be sold by Arthur Savage, To-morrow Evening, at his Vendue-Room on the North side of the Town Dock. Twelve Crates of Knot Glass of various sizes, large and small Looking Glasses, ... Leather Breeches, Desks, Tables, etc. Also, a Camera Obscura with Prints.—*Boston Gazette*, Jan. 24, 1757.

WINDOW GLASS. To be sold by Jonathan Bradish in Charlestown near the Sign of the Buck, sundry sorts of Window Glass, viz., 8 by 10, 8 by 6, 7 by 9, etc. Also Painters' Colours and Linseed oyl.—*Boston Gazette*, Nov. 12, 1751.

[131]

GLOVER. To be sold by the Maker, Ph. Freeman, who arrived in the last Ship from London, at Mr. Irish's in Bridge's Lane near Mr. Welsteed's Meeting-House, A Large Parcel of Gloves of all Sorts, viz. Men's and Women's Buck and Doe, Kid and Lamb, for Mourning and all other Sorts.—*Boston News-Letter*, Sept. 30-Oct. 7, 1742.

GLOVE MAKER. Just Imported and Sold by Philip Freeman, Norway Doe Gloves, and Makes and Sells Winter Gloves, for Men and Women: and lines Gloves with Fur, after the best Manner.—*Boston Gazette*, Nov. 26, 1754.

GUNSMITH. To be sold by John Pim of Boston, Gunsmith, at the Sign of the Cross Guns, in Anne-Street near the Draw Bridge, at very Reasonable Rates, sundry sorts of choice Arms lately arrived from London, viz. Handy Muskets, Buccaneer-Guns, Fowling pieces, Hunting Guns, Carabines, several sorts of Pistols, Brass and Iron, fashionable Swords, &c.—*Boston News-Letter*, July 4-11, 1720.

GUNSMITH. Newly imported, and sold by Samuel Miller, Gunsmith, at the Sign of the cross Guns near the Draw-Bridge, Boston: Neat Fire Arms of all sorts, Pistols, Swords, Hangers, Cutlasses, Flasks for Horsemen, Firelocks, &c.—*Boston Gazette*, May 11, 1742.

HALBERTS. A Set of Halberts for a foot Company to be sold on reasonable Terms, by Nicholas Boone Bookseller, to be seen at his House near School-House Lane, Boston.—*Boston News-Letter*, Apr. 22-29, 1706. "A Set of New-Halbards" were offered for sale in the June 3-10, 1706, issue.

HAND ENGINES. Hand Engines made after the best manner, fitted with Brass Clappers, very useful in all Families, convenient for extinguishing Fire in Chimneys, or in any Room in a House; Also very proper for Coasters to carry to sea to wet the Sails in small Winds to preserve them from Mildews; said Engine throws Water with ease 40 Feet perpendicular. Sold by Rowland Houghton, on the North side of the Town House at 25s. each.—*Boston Gazette*, June 10-17, 1734.

[132]

HATS. Daniel Jones, at the *Hat & Helmit*, South-End, Boston, ... makes and sells Beaver, Beaveret, and Castor-Hats: and has also a good Assortment of English Castor and Beaveret Hats, English and Felt ditto; Hat Linings and Trimmings of all sorts: Red Wool, Coney Wool, Camels Hair: Logwood by the 100 Wt. by Wholesale or Retail, cheap for Cash or Treasurer's Notes.—*Boston Gazette*, Dec. 10, 1759.

HOUR GLASSES. All sorts of Hour-Glasses to be made or mended on Reasonable terms, by *James Maxwell*, at his House in Water Street, near the Town House in Boston.—*Boston News-Letter*, Sept. 17-24, 1716.

IRON MONGER. To be sold by *John Winslow*, at his Warehouse, in Newbury-Street, near Summer Street: Best refined and blommery Iron, Ploughshare Moulds, Anchor Palms, Coohorns, Swivel Guns, Ten Inch Mortars and Shells, 6, 4, & 3 pound Swivel and Grape Shot.—*Boston Gazette*, Apr. 25, 1757.

IRON HEARTH. On the 11th Instant, early in the Morning, a Fire broke out at *Mr. Pierpont's* House near the Fortification, occasioned by the Heat of the Iron Hearth of one of the newly invented Fireplaces, whereby the Floor was set on Fire; the People being in

Bed, perceived a great Smoke, got up, and happily discover'd and timely distinguished [*sic*] the Fire.—*Boston Gazette*, Dec. 22, 1747.

IRON FOUNDRY. Any Person that has occasion for Forge Hammers, anvils, or Plates, Smiths' Anvils, Clothiers' Plates, Chimney Backs, Potts, Kettles, Skillets, Cart Boxes, Chaise Boxes, Dog-Irons, or any other Cast Iron Ware, may be provided with them by Richard Clarke, at his Furnace in the Gore, giving speedy Notice (of the Sizes and Quantity they want) to him there, or to Oliver, Clarke, and Lee, at their Warehouse in King Street, Boston; where they may be supplied with Swivel Guns.—*Boston Gazette*, July 13-20, 1741.

JEWELLER. This is to inform the Publick, That Mr. *James Boyer*, Jeweller, from London, living at Mr. Eustone's, a Dancing Master in King Street, Boston, setts all manner of Stones in[133] Rings, &c. and performes every thing belonging to that Trade. N.B. Said Mr. Boyer is lately recovered of a fit of Sickness.—*New England Courant*, Dec. 31-Jan. 7, 1722-3.

JOYNER. Richard Lambert of Salem, the joyner, was living there as early as 1637, and four years later was fined for drinking and also sat in the stocks for two hours.—*Essex Co. Court Records*, Feb., 1641.

LINEN PRINTER. The Printer hereof Prints Linens, Callicoes, Silks, &c. in good Figures, very lively and durable Colours, and without the offensive smell which commonly attends the Linens Printed here.—*Boston Gazette*, Apr. 18-25, 1720.

LINEN PRINTER AND DYER. John Hickey, linen-printer and dyer, from Dublin, is now settled in this town, at the linen manufactory, where he follows the business of blue and white printing, and silk or cloth dying; and takes all manner of spots out of silk or cloths, cleans gold and silver lace, and scarlet cloth, dyes linnen and cotton of a blue or London red, and all manner of country stuffs, worsteds, camlets, tammies, or leather; he dyes blacks so as they shall be sound and clean as any other colour; also dyes ribbons and makes them up again as well as ever, and English thick sets after they have been worn or faded, and blue yarn for one shilling a pound. N.B. as there has been several who have imposed upon this country in telling that they were printers; I engage myself that if my colours be not as good and as lasting as any that comes from Europe, to satisfy my employers with all charges or damages that shall be justly laid against me.

All the above articles done with expedition at the most reasonable price, by JOHN HICKEY.—*Boston Gazette*, (sup.) May 7, 1759.

LINEN MANUFACTORY. The Massachusetts General Court at its session held in the summer of 1753, passed an "Act for granting the sum of Fifteen Hundred Pounds To encourage the Manufacture of Linnen," providing for a tax on every "Coach, Chariot, Chaise, Calash and Chair" for the term of five years, the Governor, Lieutenant Governor, the President of Harvard College, and the[134] settled ministers in the Province, being excepted from its provision, at the following rates: each Coach, ten shillings annually, Chariot, five shillings, Chaise, three shillings, Calash, two shillings, Chair, two shillings. The several sums received from Time to Time were to be paid to a committee of ten appointed by the Act, "to be applied to the purchasing a Piece of Land, and building or purchasing a convenient House within the Town of *Boston*, for carrying on the Business of Spinning, Weaving, and other necessary Parts of the Linnen Manufacture." This legislation was instituted because of "the great Decay of Trade and Business the Number of Poor is greatly increased, and the Burden of supporting them lies heavy on many of the Towns within this Province, and many Persons, especially Women and Children are destitute of Employment."—*Boston Gazette*, Aug. 7, 1753.

LIME KILN. To be Sold a good Penny-worth; A good Lime-Kiln, a Lime-House, a good Well, a Wharf, and a piece of Ground, being near the Bowling-green, Boston; Inquire of Mr. Walter Browne at the Sign of the Blue Anchor in King-Street, Boston, and know further.

N. B. There is very good Lime-juice to be sold by the aforesaid Browne at his House.—*Boston News-Letter*, Mar. 28-Apr. 4, 1723.

STONE LIME. To be sold by the Hogshead or Bushel, the best eastward Stone Lime, by John Blowers of Boston, Mason, in School Street.—*Boston Gazette*, Mar. 31, 1747.

LINEN MANUFACTURE. Publick Notice is hereby given, That sundry Looms for Weaving of Linnen, of all Sorts, are set up at the Linnen-Manufacture House in the Common below Thomas Hancocks' Esq; where all Persons may have their Yarn wove in the best and Cheapest Manner, and with the utmost Dispatch. At the same Place, money will be given for all Sorts of Linnen Yarn.

And whereas the setting up and establishing the Linnen Manufacture is undoubtedly of the utmost Importance to this Province: It is propos'd by a Number of Gentlemen, very soon to open several Spinning-Schools in this Town, where children may be taught[135] Gratis. And it is to be hop'd, that all Well-wishers to their Country will send their children, that are suitable for such Schools, to learn the useful and necessary Art of Spinning; and that they will give all other proper Countenance and Encouragement to this Undertaking.—*Boston News-Letter*, Dec. 13, 1750.

LOCKSMITH. This is to inform my Customers, that I have remov'd from Middle-street, to the Bottom of Cross street, where I continue to mend all sorts of Locks, also to fit Keys to Locks, mend all sorts of Kettles, as Brass, Copper, Pewter, &c. at a very reasonable Rate, by *Reuben Cookson.—Boston Gazette*, Apr. 23, 1754 (*sup.*)

MAHOGANY AND OTHER WOODS. To be Sold behind Numb. 4, on the Long Wharffe, Lignumvitee, Box wood, Ebony, Mohogany Plank, Sweet Wood Bark, and wild Cinnamon Bark.—*Boston Gazette*, Aug. 22-29, 1737.

MAHOGANY. To be sold at publick Vendue at the Exchange Tavern, on Thursday, the first of December next, at three o'clock Afternoon; 50 Pieces of fine Mahogany in 10 Lots, No. 1 to 10, being 5 Pieces in a Lot, to be seen at the Long Wharffe before the Sale begins.—*Boston Gazette*, Nov. 21-28, 1737.

MILITARY EQUIPMENT. On Thursday the 6 of February at three of the clock Afternoon, will be sold by Publick Vendue at the Exchange Tavern, about one hundred Canvice & Ticken Tents, Poles, Mallets, and Pins to them, about five hundred Pick-Axes, fifty Axes and Hatchets, about eight hundred Tomhawks or small Hatchets, about three hundred Spades and Bills, a parcell of Shovels, Wheelbarrows, Handbarrow's, Baskets of Speaks and Nails, all to be put and sold in Lots, and to be seen at the place of sale the Morning before the Sale begins: Also a very fine Negro Woman.— *Boston Gazette*, Jan. 27-Feb. 3, 1728-9.

MILITARY EQUIPMENT. Extract from the *Act for Regulating the Militia*:—"Every listed Soldier, and other Householder shall be always provided with a wellfixt Firelock Musket, of Musket or Bastard-Musket bore, the Barrel not less than three Foot and an half long, or other good Fire Arms to the satisfaction of the Commission[136] Officers of the Company; a Cartouch Box: one Pound of good Powder: Twenty Bullets fit for his Gun, and twelve Flynts; a good Sword or Cutlass; a Worm, & priming Wire, fit for his Gun, on Penalty of six Shillings...."—*Boston News-Letter*, Feb. 7-14, 1733-4.

BREECH-LOADING GUN. Made by John Cookson, and to be Sold by him at his House in Boston: a handy Gun of 9 Pound and a half Weight; having a Place convenient to hold 9 Bullets, and Powder for 9 Charges and 9 Primings; the said Gun will fire 9 Times distinctly, as quick, or slow as you please, with one turn with the Handle of the said Gun, it doth charge the Gun with Powder and Bullet, and doth prime and shut the pan, and cock the Gun. All these Motions are performed immediately at once, by one turn with the said Handle. Note, there is Nothing put into the Muzzle of the Gun as we charge other Guns.—*Boston Gazette*, Apr. 12, 1756.

MATHEMATICAL BALANCEMAKER. Jonathan Dakin, Mathematical Balance maker, at the Sign of the Hand & Beam, opposite to Dr. *Colman's* Meeting House, makes all sorts of scale Beams, and likewise mends all that can be mended; where all Gentlemen may be supplied with Beams ready adjusted and scaled, as the Law directs.—*Boston Gazette*, Nov. 12, 1745.

MATHEMATICAL INSTRUMENTS. Stephen Greenleaf, Mathematical Instrument-Maker, in *Queen Street*, Boston, opposite to the Prison, Makes and Mends all Sorts of Mathematical Instruments, as Theodolites, Spirit Levels, Semi circles, Circumferences, and Protractors, Horizontal and Equinoctial Sun Dials, Azimuth and Amplitude Compasses, Eliptical and Triangular Compasses, and all sorts of common Compasses, drawing Pens and Portagraions, Pensil Cases, and parallel Rulers, Squares and Bevils, Free Masons Jewels, with sundry other articles too tedious to mention.

N.B. He sets Load Stones on Silver or Brass, after the best manner.—*Boston Gazette*, June 18, 1745.

MUSICIAN. Thomas Androus, "the scholar musician, was there[137] with his music," at John Androus house in Ipswich, in the summer of 1656, at a merriment.—*Essex Co. Court Records*, April, 1657.

MUSTARD MAKER. John Ingram, the Original Flower of Mustard Maker, from Lisbon, now living at the House of Mrs. Townsend, near Oliver's-Dock, Boston, Prepares Flower of Mustard to such Perfection, by a Method unknown to any Person but himself, that it retains its Strength, Flavour and Colour Seven Years; being mix'd with hot or cold water, in a Minute's Time it makes the strongest Mustard ever eat, not in the least Bitter, yet of a delicate and delightful Flavour, and gives a most surprizing grateful Taste to Beef, Pork, Lamb, Fish, Sallad, or other Sauces. It is approved of by divers eminent Physicians as the only Remedy in the Universe in all nervous Disorders, sweetens all the Juices, and rectifies the whole Mass of Blood to Admiration. If close stopt it will keep its Strength and Virtue Seven years in any Climate. Merchants and Captains of Ships shall have good Allowance to sell again.—*Boston Gazette*, Sept. 19, 1752.

NAILMAKING. Any Gentleman that hath a mind to set up the nailing Business, which may be done to very great Advantage in this Country, may by inquiring of the Printer be informed of a Man that will carry it on to Perfection for him.—*Boston Gazette*, Mar. 2, 1742.

NEEDLE MAKER. Simon Smith, Needle maker from London, is removed from the Rainbow and Dove in Marlborough Street, now in Union Street near the Corn fields; continues to make and sell all sorts of white Chapple Needles, and all other sorts round and square.—*Boston News-Letter*, Apr. 15-22, 1742.

Oil Lamp. A New England vessel having "30 Tons of Lamp Oyl" on board was captured by French and Indians in Newfoundland.— *News-Letter*, Oct. 2-9, 1704.

OIL LAMP. Best Refin'd Sperma-Ceti Oil for Lamps, to be sold next Door to the *Salutation*, near the North Battery.—*Boston Gazette*, July 17, 1758.

PAPER MILL. Whereas some Gentlemen design to set up a Paper-Mill in New England, if a supply can be had to carry on[138] that Business: These are therefore to give Notice, that James Franklin, Printer in Queen Street, Boston, buys Linen Rags, either coarse or fine, at a Peny a Pound.—*New England Courant*, June 1-8, 1724.

PAPER MAKER. This is to give Notice, That Richard Fry, Stationer, Bookseller, Paper-maker, and Rag Merchant, from the City of London, keeps at Mr. Thomas Fleet's Printer at the Heart and Crown in Cornhill, Boston; where the said Fry is ready to accommodate all Gentlemen, Merchants, and Tradesmen, with sets of Accompt-Books, after the neatest manner; and whereas, it has been the common Method of the most curious merchants in Boston, to Procure their Books from London, this is to acquaint those Gentlemen, that I the said Fry, will sell all sorts of Accompt-Books, done after the most accurate manner, for 20 per cent. cheaper than they can have them from London.

I return the Publick Thanks for following the Directions of my former advertisement for gathering of Rags, and hope they will continue the like Method; having received seven thousand weight and upwards already.

For the pleasing entertainment of the Polite part of Mankind, I have Printed the most Beautiful Poems of Mr. Stephen Duck, the famous Wiltshire Poet; It is a full demonstration to me that the People of New England, have a fine taste for Good Sense & Polite Learning, having already sold 1200 of these Poems, Richard Fry.—*Boston Gazette*, May 1-8, 1732.

PEWTERER. This is to give notice, that a Journeyman Pewterer, who is a good workman in Hollow-ware, may have constant work, and good Wages, if they will go to New York, and apply themselves to Mr. *David Lyell*, or they may write to him and know further.—*Boston News-Letter*, Aug. 23-30, 1714.

POTASH WORK set up at Charlestown Ferry in Boston, at the House of John Russell, Ferryman, 6d. in money paid per Bushell to any that have ashes to spare.—*Boston News-Letter*, Nov. 27-Dec. 4, 1704.

POTTERY. John Pride owned a pottery in Salem as early as[139] 1641. William Vincent owned a pottery there in 1681. At a later date several potteries existed at what is now the town of Peabody.

POTTERY AT CHARLESTOWN. John Webber, a potter, at Charlestown, was injured by the explosion of a cannon while celebrating the marriage of the Princess Royal.—*Boston News-Letter*, May 16-23, 1734.

EARTHEN WARE. To be sold on reasonable Terms, A Dwelling-House & Land in Charlestown, near the Swing-Bridge, with a House & Kiln for the making of Earthen Ware; as also a Warehouse and other Conveniences necessary for that Business, Inquire of the Printer.—*Boston News-Letter*, Nov. 1, 1744.

POTTERY. Made and Sold reasonably by *Thomas Symmes* and Company at *Charlestown* near the Swing Bridge, blue and white stone Ware of forty different sorts; also red and yellow ware of divers sorts, either by Wholesale or Retale.—*Boston Gazette*, Apr. 16, 1745.

POTTER'S KILN. To be sold by publick Vendue on Tuesday the 16th Currant, two o'Clock Afternoon, at the Three Crane Tavern at

Charlestown, a Dwelling House, Potter's Kiln House and Kiln in Wapping Street in Charlestown aforesaid, any Person minding to purchase the same before said Time may inquire of Michael Brigden or Grace Parker.—*Boston Gazette*, Dec. 9, 1746.

POWDER MAKER. Any Gentlemen, Merchants or others, that have any damnifyed Powder, or dust of Powder, either to sell, or to be made of New, They may repair with the same unto Walter Evenden, Powder-maker, at his House in Dorchester, who will either buy it or make it of New for them, on reasonable terms.—*Boston News-Letter*, Nov. 25-Dec. 2, 1706.

PRINTED FABRICS. The Printer hereof Prints Linens, Callicoes, Silks, etc., in good Figures, very lively and durable Colours, and without the offensive Smell which commonly attends the Linens printed here.—*Boston Gazette*, April 18-25, 1720.

The Printer hereof having dispers'd advertisements of his Printing Callicoes, etc. a certain Person in Charlestown, to rob him of the Benefit of said advertisements and impose upon strangers,[140] calls himself by the Name of Franklin, having agreed with one in Queen Street, Boston, to take in his work. These are to desire him to be satisfyed with his proper Name, or he will be proceeded against according to Law.—*Boston Gazette*, May 2-9, 1720.

PUMPS. Pumps erected or altered after a new and Easy Method, whereby they will deliver more Water, and with less strength, not being apt to loose water, not at all liable to Freeze, tho' fixed in the most Bleak Places; by the Directions of Rowland Houghton.—*Boston News-Letter*, Sept. 14-21, 1732.

ROASTING JACKS. To be sold by John Jackson, Jack-maker, at his shop, being the corner shop at the Draw bridge, in Boston, all sorts of Jacks, reasonably, and makes, mends and Cleans all sorts of Jacks; also makes & mends Locks, Keys, and Ironing Boxes, at a reasonable rate.—*Boston Gazette*, May 2-9, 1737.

SCALES. All Sorts of Weights and Skales of the best sort for weighing Money or other Merchandize. Made and Sold by Caleb

Ray, Chief Skale-maker of New England; or Skales to be new strung and mended; at the sign of the Skales and Weights in the Alley near to Governours Dock in Boston, at reasonable Rates.—*Boston News-Letter*, Apr. 26-May 3, 1708.

SCALES AND BALANCES. Jonathan Dakin, Mathematical Balance-maker, at the sign of the Hand & Beam opposite to Dr. Colman's Meeting House, Makes all Sorts of Scale Beams, and likewise mends all that can be mended; where all Gentlemen may be supplied with Beams ready adjusted and sealed as the Law directs.—*Boston Gazette*, Nov. 26, 1745.

SHOEMAKER. Francis Dowse, a shoemaker, was in the employ of George Burden of Boston, in 1640.

SLITTING MILL AND IRON FORGE. To be Sold a good Penniworth, a Slitting Mill compleatly finished and furnished, scituated in the middle of near 20 Forges in the Compass of 12 Miles, with a well built Forge with Two Fires, and conveniency for a third; together with a well built and well accustomed Grist Mill, all standing on one Dam; on as constant a stream as this Land affords; with accommodations for other Water Works; A good[141] Dwelling House, Coal House, and above 6 Acres of Land, and a good Orchard upon it, said Works stand on Namasket River in Middleborough, 13 Miles from Plymouth, and 10 from Taunton. All finely scituated for a Country Seat; and now Lets for 379 Pounds per Annum. Any Person or Persons minded to purchase the same, may inquire of the Rev. Mr. Peter Thacher of Middleborough aforesaid, or of the Printer hereof, and know further.

N.B. The Reason of this Sale is because the Person wants the money for it, and intending to leave off that Business.—*Boston Gazette*, May 11, 1742.

STAMPED LINEN. These are to Inform the Publick, that I the Subscriber propose to come once more to Boston; if any Person or Persons have old sheets or Linnen to stamp, they are desired to leave them at the House of *James Nichol* in School Street, next door to the French Meeting House; and if they send them in four Weeks from this Date, they shall have them in March next without fail. As Witness my Hand, *Sarah Hunt.—Boston Gazette*, Dec. 22, 1747.

STOVES. New-fashion Fire-Places or Stoves from Philadelphia, to be sold by *Thomas Wade.—Boston News-Letter*, Jan. 31, 1745.

JUST PUBLISHED. An account of the new-invented Pennsylvania Fire-Place: Wherein their construction and manner of operation is particularly explained; their Advantages above every other method of warming Rooms demonstrated; And all objections that have been raised against the Use of them, answered and obviated. Sold by *C. Harrison*, over against The Brazen-Head in Cornhill.—*Boston News-Letter*, Feb. 7, 1745.

TAILOR. William Jones, a tailor, had one half of his fine remitted at Salem Court.—*Essex Co. Court Records*, December, 1642. Daniel Gaines of Lynn, aged 11 years, was apprenticed for 8 years to Luke Potter of Concord to learn the "skill and mistery" of a tailor.—*Essex Co. Court Records*, March, 1649. John Bourne, a tailor, was making clothes in Gloucester, in 1652. John Annable of Ipswich, tailor, was living there as early as 1641.

WATER ENGINE. There is newly erected in the Town of Boston,[142] by Messieurs John and Thomas Hill, a Water-Engine at their Still-house, by the Advice and Direction of Mr. Rowland Houghton, drawn by a Horse, which delivers a large quantity of Water twelve Feet above the Ground. This being the first of the kind in these Parts, we thought taking Notice of it might be of Publick Service, inasmuch as a great deal of Labour is saved thereby.—*Boston Gazette*, Jan. 15-22, 1733.

WHEELWRIGHT. John Robinson, a wheelwright, was living in Ipswich as early as 1635, only two years after the settlement of the town.

[143]

CHAPTER XI

CONCERNING SHIPPING AND TRADE

New England, with its many rivers and indented coastline, until recent years, has been a breeding place for sailors and a location for shipbuilding. During the first century following the settlement, the larger part of the population lived near the coast, and as roads between towns were poor, it naturally followed that craft of small tonnage were constantly employed for transport on the ocean and the navigable rivers, and as no extent of rich soil was found awaiting cultivation, many settlers, of necessity, turned to fishing and to trade. A ship carpenter was brought over to Plymouth, in 1624, who "quickly builte them 2 very good and strong shalops ... and a great and strong lighter, and had ... timber for 2 catches" framed when he fell sick of a fever and soon died.[44] These shallops were used in opening a fur trade among the Indians on the Kennebec River that eventually discharged the indebtedness of the Pilgrims to the London adventurers.

Six shipwrights were sent over by the Company of the Massachusetts Bay, in the spring of 1629, together with a considerable stock of ship stores, such as pitch, tar, cordage and sail cloth.[45] Doubtless these men were employed at the outset in housing the settlers and in building small fishing boats, as the first vessel of any size in the Bay, of which there is record, is Governor Winthrop's trading bark, *The Blessing of the Bay*, of thirty tons, built mainly of locust, which went to sea, August 31, 1631, on a voyage to the eastward and afterwards traded with the Dutch at New Amsterdam.[46]

In January, 1633, Emanuel Downing wrote to the Council for[144] New England that he had made enquiries of Mr. Winthrop respecting the ship carpenters employed in New England and found that the plantation was able to build ships of any burden. Their most competent shipwright was William Stephens, who had built in England, the *Royal Merchant*, a ship of six hundred tons.

The General Court, in 1639, exempted ship carpenters and fishermen (during the fishing season) from compulsory military training.[47] Two years later the Court was informed that some shipwrights were scanting their work and an order was adopted providing for a survey of all ship construction as was usual in England at that time.[48]

The coasting trade led to the building of small shallops and sloops and the need for firewood in Boston and Charlestown brought about the building of sloops, broad of beam, intended especially for that trade. Fishing craft and wood sloops were soon being built all along the coast. As early as 1634, one merchant in Marblehead owned eight fishing craft, and Portsmouth, N. H., had six great shallops, five fishing boats, with sails and anchors, and thirteen skiffs, in the trade as early as 1635. Richard Hollingsworth, in 1637, had a shipyard at Salem Neck and in 1641, built "a prodigious ship of 300 Tons."

The number of New England vessels used in foreign trading during the seventeenth century was considerable and the mainstay of the trade was the fishing business. Off-shore fishing in the early days was carried on in shallops—capacious, open boats carrying several pairs of oars and also fitted with masts and sails. They were sometimes decked over, in whole or in part, and usually carried one mast with a lug sail. Many of these small craft were built in the winter time by the fishermen and their sons, as a fisherman is always more or less of a boatbuilder by virtue of his calling. The lumber for the boat would be cut in the common woods and got out, a little at a time, and the boat when built would actually cost its owner little more than the outlay for certain necessary fittings. These boats might be framed-in anywhere—on the beach in front[145] of the fisherman's cottage; in his dooryard or in the woods, some distance from the shore, to which the hull would be dragged by oxen, on sledges of timber. The first vessels sent to "the banks," from Massachusetts, for deep-water fishing, were "a ship and other vessels," rig unknown.[49] That was in 1645.

By 1665 there were three hundred New England vessels trading with Barbadoes, Virginia, Madeira, Acadia, etc., and 1,300 smaller craft were fishing at Cape Sable. Cod and mackerel were caught and salted. The best fish were sent to Malaga and the Canaries, the second sort to the Portugal Islands, and the worst to the Barbadoes there to be used in the diet of the negro slaves. At that time, the principal commodities produced in the Massachusetts Bay were fish and pipe-staves, masts, fir-boards, pitch, tar, pork, beef, and horses and corn which were sent to Virginia, Barbadoes, &c. Tobacco and sugar were taken in payment and shipped to England. Excellent masts were shipped from the Piscataqua River, and many pipe-staves. There were more than twenty sawmills located on that river and "much good timber was spoilt," reported an agent of Lord Arlington, the Secretary of State.[50] New England masts, 33 to 35 inches in diameter, at that time cost the Navy Commissioners from £95 to £115 per mast. The agent also reported that Boston, the chief town, was "built on a peninsula in the bottom of a bay, which is a good harbour and full of fish. The houses are generally wooden, the streets crooked, and neither days, months, seasons, churches, nor inns are known by their English names."

During the middle years of the seventeenth century the waters of the West Indies were covered with privateers commissioned to prey upon Spanish commerce. Not only did the home government issue these commissions but every Colonial governor as well, and not infrequently it was difficult to separate privateering from piracy. John Quelch, who was hanged in Boston for piracy, in 1704, preyed upon Portuguese commerce as he supposed in safety and not until he returned to Marblehead did he learn of the treaty[146] of peace that made him a pirate. In 1653, Thomas Harding captured a rich prize sailing from Barbadoes and in consequence was tried in Boston for piracy, but saved his neck when he was able to prove that the vessel was Dutch and not Spanish.

The town of Newport, R. I., frequently profited from the visits of known pirates, as in 1688, when Peterson, in a "barkalonga" of ten guns and seventy men, refitted at Newport and no bill could be obtained against him from the grand jury, as they were neighbors and friends of many of the men on board. Two Salem ketches also traded with him and a master of one brought into "Martin's Vineyard," a prize that Peterson, "the pirate, had taken in the West Indies."[51] Andrew Belcher, a well-known Boston merchant, and master of the ship *Swan*, paid Peterson £57, in money and provisions, for hides and elephants' teeth, taken from his plunder.

The ill-defined connection between privateering and piracy was fully recognized in those days and characterized publicly by the clergy. In 1704 when Rev. Cotton Mather preached his "Brief Discourse occasioned by a Tragical Spectacle in a Number of Miserables under Sentence of Death for Piracy," he remarked that "the Privateering Stroke so easily degenerates into the Piratical; and the Privateering Trade is usually carried on with an Unchristian Temper, and proves an Inlet unto so much Debauchery and Iniquity."

Another strong influence that led to insecurity on the high seas and eventually to outright piracy was the operation of the English Navigation Acts. European nations were in agreement that the possession of colonies meant the exclusive control of their trade and manufactures.

In 1696, Col. Charles Lidgett, a New England merchant, in "Some Considerations Offered to the Board of Trade," wrote that "all the American Colonies are generally esteemed according to the Conveniency and benefit they bring to England, their Mother."[52] Lord Chatham wrote, "The British Colonists in North[147] America have no right to manufacture so much as a nail for a horse shoe," and Lord Sheffield went further and said, "The only use of American Colonies, is the monopoly of their consumption, and the carriage of their produce."[53]

English merchants naturally wished to sell at high prices and to buy colonial raw materials as low as possible and as they were unable to provide a market for all that was produced, the Colonies were at a disadvantage in both buying and selling. By the Acts of Navigation certain "enumerated articles" could be marketed only in England. Lumber, salt provisions, grain, rum and other non-enumerated articles might be sold within certain limits but must be transported in English or plantation-built vessels of which the owners and three-fourths of the mariners were British subjects. Freight rates also advanced, as other nations, notably the Dutch, had previously enjoyed a good share of the carrying trade.

The first Navigation Act was passed in 1645. It was renewed and its provisions enlarged in 1651, 1660, 1663 and later. Before long it was found that these attempts to monopolize the colonial markets resulted in a natural resistance and smuggling began and also an extensive trade with privateers and pirates who brought into all the smaller ports of New England captured merchandise that was sold at prices below the usual market values. Matters went from bad to worse and servants of the Crown frequently combined with the colonists to evade the obnoxious laws. Even the Royal Governors connived at what was going on. This was particularly true in the Colonies south of New England.

There were pirates and pirates. Some were letters-of-marque and illegitimate traders and enjoyed the protection of merchants and officials on shore, while others were outlaws. In 1690, Governor Bradstreet of the Massachusetts Colony was complaining of the great damage done to shipping by "French Privateers and Pirates," and four years later, Frontenac, the Governor of Canada, was asking for a frigate to cruise about the St. Lawrence against the New England *"corsaires and filibusters."* There is no doubt[148] these French privateers were a considerable menace to New England shipping and that there was need for privately armed vessels to protect the coast, a task not easy or desirable; so why should one scrutinize too closely semi-piratical captures made by so useful friends?

The profits of piracy and the irregular trade practiced at that time were large, and twenty-nine hundred per cent profit in illicit trade was not unusual, so there is little wonder that adventurous men took chances and honest letters-of-marque sometimes seized upon whatever crossed their course. The pirate, the privateer and the armed merchantman often blended the one into the other.[54]

Edward Randolph landed in Boston on June 10, 1676, and during the next week the following vessels arrived: "a Bostoner, 100 tons, Clutterbuck, master, from Nantes, laden with 50 butts of brandy and French commodities; a pink, of Boston, from France, of 70 tons, with 12 tun of brandy, wine, etc.; a Scotsman, 130 tons, from the Canaries, with 80 pipes of Canary; a Bostoner, 80 tons, from the Canaries, with 50 pipes of Canary, and a ketch of Southampton, from Canary, with wine."[55] He reported to Secretary Coventry that the fishermen had made good voyages notwithstanding the war with the Indians. He estimated that the fish exported amounted to about £50,000 yearly with profitable returns in barter on masts and timber for shipping sent to Barbadoes and other of the Carib Islands. The Bay of Campeachy supplied about 1,000 tons of logwood annually. The maritime towns were well stored with sailors, fishermen and carpenters, and yearly several ships of good burthen were built, besides ketches and barques. In 1676 thirty vessels had been ordered set on the stocks by merchants in England, but the Indian War had prevented building the full number. However, twelve were in process of construction at Boston, Charlestown, Salisbury and other places, some of which were upwards of 160 tons burthen.

In October he wrote that there were about thirty merchants in[149] Massachusetts, New Hampshire and Maine estimated worth from £10,000 to £20,000. Local commodities consisted of naval stores, cattle and provisions, exported to Virginia, Maryland and the West Indies—(to the latter were also sent "houses ready framed"), to Spain, Portugal, the Straits and England. Tobacco, sugar, indigo, cotton, wool, ginger, logwood, fustic, cocoa and rum were imported and again exported. "They trade with most parts of Europe from which they import direct all kinds of merchandise, so that little is left for English merchants to import," wrote Randolph. "Some ships have been sent to Guinea, Madagascar, etc., and some to Scanderoon; there are built in the Colony, 730 ships varying from 6 to 250 tons, by thirty master shipbuilders." Duties were imposed on provisions and wines imported, and on ships, but there was no custom on exports, except on horses.[56]

In April, 1675, William Harris wrote from Boston that "The merchants seem to be rich men, and their houses [are] as handsomely furnished as most in London. In exchange of fish, pipe-staves, wool and tobacco, they have from Spain, Portugal, and the islands, the commodities of those islands; their wool they carry to France and bring thence linen; to England they bring beaver, moose, and deer skins, sugar and logwood, and carry hence cloth and ironwares; to Barbadoes, in exchange for horses, beef, pork, butter, cheese, flour, peas, biscuit, they have sugar and indigo; when they trade with Jamaica; as they do sometimes, they bring home pieces of eight, plate, and pigs of silver.... As to cloth, there are made here Linsey woolseys, and other of cotton and wool, and some all sheep's wool, but the better sort of linen is brought from England; they have many woolcombers, and some make tammeys, but for their private use. Salt they get from Tortudas, not far from Barbadoes. It is sold at 10s. the hogshead, and is clear and white as alum, very sharp and much stronger than ordinary bay salt."[57]

Governor Simon Bradstreet wrote in 1680, in answer to an enquiry[150] from the Lords of the Privy Council: "There may bee near twenty English merchants within our Government bred up to that calling, and neere as many others that do trade and merchandize more or less; but Foreign merchants of other Nations Wee have none ... there are two or three [merchants] in our Corporation that may bee worth sixteen or eighteen thousand pound a piece, some few others worth eight or ten Thousand pounds a piece, a third sort worth four or five thousand pounds a piece.... Hee is accounted a rich man in the Country that is worth one thousand or Fifteen hundred pounds. There are about one hundred or one hundred and twenty Ships, Sloopes, Katches and other Vessells that trade to and from hence yearly of our own or English built, most of them belonging to the Colony, wee have eight or ten ships of one hundred tons or upwards, three or four of two hundred tons or more, and about Forty or Fifty Fishing Katches of betwixt twenty and Forty tons; Six or eight

English ships do usually come hither yearly belonging to the Kingdom of England, bringing commodities of all sorts from thence.

"The obstructions wee [encounter] within our trade are the generall decay of any profitable trade in the places wee mostly trade unto. Vizt. to all his Majesties plantations in America, where wee send our horses, beasts, timber, provisions, mackeril, fish, etc. For the commodities of those places which are spent here or transported into England wee finde those markets many times so overlaid and clogged with the like comoditys from England, Ireland and other places, that many of our commodities are sold at cheaper rates many times then they were worth at home. 2dly The Algeir men of warr infesting the seas in Europe have taken some of our Ships and men which is a discouragement to our trade and Navigation. 3dly the French at Nova Scotia or Acadia (as they call it) do interrupt our Fishers in those parts and Sr. Edmond Andros, Governor of New-Yorke for his highness the Duke of Yorke, doth the like betwixt the French and Pemaquid requiring duty to bee paid to them by all our Vessells that fish in those Seas, otherwise threatening to make prizes of them, which hath been alwaies Formerly[151] free For his Majesties Subjects for Fishing ever since wee came hither. The double custom which our merchants pay for Sugar, Indigo, Cotton Wool, Tobacco, etc. First at the places from whence they fetch these commodities, the greatest part whereof is transported from hence to England, where they pay the full custome again.

"Wee impose no rates or dutys upon Goods exported they being generally the produce of the Country got with hard labour and sold at low prices ... and but one penny pr pound upon Goods imported, when they come into the Merchant's hands, which is the taxe wee have set upon houses, Lands, cattle and other estate of the Country yearly."[58]

By this time the Colonists were all comfortably housed according to the standards of the period and were producing all the foodstuffs needed and more. Wines and spirit were imported in considerable quantity to give variety to the native beer and cider. Much butter and cheese were brought from abroad and also luxuries such as spices, chocolate, raisins of the sun, almonds, figs, oranges, etc. Our English ancestors were gross eaters and drinkers. Mulled and spiced wines were drunk in the absence of tea and coffee, and highly-seasoned dishes were popular. The absence of a variety of root-crops made it necessary to pickle meat and pepper and spice were used to a considerable extent. There was a very comfortable and varied diet among the merchant and governing class but the farmers and common people lived much on salt pork, beans, fish and boiled foods. As for clothing—home industry, of course, provided a certain amount but as yet the loom was not in common use. Between 1665 and 1675 over three hundred estates were settled in Essex County, Massachusetts, with only nine looms listed in the inventories. Eighty-three of these homes, however, possessed spinning wheels—cotton, linen and wool—for every good wife and child could knit stockings, mittens and tippets. Among those who died during this ten years were two tailors, five shoemakers, a cloth worker and eight weavers.[59]

[152]

Much clothing was brought from overseas, particularly for the town dwellers. John Hull, the mintmaster, records in his diary in June, 1657, that three ships arrived from London bringing supplies of clothing, "for, as yet," he writes, "our chief supply, in respect of clothes, is from England." He owned a number of vessels and his little ketches were constantly on the go between Boston and the Barbadoes and thence to Bilboa, London or Bristol. He shipped salted fish, logwood, tobacco, furs and plantation products and received iron in bars, salt, wines and fruits from Spain, while from England came dress goods, lead, shot, etc. His serges he wanted "sad coloured," none above 42 shillings, nor under 30 shillings. He also instructed one of his captains to load "dowlass and good nowell convass [which was used for sails], Dutch duffalls, red penystones and flanils, no such scalet cloth as you brought me before." He looked askance at calicoes. Another time he called for duffalls, white, striped or blue, with red and blue stockings, none above 16 shillings and under if possible. He wanted no "kersey" that cost above 46 pence per yard and the black stuff, either of "hair or wosted," must be cheap.

A cousin once advised him to ship a cargo of pipe-staves, hoops and fish to the Canaries, but he declined the venture and wrote in reply that he "would more and more affect and imbrace opportunity of getting out rather than running into the businesses of this world Speacially forraigne trafficque as desirous to be more thoghtfull of Lanching into that vast ocian of Eternity whither we must all shortly bee carried yt soe I might bee in a prepared posture for my Lord's Comeing."[60]

His sea captains were carefully instructed "to see to the worship of God every day in the vessel and to the santification of the Lord's day and suppression of all prophaness that the Lord may delight to be with you and his blessing be upon you which is the hearty prayer of youre frind and own^r." The sailors were not all to this way of thinking, however, but Mintmaster Hull rode with the ruling party which saw to it that the Quarterly Courts were kept[153] busy measuring out the metes and bounds. In the journal of the voyage over kept by the Reverend Higginson in 1629, he records a visitation of avenging Providence; a just retribution inflicted upon the ungodly. He writes, "this day a notorious wicked fellow yt was given to swearing and boasting of his former wickednes and mocked at ye daies of fast, railing & jesting ag^t puritans, this fellow fell sicke of ye [small] pocks and dyed."

It is interesting to discover at how early a date it was possible to purchase in the shops in New England, the manufactured products of Old England. It is known that George Corwin set up a shop in Salem, for the sale of fabrics and hardware, as early as 1651, or only twenty-five years after the first immigration. His shop was well stocked and at the outset he was selling such luxuries as children's toys. Undoubtedly stocks of manufactured goods were on sale in the Colony years before this time. In the matter of house hardware Corwin sold a considerable variety of locks. He carried stock locks of several sizes, spring locks with screws, single and double chest locks, warded outside chest locks, outside box locks, plain cupboard locks and small and large padlocks—by no means a poor assortment for a small shop tucked into a corner in the American wilderness.

This shop, a few years later, was supplying the town with such articles as combs, white haft knives, barbers' scissors, flour boxes, carving tools, carpenter's tools of all kinds, door latches, curry combs and brushes for horses, and a great variety of earthen and woodenware. Its shelves held broadcloth, red cloth rash, perpetuana, red cotton, sad colored rugs, green rugs, green Tammy, blue calico, crape, curley duroy, prunella, silk barronet, peniston, Persian silk, worsted faradeen, camblet, St. Peter's canvas, hall cloth, vittery, blue linen, noyles, together with a great variety of hose, stomachers, ribbons, tape, fileting, silk and gimp laces, needles, pins, thread, buttons, etc., etc.[61]

The invoice of an importation made into Boston in 1690, contains such items as brass curtain rings, dressing glasses, square[154] monument candlesticks, iron spring candlesticks, brass extinguishers and save-alls, tin lanterns, pocket nutmeg graters, bread graters, wooden rat traps with springs and a great variety of woodenware. It seems strange that New England should import from across seas wooden plates and bowls, yet here they are:

9 doz. best Maple Trenchers @ 30/ per dozen 1 doz. Porridge Dishes at 11/4.

Here also are carved spoons, beer taps, hair sieves, sucking bottles and milk trays.[62]

From the returns of outward and inward entries at the Colonial ports, the records of which are now preserved in the Public Record Office in London, much may be learned concerning early shipping and trade in the Massachusetts Bay. Let us take, for example, the last six months in the year 1714, covering the outward entries of shipping at the port of Boston. During that time there were 236 clearances not including, of course, fishermen and coasting craft. The rig is not stated in the first part of the register but between Sept. 21st and December 31st there were cleared 49 ships, 18 brigantines, 64 sloops, two barques, one snow, one pink, and a "ship or snow" of 40 tons. Not a schooner is mentioned. The largest ship measured 210 tons and the smallest was the *Grayhound* of London, a British-built vessel of 33 tons, carrying a crew of five men and a cargo of dyewood, turpentine, whale oil, barrel staves and sugar. With the exception of five ships hailing from London, every vessel cleared was "plantation built," that is, it had been built in one of the American colonies. Of the 236 entries, 147 of the vessels hailed from Boston; 18 were owned in London; six in Bristol; four came from the West Indies; and the rest hailed from New York, Virginia, Maryland, and other colonies. Most of them were small craft averaging from thirty to sixty tons burthen.[63]

The *Hopewell*, of North Carolina, five tons, and a crew of two men, was loaded with rum and salt.

The *Swallow*, of Boston, 20 tons, and three men, sailed for[155] Annapolis Royal with a cargo of tobacco, pitch, molasses, rum, pork, and English goods for the garrison.

The sloop *Success*, owned in New York, 20 tons, with four men, sailed for home carrying four hhds. rum, pewter ware, a cart, chairs, boxes, etc.

The sloop *Pelican* of Boston, 25 tons, with four men, sailed for Virginia, loaded with 42 bbls. salt, three hhds. rum, iron pots, etc.

The sloop *Sea Flower* of Boston, 40 tons, with six men, entered out, the 3d day of November, carrying bread, butter, beer, onions, and peas for the logwood cutters in the Bay of Campeachy.

The brigantine *William and Susanna*, owned in Salem, 40 tons, and eight men, sailed for Virginia, carrying rum, lime juice, salt, earthen ware, etc.

The sloop *Branch* of Boston, 50 tons, with six men, sailed for South Carolina, carrying rum, blubber, onions, etc.

The brigantine *Speedwell* of Boston, 60 tons, with seven men, cleared for Surinam, carrying 10 pipes of wine and twenty horses.

The ship *Brunswick* of Boston, 65 tons, two guns and ten men, sailed for Barbadoes, carrying 37 hhds. fish, 50 boxes candles, and 15 boxes of soap.

The ship *Mary Ann* of London, 80 tons, with four guns and ten men, entered out, bound for Lisbon, carrying 240 quintals of salted fish, "which is the whole cargo," states the register.

The ship *Bedmunster* of Bristol, 100 tons, with ten men, returned home with 18½ tons of logwood, 507 bbls. tar, 307 bbls. pitch, 7 bbls. whale oil, and 40½ bbls. cranberries.

The ship *Amity* of London, 130 tons, six guns and fourteen men, returned with a cargo of 20 hhds. sugar, 5 bags of cotton, 168 tons, 9 cwt. 1 qr. and 14 lbs. logwood, 10 bbls. pitch, pimento, wines, furs and staves.

The largest ship to clear was the *Sophia* of Boston, 310 tons, built in New Hampshire, armed with 18 guns and carrying a crew of twenty men. She sailed for Barbadoes carrying fish, corn, candles and lumber.

Among the more unusual articles of merchandise enumerated in[156] the cargo lists are "2 cases of returned pictures," shipped to London; pots and frying pans, to Maryland; apples, cider, Indian meal, and six sheep, shipped to Newfoundland; 230 barrels of cider shipped to Philadelphia; and rum, cider, iron and brass, saddles and bridles, etc. to North Carolina. Bricks, shingles, iron and woodenware, hops, pickled sturgeon, beeswax, rice, furs, washed leather, linens and calicoes are mentioned.

The West India trade called for lumber, horses, rum, food, and luxuries; and supplied sugar and molasses. Salt fish and pickled sturgeon were sent to Spain, Portugal and the Western Islands— Roman Catholic countries. The important dyewood trade in the Bay of Campeachy required foodstuffs; and the coasting trade with the Southern colonies called for manufactured goods of all sorts and supplied in return tobacco, pitch, turpentine and tar, which were used in the New England shipyards and also reshipped to England.

The fisheries in Newfoundland called for foodstuffs and London and Bristol supplied markets for dyewoods, naval stores, furs, whale oil, sugar, manufactured lumber, and wines brought from Portugal and the Western Islands.

During the months of April, May and June, in the year 1717, there were twenty-seven inward entries at the Salem customhouse. All but three were plantation built. Seventeen were owned in Salem; two hailed from London; two from Liverpool, and one from Bristol. There were eight ships, four brigantines, twelve sloops and three schooners. The first of these schooners to enter was the schooner *Fisher*, 30 tons, Timothy Orne, master, registered at the Salem customhouse, Oct. 27, 1715. This is the earliest authentic record of a schooner I have ever found. Those vessels having the largest tonnage were the ship *Patience and Judith*, 100 tons, owned in London, England, and carrying six guns and a crew of fourteen men, entering from the Isle of May, with a cargo of 140 tons of salt; and, second, the ship *Friendship*, Capt. Samuel Crow, 100 tons, owned in Salem, carrying two guns and a crew of ten men, also entering from the Isle of May with 90 tons of salt. Ten out of the twenty-seven entries brought in salt for the Salem[157] fisheries. Rum and lignumvitae wood came from the West Indies, and wheat, corn, beans, flour, flax, hides, pork and lard came from Maryland, Virginia and North Carolina. The ships from English ports brought European goods.

During the last three months of 1754, eighty-seven vessels cleared outward at the Salem customhouse and sixty-eight were schooners. The largest tonnage was the snow *Aurora* of Salem, 130 tons, built at Newbury that year, sailing for Liverpool with a cargo of 15,000 staves and 40 tons of pine timber. Of the ten European clearances, seven were for Bilboa, with salted fish; thirty-three cleared for ports in the West Indies; forty for southern colonies; and two for Newfoundland. The principal cargoes were salted fish, manufactured lumber, rum, sugar, molasses, salt, horses, sheep, and salted meats. Nearly all clearing for Maryland, Virginia and the Carolinas carried cargoes of wooden, earthen and iron wares, probably manufactured in Salem or its immediate vicinity. Twenty-six thousand bricks were shipped to the West Indies and 20 bales of hay to South Carolina. The two schooners clearing for Halifax were loaded with "dead meat," probably intended for the garrison.

During the first three months of the year 1762, fifty-three vessels cleared from Salem, bound for foreign ports and the southern colonies; thirty-four were schooners. The largest vessel was the ship *Antelope*, 150 tons, a prize, registered at Salem in 1761 and owned by Richard Derby. She cleared for Guadaloupe with lumber, fish, train oil, and Fyall wines. There were nineteen clearances for Guadaloupe during those three winter months. Listed with the staples were the following curious items, viz.: 7½ tons prize soap, illegally imported, shipped to Guadaloupe; and 12,000 feet of oars, shipped to St. Christophers. There is a surprising diversity of ownership among these fifty-three vessels. No large shipowner had a considerable interest. Richard Derby of Salem owned three vessels; Robert Hooper of Marblehead, two; Jeremiah Lee of Marblehead, two; Nathaniel Ellery of Gloucester, owned two and the rest were owned by men who cleared only one vessel.

The ships, that plied between English and American ports, at[158] more or less regular intervals during the eighteenth century, not only brought an exchange of merchandise, but also carried passengers. Officials connected with the government—the customs service and the military establishment, with a sprinkling of clergymen and scholars, were crossing on nearly every ship and the New England merchant sailing to London to buy a new stock of goods for his shop and the Englishman who came to the colonies bringing adventures of goods in great variety, all helped to maintain the service. In the year 1737, the Boston newspapers mention by name eighteen persons who had arrived by ship or were about departing. On January 31st, John Banister, late in business with his uncle Samuel Banister, at Marblehead, advertised in the *Gazette* that he designed speedily to embark for Great Britain and requested a settlement of all accounts. John Jeykill, the collector of the Port of Boston, arrived from London, April 18th, in Captain Shepardson; early in May,

Thomas Phillips of Boston, merchant, advertised that he would sell his household furniture by vendue, as he intended speedily for London, and a week later Major Martin and family arrived from Antequa, in the West Indies. He proposed to reside in Boston for a few years. Toward the last of the month, the Lieutenant-Governor of New Hampshire sailed from Portsmouth, bound for England, and about the middle of June, the Rev. Doctor McSparrow and lady arrived in Boston. As late in the year as December 20th, Edmund Quincy, Esq., the agent of the Province at the Court of Great Britain, was sailing for London, in Captain Homans, with several other unnamed gentlemen.

Very little is known at the present time concerning the intimate details of life on board ship in the early times and especially as to the accommodations provided for passengers. On the vessels that brought over emigrants in any number, the living conditions must have been well-nigh intolerable because of crowding many people into limited space and also by reason of a meagre equipment and lack of necessary conveniences. During the period of the German emigration and that from northern Ireland in the mid-eighteenth century, there was frequently a high mortality during[159] the voyage and sometimes, when it was of unusual length, the supply of food and water ran short and there was terrible suffering. Doubtless some attempt was made to separate the sexes and the families but from time to time cases are found in the court records in which depositions or testimony clearly show that living conditions on board ship in the early days were decidedly of a miscellaneous character.

It isn't necessary to delve into the very remote past in order to discover casual social relations between the sexes on board ship. In 1888, I went the length of Cape Breton and while sailing up the Bras d'Or lakes on the steamer that plied regularly during the summer, I came on deck early one morning to see the sun rise and then began an exploration of the boat. On the lower deck I suddenly came upon some twenty or more barefooted and half-clothed men and women lying in a long row, side by side, stretched out on mattresses placed on the deck. They were probably waitresses, cooks, stewards, and the like, but may have been second-class passengers. However that may be, they were unconscious of the presence of any passer-by and slept quietly together like so many puppies.

In the olden time it is known that in the more regular passenger service the main cabin was parted off at night by means of curtains. Small cabins or staterooms were also built and especially on the larger ships. It is impossible to imagine that it could be otherwise, when the official station or wealth of the passenger is considered.

The captain's cabin had its steward and there the food and service were undoubtedly better than that provided forward where all slept in canvas hammocks slung from hooks in the deck timbers overhead, or lay upon pallet beds on the deck. Here they served themselves from the ship's galley. The foul odors below deck and the unsanitary conditions are part of the lore of the sea. "Ship feaver" was well known to all physicians practicing in seaport towns. In those days the cooking was done in an open fireplace. So, too, on shipboard there was provided an open "hearth" made of cast iron and weighing from four to eight hundred pounds. This[160] was fastened to the deck and its "chimney" was screened by a "smoke sail." A smaller "hearth" was in the captain's cabin and supplied all the heat below. It must have been bitterly cold on board ship during a winter crossing. The coals in these "hearths" were a menace to safety and required constant attention.

A communication printed in the *Boston News-Letter* describes an escape from fire on board one of these English packets. The writer, a good New England puritan, first declares his suspicion that a certain military gentleman, a fellow passenger from Boston, had brought on board a fair lady who was not his wife. The couple occupied a small cabin, partitioned off from the main cabin, which had a curtained window looking into it. There were other curtains about. As the Boston shopkeeper sat near the "hearth," musing over his suspicions, a sudden lurch of the vessel brought a carelessly placed curtain swinging into the coals on the "hearth" and in an instant it was aflame. The shopkeeper shouted "Fire! Fire!" which brought the major's inamorata to her cabin window and an instant later she rushed into the main cabin with a certain necessary receptacle in her hands. One splash and the worst was over. The charred curtain was soon torn from its fastenings and the fire stamped out on the cabin floor.

In 1760, Jacob Bailey, a native of Rowley, Mass., and a graduate of Harvard College, having prepared for the ministry and been licensed to preach, determined to obtain orders in the Church of England and so, through the intervention of friends, took passage from Boston for London in the ship *Hind*, carrying twenty guns, which sailed in company with six other vessels. Mr. Bailey kept a diary of the voyage and his description of the accommodations which the ship supplied, the life on board, and the men with whom he was brought in contact, is a surprisingly vivid picture of strange and uncouth conditions attending passenger service to England in the mid-eighteenth century. The ship lay at anchor in the harbor and Mr. Bailey went out to her in a small boat.

"The wind was blowing strong, and it was some time before we could get on board ship. At length, with difficulty, I clambered up[161] the side and found myself in the midst of a most horrid confusion. The deck was crowded full of men, and the boatswain's shrill whistle, with the swearing and hallooing of the petty officers, almost stunned my ears. I could find no retreat from this dismal hubbub, but was obliged to continue jostling among the crowd above an hour before I could find anybody at leisure to direct me. At last, Mr. Letterman, the Captain's steward, an honest Prussian, perceiving my disorder, introduced me through the steerage to the lieutenant. I found him sitting in the great cabin. He appeared to be a young man, scarce twenty years of age, and had in his countenance some indications of mildness. Upon my entrance he assumed a most important look and with a big voice demanded to know my request. I informed him that I was a passenger on board the *Hind*, by permission of Capt. Bond, and desired that he would be civil enough to direct me to the place of my destination. He replied in this laconic style: 'Sir, I will take care to speak to one of my mates.' This was all the notice, at present. But happily, on my return from the cabin, I found my chest and bedding carefully stowed away in the steerage. In the meantime the ship was unmoored and we fell gently down to Nantasket....

"I observed a young gentleman walking at a distance, with a pensive air in his countenance. Coming near him, in a courteous manner he invited me down between decks to a place he called his berth. I thanked him for his kindness and readily followed him down a ladder into a dark and dismal region, where the fumes of pitch, bilge water, and other kinds of nastiness almost suffocated me in a minute. We had not proceeded far before we entered a small apartment, hung round with damp and greasy canvas, which made, on every hand, a most gloomy and frightful appearance. In the middle stood a table of pine, varnished over with nasty slime, furnished with a bottle of rum and an old tin mug with a hundred and fifty bruises and several holes, through which the liquor poured in as many streams. This was quickly filled with toddy and as speedily emptied by two or three companions who presently joined us in this doleful retreat. Not all the scenes of horror about[162] us could afford me much dismay till I received the news that this detestable apartment was allotted by the captain to be the place of my habitation during the voyage!

"Our company continually increased, when the most shocking oaths and curses resounded from every corner, some loading their neighbors with bitter execrations, while others uttered imprecations too awful to be recorded. The persons present were: first, the captain's clerk, the young fellow who gave me the invitation. I found him a person of considerable reading and observation who had fled his native country on account of a young lady to whom he was engaged. Second, was one John Tuzz, a midshipman and one of my messmates, a good-natured, honest fellow, apt to blunder in his conversation and given to extravagant profaneness. Third, one Butler, a minister's son, who lived near Worcester, in England. He was a descendant from Butler, the author of *Hudibras*, and appeared to be a man of fine sense and considerable breeding, yet, upon occasion, was extremely profane and immodest, yet nobody seemed a greater admirer of delicacy in women than himself. My fourth companion was one Spear, one of the mates, a most obliging ingenious young gentleman, who was most tender of me in my cruel sickness. Fifth: one of our company this evening was the carpenter of the ship who looked like a country farmer, drank excessively, swore roundly, and talked extravagantly. Sixth: was one Shephard, an Irish midshipman, the greatest champion of profaneness that ever fell under my notice. I scarce ever knew him to open his mouth without roaring out a tumultuous volley of stormy oaths and imprecations. After we had passed away an hour or two together, Mr. Lisle, the lieutenant of marines, joined our company. He was about fifty years of age, of gigantic stature, and quickly distinguished himself by the quantities of liquor he poured down his throat. He also was very profane.

"About nine o'clock the company began to think of supper, when a boy was called into the room. Nothing in human shape did I ever see before so loathsome and nasty. He had on his body a fragment only of a check shirt, his bosom was all naked and greasy, over his[163] shoulders hung a bundle of woolen rags which reached in strings almost down to his feet, and the whole composition was curiously adorned with little shining animals. The boy no sooner made his appearance than one of our society accosted him in this gentle language. 'Go you —— rascal, and see whether lobscouse is ready.' Upon this the fellow began to mutter and scratch his head, but after two or three hearty curses, went for the galley and presently returned with an elegant dish which he placed on the table. It was a composition of beef and onions, bread and potatoes, minced and stewed together, then served up with its broth in a wooden tub, the half of a quarter cask. The table was furnished with two pewter plates, the half of one was melted away, and the other, full of holes, was more weather-beaten than the sides of the ship; one knife with a bone handle, one fork with a broken tine, half a metal spoon and another, taken at Quebec, with part of the bowl cut off. When supper was ended, the company continued their exercise of drinking, swearing and carousing, till half an hour after two, when some of these obliging gentlemen made a motion for my taking some repose.

Accordingly, a row of greasy canvas bags, hanging overhead by the beams, were unlashed. Into one of them it was proposed that I should get, in order to sleep, but it was with the utmost difficulty I prevented myself from falling over on the other side....

"The next day, towards evening, several passengers came on board, viz: Mr. Barons, late Collector, Major Grant, Mr. Barons' footman, and Mrs. Cruthers, the purser's wife, a native of New England. After some considerable dispute, I had my lodgings fixed in Mr. Pearson's berth, where Master Robant, Mr. Baron's man, and I, agreed to lie together in one large hammock."[64]

Such were the accommodations of the petty officers' mess on board a twenty-gun ship of 1760 in the New England service.

In October, 1774, Miss Janet Schaw set sail from the Firth of Forth, Scotland, in the brig *Jamaica Packet*, of eighty tons burden, built in Massachusetts two years before. With her sailed a girl[164] friend, two young nephews, her brother and her maid. They arrived on board in the evening and turned in at once. In Miss Schaw's journal of the voyage, now in the British Museum, we read:

"Our Bed chamber, which is dignified with the title of *state room*, [there were only two staterooms: the captain occupied the other] is about five foot wide and six long; on one side is a bed fitted up for Fanny and on the opposite side one for me. Poor Fanny's is so very narrow, that she is forced to be tied on, or as the Sea term is *lashed in*, to prevent her falling over. On the floor below us lies our Abigail. As she has the breadth of both our Beds and excellent Bedding, I think she has got a most envyable Berth, but this is far from her opinion, and she has done nothing but grumble about her accommodations." The two had been asleep about an hour when her brother came to the stateroom and let down "the half door" to enquire after their healths. His "Cott" swung from the ceiling of the cabin of the brig and the two boys slept on a mattress on the deck beneath the hammock. The hencoop was located on deck just over his head and in the morning the rooster and hens kept up such a pecking that it was impossible for him to sleep. The brig was making a northerly course in a heavy sea and Fanny and the maid were both seasick and lying flat on their backs in their five by six foot cubicle, dimensions probably somewhat underestimated by Miss Schaw, although later she records that "we sit in bed till we dress, and get into it whenever we begin to undress."

In the cabin, in which Schaw hung his "cott," was a small cast-iron stove and here, too, was the case containing the Captain's gin, which he frequently opened and the odor of which set their stomachs topsy-turvy and sent poor Fanny to her bed, and Schaw flying on deck for fresh air. This cabin was furnished with joint stools, chests, table, and even an elbow chair which Miss Schaw had lashed to a mooring near the fireside.

A few days after sailing the brig ran into a storm and the water finding its way into the cabin almost reached the beds in the stateroom—(which was located beside the companion stair)—forcing[165] the maid to "peg in with the boys who could easily let her share with them." The gale also washed away most of their private store of provisions so they were forced to depend upon the ship's stores which consisted mainly of neck-beef, several barrels of New England pork, then on its third voyage across the Atlantic, oatmeal, stinking herrings and excellent potatoes. Lobscouse was a favorite dish made from salt beef that had been hung by a string over the side of the ship till tolerably fresh and then cut up in little pieces and stewed for some time with potatoes, onions and peppers. They also varied their diet by "chowder, scratch-platter and stir-about."[65]

Just forward of the cabin was the steerage filled with immigrants of all ages. Their beds were made up on the deck where they lay alongside of each other and in this low-studded space they existed when the hatches were battened down in stormy weather. "They have only for a grown person per week, one pound neck beef, or spoilt pork, two pounds oat meal, with a small quantity of bisket, not only mouldy, but absolutely crumbled down with damp, wet and rottenness. The half is only allowed a child, so that if they had not potatoes, it is impossible they could live out the voyage. They have no drink, but a very small proportion of brakish bad water."

It is quite plain that eighteenth-century trans-Atlantic voyaging was full of discomfort to the average traveler, and to the unfortunate in the steerage a fearful adventure.

---

[166]

CHAPTER XII

FROM WAMPUM TO PAPER MONEY

The early settlers of New England had little coinage for circulation and were driven to the necessity of using the produce of the soil and the live stock from their pastures as their media of exchange. Peltry also was one of the first and for many years the principal article of currency. It was offered in great abundance by the Indians who were very ready to barter it for beads, knives, hatchets and blankets and especially for powder, shot, guns and "strong water."

In most of the Colonies the wampum of the Indians also was extensively used and frequently was paid into the treasury in payment of taxes. So, also, were cattle and corn as is shown by numerous enactments of the Great and General Court of the Massachusetts Bay. Musket balls were also current and were made legal tender by order of the Court which decreed "that musket bullets of a full bore shall pass current for a farthing a piece provided that no man be compelled to take more than 12 pence at a time of them." In Virginia, tobacco was used for currency and "from 100 to 150 pounds of it bought many a man a good wife."

The Indian wampum was perhaps the most convenient currency available. It is described by Roger Williams who, perhaps, had a better knowledge of it than most of the early colonists. He says: "It is of two kinds which the Indians make of the stem or the stock of the periwinkle after all the shell is broken off. [The periwinkle is a mollusc, more common south of Cape Cod than along the shores of Massachusetts Bay.] Of this kind, six of the small beads, which they make with holes to string upon their bracelet, are current with the English for a penny. The other kind is black, inclined to a blue shade, which is made of the shell of a fish [that is, a mollusc] which some of the English call henspoquahoc [now known as the hen-clam or quahaug] and of this description three[167] are equal to an English penny. One fathom of this stringed money is worth five shillings."

To show the intimate relation of this Indian money to our early history, it appears that even Harvard College accepted it for tuition fees and otherwise; for in 1641 a trading company, chartered to deal with the Indians in furs and wampum, was required to relieve the College of its super-abundance of this odd currency and redeem it, "provided they were not obliged to take more than £25 of it at any one time." The thrifty Dutch at New Amsterdam, however, took advantage of the scarcity of legitimate currency and the corresponding demand for wampum and established factories where they made it in such vast quantities that the market was broken and the value of wampum rapidly decreased.

The great source of metallic currency for New England in those earliest days was the West India Islands and much silver brought from there was later coined into "pine tree" shillings and sixpences. Governor Winthrop, in 1639, tells of a "small bark from the West Indies, one Capt. Jackson in her, with a commission from the Westminister Company to take prizes from the Spanish. He brought much wealth in money, plate, indigo and sugar." But metallic money became so scarce that by 1640 there was but little in the colonies and the greatest difficulty existed in making payments for goods or the wages of servants. In one instance, in Rowley, "the master was forced to sell a pair of his oxen to pay his servant's wages and so told the servant he could keep him no longer, not knowing how to pay him the next year. The servant answered him that he would [continue to] serve him for more of his cattle. But how shall I do, said the master, when all my cattle are gone? The servant replied, why, then you shall serve me and you shall then have your cattle again."

Various attempts were made to establish values to certain coins, more or less ficticious, but this failed to relieve the situation and finally, to obtain a more stable basis the Massachusetts General Court adopted a currency of its own and the "pine tree" money appeared, shortly preceded by the more rude and more easily counterfeited[168] New England shillings and sixpences, that bore on one side the letters "N. E." within a small circle and on the other side the denomination in Roman numerals. These primitive coins were made between 1650 and 1652 and were superseded by the true oak and pine tree pieces after that date. The simple irregular form of the "N. E." coins rendered them an easy prey to the counterfeiter and the clipper, and the design of the newer coins, covering the whole surface of the planchet, was a protection against both dangers. The "N. E." shilling is now a rare coin and likewise the sixpence, while the threepence is rarer still, but two or three genuine examples being known to exist.

There are two distinct forms of the so-called "pine tree" currency, the one bearing on the obverse a representation of a tree resembling an oak, or as some say, a willow; the other with the true pine-tree. It is thought that the ruder pieces bearing the oak tree design were the first coined and that the more perfect pine tree money was issued later. At any rate both "oak" and "pine tree" pieces, shillings, sixpences and threepences, all bear the same date, 1652. But this money was issued continuously until 1686 without a change of the date, it is said, to avoid interference from the English government, the coining of money by the colonists being a distinct violation of the royal prerogative. By the retention of the original date it was thought to deceive the authorities at home into the belief that the violation of the laws ceased as it began, in 1652. In 1652, however, a two-penny piece was minted bearing the oak tree design and hence it is natural to suppose that the pieces bearing the true pine tree design were the last coined and not issued until after 1662.

One of the traditions connected with the pine or oak tree money is the story that Sir Thomas Temple, who was a real friend of the colonists, in 1662, showed some of the pieces to the King at the council table in London, when King Charles demanded upon what authority these colonists had coined money anyway and sought to have orders sent to prohibit any further issues. "But," responded Sir Thomas, "this tree is the oak which saved your majesty's life[169] and which your loyal subjects would perpetuate." Sir Thomas of course referred to the episode of Boscobel in which Charles II escaped his enemies by hiding in the branches of an oak. This it is said so pleased the King that he dropped the subject and the coining of "pine tree" money proceeded merrily, as before, for twenty-five years longer.

The master of the mint was John Hull who lived in Boston where Pemberton Square now opens from Tremont Street and where later was the famous garden and residence of Gardner Green, Esq. The mint house, sixteen feet square and ten feet high, was built on land belonging to Hull in the rear of his house. Robert Sanderson, a friend of Hull, was associated with him in making the "pine tree" money. It is not known how they divided their profit, but they received one shilling sixpence for each twenty shillings coined, and as it is estimated that "pine tree" money to the amount of five millions of dollars in value was made during the thirty-four years it was issued, the commissions received must have been very large and the statement that the dowry, said to have been £30,000, given to Hull's daughter at her marriage, appears reasonable. That the girl, plump as she is reported to have been, actually weighed down the dowry in shillings, is, of course, absurd as that amount in silver would weigh over 6,000 pounds rating a silver £ as weighing 4 oz. at that time.

Hawthorne's description of what is said to have taken place on that occasion is too vivid a picture to be overlooked. He relates that Captain John Hull was appointed to manufacture the pine tree money and had about one shilling out of every twenty to pay him for the trouble of making them. Hereupon all the old silver in the colony was handed over to Captain John Hull. The battered silver cans and tankards, I suppose, and silver buckles and broken spoons, and silver hilts of swords that figured at court—all such articles were doubtless thrown into the melting pot together.

The magistrates soon began to suspect that the mint-master would have the best of the bargain and they offered him a large sum of money if he would but give up that twentieth shilling[170] which he was continually dropping into his own pocket. But Captain Hull declared himself perfectly satisfied with the shilling. And well he might be, for so diligently did he labor that in a few years, his pockets, his money bags, and his strong box were overflowing with pine tree shillings.

Then Samuel Sewall, afterwards the famous Judge Sewall of the days of witchcraft fame, came a courting to Hull's daughter. Betsy was a fine and hearty damsel and having always fed heartily on pumpkin pies, doughnuts, Indian puddings and other Puritan dainties, she was as round and plump as a pudding herself.

"Yes, you may take her," said Captain Hull, to her lover, young Sewall, "and you'll find her a heavy burden enough." Hawthorne describes the wedding and the costumes of the contracting parties and their friends, and Captain Hull he "supposes," rather improbably one would think, however, "dressed in a plum colored coat all the buttons of which were made of pine tree shillings. The buttons of his waistcoat were of sixpences and the knees of his small clothes were buttoned with silver three-pences ... and as to Betsy herself, she was blushing with all her might, and looked like a full-blown peony or a great red apple."

When the marriage ceremony was over, at a whispered word from Captain Hull, a large pair of scales was lugged into the room, such as wholesale merchants use for weighing bulky commodities, and quite a bulky commodity was now to be weighed in them. "Daughter Betsy," said the mint-master, "get into one side of these scales." Miss Betsy—or Mrs. Sewall as we must now call her—did as she was bid and again the servants tugged, this time bringing in a huge iron-bound oaken chest which being opened proved to be full to the brim with bright pine tree shillings fresh from the mint. At Captain Hull's command the servants heaped double handfuls of shillings into one side of the scales, while Betsy remained in the other. Jingle, jingle, went the shillings as handful after handful was thrown in, till, plump and ponderous as she was, they fairly weighed the young lady from the floor. "There, son Sewall," cried the honest mint-master, resuming his seat, "take these shillings for[171] my daughter's portion. Use her kindly and thank Heaven for her. It's not every wife that's worth her weight in silver."

However interesting the story may be of the plump girl sitting in one pan of the scales as shillings were thrown into the other, as depicted in Hawthorne's version of the affair, we must be permitted to consider that time has cast a halo around the mint-master's daughter and increased both her avoirdupois and her dowry.

Massachusetts was the only New England colony to coin silver but close upon the date of the issue of the first "pine tree" money came the Maryland shilling, sixpence, groat and penny, the last in copper. These bear no date but appeared about 1659, the dies having been made in England.

Numerous coins were later made in the colonies, either intended for regular circulation or as tokens privately issued, among which are the Granby coppers—rude half-pennies—made in 1737 by one John Higley, the blacksmith, at Granby, Conn. They were made of soft copper which was dug at Granby and are never found in very good condition.

The word dollar is the English form of the German word thaler, and the origin of the thaler is as follows: In the year 1519, Count Schlick of Bohemia issued silver coins weighing one ounce each and worth 113 cents. They were coined at Joachimsthal, that is, James's Valley or dale, hence they became known as "Joachimsthalers," soon shortened to thalers. Through trade with the Dutch these coins came into England in the sixteenth century and are referred to sometimes as "dalers."

But the dollar came to the American continent not through the Dutch or English but through the Spanish. This was due to the extent of the Spanish Empire in the sixteenth and seventeenth centuries and also to the great quantities of silver which Spain drew from her mines in Mexico and South America. The Spanish coin was, strictly speaking, a peso, better known as a piece of eight, because it was equal to eight reals (royals). As it was of the same value, the name dollar was given to the piece of eight about the year 1690.

[172]

The most famous Spanish dollar was known as the pillar dollar, because it had on one side two pillars, representing the pillars of Hercules, the classical name for the Straits of Gibralter, and this Spanish dollar was common in America at the time of the War of Independence.

In 1690 the treasury of the colony was so nearly exhausted that the Great and General Court decided to issue promises to pay, the first paper money minted by any Colony. The values were ten shillings, one pound and five pounds. The occasion for this issue was primarily the expenses of Governor Phips's expedition against Quebec, which was thriftily expected to more than pay costs. The French and Indians, however, were too strong for Sir William, and the colonial treasury was faced with costs to the amount of £50,000, instead of the anticipated loot. These "Colony" or "Charter bills" obtained a wide circulation and were called in annually and redeemed and reissued as need arose, but after a few years, confidence in them decreased and before long they passed at a discount as great as 30 per cent.

In 1722, Massachusetts tried to relieve the scarcity of small change by issuing five hundred pounds worth of tokens of the value of one, two and three pence. They were printed on parchment to make them more durable but apparently were not a success as there were no more printed.

As the years went by, monetary conditions became more and more unstable, and in 1740 an attempt was made to establish a bank in the hope of placing the currency on a firmer basis. The fight lay between a silver bank with bullion behind its notes and a land bank issuing notes guaranteed by mortgages and manufactured articles. These notes were to come due in twenty years and at that time the holders instead of receiving coin might be forced to take their pay in cast iron, bayberry wax, leather, cordwood, or other articles of trade that might be difficult to dispose of. One of these notes preserved in the cabinets of the Massachusetts Historical Society has written on its back, in old-time handwriting, "A[173] Land Bank bill reserved as a specimen of ye mad humour among many of ye people of ye Province, 1740."

Money matters now went from bad to worse. The value of silver was called tenor. In 1740 silver was worth six shillings, eight pence per ounce and in 1746 seven shillings, sixpence, and the buying value of bills varied from year to year.

"Imagine having to keep in mind the relative values of bills of old tenor, with silver at 6/8, or middle tenor; or new tenor firsts at 6/8, but passing current at 7/8; or new tenor seconds, all of which were laboring under fluctuating but constantly increasing rates of depreciation, while there were also to be remembered Connecticut bills of new tenor at 8/. and Rhode Island bills at 6/9 an ounce, and also £110,000 worth of private bills of the issue of 1733, which were worth a third more than the Colony bills, and also £120,000 in notes issued in 1740, "on a silver basis," to stifle the land bank and equivalent to cash, and in addition "public bills of the four promises at 29/. an ounce," whatever that means, and you will not wonder that there was confusion worse confounded."[66]

In 1749 Parliament voted to reimburse Massachusetts to the amount of nearly one million dollars, for expenses incurred in the expedition against Louisburg and this money was used to redeem outstanding paper bills at the rate of ten in paper to one in cash. The next year old tenor ceased to be lawful money amid general rejoicing and much doggerel verse.

"Now old tenor fare you well, No man such tattered bills will tell, Now dollars pass and are made free, It is the year of jubilee."

---

[174]

CHAPTER XIII

HERB TEA AND THE DOCTOR

At a meeting of the Massachusetts Bay Company held in London on March 5, 1628-29, it was proposed that the Company "Intertayne a surgeon for the plantation" and one Abraham Pratt was sent over soon after. He lived in Roxbury, Charlestown and Cambridge. While returning to England with his wife in the fall of 1644, their ship was wrecked on the coast of Spain and both were drowned. At the same meeting the Company selected a barber-surgeon, Robert Morley, to go to New England and practice his calling on "aney of the Company that are planters or there servants." In those days a barber-surgeon employed himself in pulling teeth, bleeding and cupping.

Earlier than this, however, Doctor Samuel Fuller had come over in the *Mayflower* and was of the greatest service to the sickly foundation at Plymouth. When John Endecott's wife lay dying at Naumkeak (Salem), in 1629, Doctor Fuller was hastily sent for, and the next year he was called to Matapan (Dorchester) where he "let some twenty of these people blood: [and] had conference with them till I was weary."[67] A month later he was at Charlestown writing "I here but lose time and long to be at home, I can do them no good, for I want drugs, and things fitting to work with." Three years later he was dead of an infectious fever.

A large portion of the physicians in the early days of the Colony were Puritan ministers who had studied medicine in England in anticipation of removal to New England, as a hasty preparation for such necessities as might arise. Each practised in his own flock and Cotton Mather in his *Magnalia* (Book III, Chap. 26), speaks of this union of the two professions as an "Angelical Conjunction."[175] When Rev. Michael Wigglesworth died in 1705, his weeping parishioners in the town of Malden, erected a stone to mark his grave and on it may still be read the words

"Here lies intered in silent grave belowMaulden's physician for soul and body two."

In colonial times there was little regulation of medical practice, although an ineffective law was passed in 1649. Any one might come into a town and announce himself as a physician and if able to cure patients of their maladies, his success was assured. Several unfortunate failures, however, would seriously effect his standing. As a natural result quacks appeared and disappeared in all the larger towns.

In the seventeenth century, and later, there were two classes of medical practitioners of which one prescribed vegetable substances only, together with a free use of the lancet, and followed the teachings of Galen, the Greek physician. The other school followed the doctrines of Paracelsus and prescribed for the most part mineral preparations, and oftentimes were styled "chemists." Of course there was bitter rivalry between the two schools, each maintaining so far as possible, a superstitious mystery concerning their profession. There were few regular graduates from any recognized medical school. Until after the Revolution most practitioners gained their scanty store of medical knowledge by studying with some family physician and in the homely school of experience. Dr. William Douglas, a young Scotchman, began to practice in Boston in 1716. In 1721 he wrote "we abound with Practitioners, though no other graduate than myself. We have fourteen Apothecary shops in Boston. All our Practitioners dispense their own medicines.... In general the physical practise in our colonies is so perniciously bad that excepting in surgery and in some very acute cases, it is better to let nature under a proper regimen take her course than to trust to the honesty and sagacity of the practitioner. Our American practitioners are so rash and officious that the saying in Ecclesiasticus may with much propriety be applied to them, 'He[176] that sinneth before his Maker let him fall into the hands of the physician.'"[68]

Governor John Winthrop was versed in medicine and his son, John, Jr., and his grandson Wait Winthrop, both were proficient in the profession. With Winthrop came Richard Palgrave and William Gager, both physicians, and two years later arrived Giles Firman, Jr., whose father was "a godly man, an apothecary of Sudbury in England." Giles, Jr., studied at the University of Cambridge and later settled at Ipswich, Mass., where he practiced medicine, but found it "a meene helpe" and later studied theology and eventually was ordained rector of Shalford, co. Essex, England.

Toward the end of the century there were two physicians practicing in Boston, Dr. Thomas Oakes and Dr. Benjamin Bullivant, of whom Dunton, the London bookseller gossiped in his "Letters Written from New England."[69]

Of Oakes he wrote that—

"His wise and safe Prescriptions have expell'd more Diseases and rescu'd Languishing Patients from the Jaws of Death, than Mountebanks and Quack-Salvers have sent to those dark Regions."

Concerning Dr. Bullivant he commented that—

"His Skill in Pharmacy was such, as rendered him the most compleat Pharmacopean, not only in all Boston, but in all New England ... to the Poor he always prescribes cheap, but wholesome Medicines, not curing them of a Consumption in their Bodies, and sending it into their Purses; nor yet directing them to the East Indies to look for Drugs, when they may have far better out of their Gardens."

Doctor John Clarke, said to have been a younger son of a good family in the north of England, with a collegiate education, and late of London, was granted a four-hundred acre farm in the town of Newbury, in January, 1638, and September 28th, following, the town also granted that

[177]

"Mr. Clarke in respect of his calling should be freed and exempted from all public rates either for the country or the towne so long as he shall remayne with us and exercise his calling among us."

He exercised his calling in Newbury until 1647, when he removed to Ipswich and two or three years later settled in Boston where he died in 1664. Soon after removing to Boston he invented a stove "for the saving of firewood & warming of howses," which the Great and General Court confirmed for a term of three years. Nothing further is known of this invention and the fireplace persisted until recent times.

When Doctor Clark removed from Newbury he was followed by Dr. William Snelling who seems to have been a merry fellow in times of drinking healths. On an occasion during the winter of 1651 he drank to his friends in the following toast,—

"I'll pledge my friends,And for my foes,A plague for their heelsAnd a pox for their toes,"

which e'er long led to sorrowful acknowledgment of his weakness before the Quarterly Court at Salem, and a fine of ten shillings for cursing. This doubtless helped sustain the dignity of the Court and strengthened virtue among the good men of the town of Newbury at times when ribald mirth prevailed.

Dr. John Perkins who practised in Boston during the first half of the eighteenth century, is said to have gone to London for two year's study but his medical notebooks show that in his Boston practise he prescribed for scrofula, syrup made of sow bugs drowned in white wine. Castile soap boiled in strong beer he used as a remedy for a "heavy load at the Stomac." For numb palsy he prescribed "a bath of absinthe in *urina hominis*, used hot," and his cure for a nervous weakness of the eyes was "shaving the head." He noted that "Widow Alcock [died] of a hot bread supper. Jus. Billings did so of eating Brown Bread for breakfast, a Thing he never used before," and Reverend McGee's wife died by eating a[178] supper of roast chickens at 13 days after childbirth and drinking strong beer flip on it. "Wonderful that in learned and elevated situations among ye great, should be such ignorance."

"Samuel Bent, Goldsmith, tender constitution and lax nerves, upon a change of a linnen for a woolen cap to sleep in was affected with a running of Bloody Water from ye nose, which staunched when he wore linnen.

"Nathaniel Parkman's Daughter, scrophulously affected, had a blow on the Head, on which the scrophula immediately left her and Chorea St. Viti succeeded and followed her every Spring till she turned consumptive and died."[70]

Doctor Perkins was quite modern in some of his theories. He entered in his notebook—

"Exercise is good [for pains in the stomach] in young girls and others that use a sedentary life. So Sarah Bergers was cured by learning country dances.

"Wheat, ye Shoemaker, was cured [of hemorrhoids] by taking to ye portering with a wheelbarrow."

Doctor Ball of Northboro had a medicine called, "Receipt for the Scratches. One Quart fishworms, washed clean; one pound hog's lard stewed together, filtered through a strainer and add one-half pint oil of turpentine; one-half pint good brandy. Simmer it well and it is fit for use."[71]

Obstetrics at that period was also a jolly pastime, as the doctor and his volunteer assistants were regaled by a special brew known as "groaning beer" and by freshly baked "groaning cakes."

In Salem lived Zerobabel Endecott, son of Governor John Endecott, who practiced the healing art and who left behind him a remarkable collection of medical recipes from which we include selections illustrating the practice of the physician in colonial days. His brother John, afterwards Governor of Connecticut, also seems to have had some medical training as appears from a bill preserved in the Massachusetts Archives, where under date of[179] 1668, he charged five shillings for "a Vomit and atendans" on one John Clark, "weak and sike by reason of a scurvy and a dropsy." Doctor Zerobabel died in 1684 and bequeathed to his son John, who also was a physician and who died in England, "al my Instruments and books both of phisicke and chirurgery." The inventory of the estate shows "a case of lances, 2 Rasors, a box of Instruments, 10 bookes in folio, 16 in quarto, a saw with six Instruments for a chirurgion and a chest of bookes & writings."

Other Salem physicians were George Emery who settled in the town in 1636 and sat on the gallows with a rope around his neck, in 1668, for an unnatural crime; Rev. John Fiske, a graduate of Cambridge, who had studied divinity and also physic, and came to Salem in 1637; and Daniel Weld, who was chief surgeon during the Narraganset campaign in King Philip's War; Col. Batholomew Gedney, who left at his death drugs and instruments inventoried at £60; Dr. John Barton, who died of yellow fever; Dr. John Swinnerton, made famous by Hawthorne's romance, and others followed.

William Salmon, in his "Compendium of Physick," published in London in 1671, estimates the necessary qualifications of the seventeenth-century physician as follows: "He that would be an accomplished physician, ought to be furnished with three things, 1. honesty and a good conscience; 2. a substantial, real, and well-grounded understanding through the whole Art of Medicine; 3. with all such Instruments and Necessaries which are ordinarily made use of in the performance of any medical operation," and these instruments are listed as follows:

"The Parascuological Instruments, wherewith medicines are prepared, whether Galenical or Chymical, are chiefly these: A brass Kettle; an Alembick; a Circulatory; a Sieve; a Gourd; a Balneum Mariae; Tongs; a Cauldron; a File; a Hippocras Bag; an Iron Mortar; a Pestle; a Pitcher; a Marble; a glass Mortar and Pestle; a Seperator; a Funnel; a Seirce; a Press; a Tile; a pair of Sheers; Vials; Boxes; Crucibles; Gally-pots; Corks; Spoons; Strainers; Retorts; Receivers; Bags; Spatulas; Weights and[180] Scales; together with a Pair of Goldsmiths Bellows; and convenient Furnaces fitted for any operation.

"The Chyrurgical Instruments with which the Artist ought to be furnished, are chiefly these: A Plaister Box; an Uvula Spoon; a

Levatory; a Director; a pair of Forceps; a Spatula Lingua; an Incision Knife; a pair of Scizzors; a Flame; a small Razour; a stitching Quill; three square Needles; with a Case of good Launcets; and a Salvatory; letting all be kept very sharp, clean and bright."

The following medical recipes are copied from a manuscript left by Dr. Zerobabel Endecott of Salem and formerly in the possession of the late Dr. Frederick Lewis Gay of Brookline.

For y* Bloudy Flux

Stone horses Liuers[72] dried in an ouen being heat for houshould bread, made into powder & giuen a spoonfull at a time in milk.

For a Spraine

Take stronge bere este & honye, of equall quantyty & boyle them to the Consistanty of honye & so apply it hott to ye place greeued.

For Extreme Thirst & Vomiting in a Malignant Feauer

Take salt of wormwood [scruple]i and a spoonfull of the Juce of Lemonds mix them in a spoon & giue it the patient

For Stone in the Kidnes and Blader Or To Prouent It

Take wild Carret seeds & boyle in Ale & drinke Dose [dram]ii euery Night.

An Other

Take 3 Drops of oyle of Fenill once a day.

For ye Dropsie Often Prou* & Espetially Vpon One Man, Other Meanes Vsed By Men of Skill Fayled This Was Affectuall

[181]

Tak good store of Elder roots wash them & make them very Cleane then splitt & steepe them in strong ale wort & Lett them stand together while ye Ale is working then when it is 2 days old drinke of it morning Noone & at night till health be obtained Lett there be as many of ye Roots as Can well be steeped in the Ale The flowers are of the same vse & more powerfull

An Other

Take Rie flower make past with water Role it thin and with ye greene Leaues of Sage & a Littl Rosemary fill it as pye bake it very dry beat altogether & take halfe a spoonefull at a time in a wine Cupfull of your beere

For a Sore Throte[73] or Kings Euell

Take Guaiacom sliced [oz]iij ye Bark of Guaiacom [oz]i infuse in 6 quarts of fair water on hott ashes 24 hours then boyle it ouer a gentill fire till a third part be wasted then add of Epithimum Pollepodium ana [oz]ii fumitory borrage & buglose Roots flowers of Rosmary Prim Rose Cow slips Violets & sweet fenill seeds of Each [oz]fs boyle it till a quart be wasted then add Sena [oz]iij boyl it a Litle & straine it & Clarifie it with whits of Eggs sweeten it with Sugar

Giue 2 or 3 spoonfulls euery morning to a child more to a groune Person; enough to give 2 or 3 Lous stooles in a daye for 8 days together this aLone haue Cured the Kings Euill

For Paine in ye Eare[74]

Take a mithredate & put it in into the eare with a Litle wooll & Keep it warme

[182]

For a Cough[75]

Take eggs boyle them till they bee hard hold them in your hand one at a time as hott as you Can suffer it & with ye heat & strength of your hand press out the oyle, take a quantity of this oyle & a Little powder of Alloes & fine Sugar make it into a surrup take a Litle of this surrup as often as need Require this is Comended by G: as if non Could Equall it

A Balsam or Liquer That Will Heal Sores as For New in Man or Beast

Tak very strong wort 3 gallons being all ye first of a boushell of good malt then tak of Comfry roots & Elder roots of each 2 handfuls the Leaues of Crud tobacko a handful Lett the Roots be brused & boyled till halfe be wasted Put it into a Vessel & Keep for Vse Put into it 3 li of hony before you take it of the fire, if it be a deepe sore tent it, if an open sore wett a Duble Clout & Lay on the sore Dress it always warme

For ye Sciatica or Paine in ye Back or Side[76]

Tak Fetherfew & steepe it in beer & drink first at morning & Last at night

A Powder for ye Dissines of ye Head Falling Sicknes[77] *& Hart Qualms That Haue Bin Oft Vsed*

Whit amber [dram]ii Diarrhodian [dram]ii Seeds of Peony [scruple]ii miselto[183] [dram]i the fillings of a Deadmans skull [scruple]i[78] mak all into a very fine Powder & tak of it as much as will Ly on a shilling 2 or 3 nights together befor the new & befor the full moon take it in Saxony or bettony water

For Rumatick Paines & To Coole Ye Liuer

Tak the Conserue of the frut of Sweet brier as much as a good nutmage morning & Evening

For Vometing & Looseness in Men Women & Children

Take an Egg break a Little hole in one end of it & put owt ye white then put in about ½ spoonfull of baye salt then fill vp the egg with strong Rom or spirits of wine & sett it in hott ashes & Lett it boyle till ye egg be dry then take it & eat it fasting & fast an hour after it or drink a Litle distilled waters of mint & fenill which waters mixed together & drank will help in most ordinary Cases

For a Person That is Distrated If It Be A Woman[79]

Tak milk of a Nurce that giues suck to a male Child & also take a hee Catt & Cut of one of his Ears or a peece of it & Lett it blede[184] into the milk & then Lett the sick woman Drink it doe this three Times

For a Bruse In Any Part Of The Body

Take of honey a Spoonfull & yest or barme or the emptings of strong beer twice as much warm them & mix them together & apply it to the place greeued admireable effects haue bin wroght by this means it hath seldom fayled in Casses very Difficult in any part of ye boddy though ye bones haue semed to be brused though it hath ben in head & in broken bones it easeth paine & vnites the bones sodainly

For Ye [J]andis[80]

Take ye Juce of Planten and Camomell 3 or 4 spoonfuls in warme Posset ale morning & Euening it helps in few days

Mir Turmarik & safron made into fine powder & drank twice or 3 times a day in Possett ale is Excelent good Dose [scruple]i or Lett the sik Person drink their own Vrin twice a day or ye Volatile fat of Vrin [ ] morning & Euening in Posset ale

To Eas Paines in Feauers[81]

Tak Cardamoms or Graines of Paradice [dram]i Nutmegs [dram]ss Safron[185] [scruple]ij Sugar [dram]ii mak it to fine Pouder & giue at any time as much as will Ly on a shilling at a time my pill is better if the boddy be Loos

For Ye Colik or Flux in Ye Belly[82]

1	the	powder	of	Wolues	guts
2	the	powder	of	Bores	Stones

3 oyle of Wormwood a drop or 2 into the Nauell
4 3 drops of oyle of Fenill & 2 drops of oyle of mints in Conserue of Roses or Conserue of single mallows, if ye Paine be extream Vse it a gaine, & if need Require aply somthing hott to the belly

For Sharpe & Dificult Trauel in Women with Child By J C

Take a Lock of Vergins haire on any Part of ye head, of half the Age of ye Woman in trauill Cut it very smale to fine Pouder then take 12 Ants Eggs dried in an ouen after ye bread is drawne or other wise make them dry & make them to pouder with the haire, giue this with a quarter of a pint of Red Cows milk or for want of it giue it in strong ale wort[83]

[186]

A Wonderfull Balsam For Fistulos & Vlsers

Take Borax [dram]ij put it into a strong stone botle of 2 quarts; stop it Close with a good Corke & then Couer it with sealing wax very Close & sett it into the bottom of a well or Cold Spring the Space of three yeeres then take it out [when it will] al be turned to a balsam whare with you may dress Sores

To Stench Bleeding[84] in a Wound

Take a peec of Salt Beef & Rost it in the hott Ashes then make it Cleane & put it into the wound & the blood will stop imediatly

For To Make a Man Vomit Presently That Is Sick at His Stomack

Take white Copperes [dram]i in powder in a Litle Beere or Water & it will Cause one to vomit presently

For Ye Plurisie[85]

Take the Leaues of wild mallows & boyl them in Oyle & being taken out bray them in a morter & put them into a peece of Lining Cloth & applie it to the greue and presently it will Cause the paine to Cease Don Alexis

[187]

For the Plurisies

Take an Apple that is of a Sweete sente & taste in it a hole taking out the Core so that the hole goeth not thorow & put into the hole 3 or 4 graines of Frankincense of the male Kind Otherwise Called olibanum then Couer againe the saide hole with the Little Pece of Apple that you tooke of first & rost it apon the Embers so that it burne not but that it may waxe tender then take it from the fire and breake it into fower parts with all the frankencense in it & so giue the patient it to eate it will by & by make the Impostume to break & heale him

For the Shingles

Take howse leeke Catts blod[86] and Creame mixed together & oynt the place warme or take the moss that groweth in a well & Catts blod mixed & so aply it warme to the plase whare the shingles be

For the Goute[87]

Take Ligmamuita [oz]xvi Sarssaparilla [oz]viii fennel Seeds [oz]vi Boyle them in 2 Gallonds of water in a Pott Close Stopped till halfe be Consumed then put it vp in a glasse Botle well Stopped & Every morning take Sumthing Less than a gill & so in the Euening

Then take those Jngredients & Boyle it ouer againe in 2 or 3[188] Gallonds of water more & So Keepe it for your Continiall Drinking at any time During the time of your Jllnes Proued Very Affectial apon a man at Dunkerck

Oyl of Roses[88]

Take Roses and Jnfuse them in good olliue oyle in a glasse in the heat of the sun for sartaine Days while the oyl smeles like Roses; oyl of Hipericon is made after the same manner

For a Fractur of the Scull

After the Scull is Layed open + and the Bones taken out By a Leuetur or Cut By a trapan then fitt a pece of Parchment of the same Bignes that the fractur is and oynt it with mell Rosarie or huny of Roses and also the Edges of ye Bone & so put it in gently on apon the Dura mater that Ciuers the Braines and apon that a good Plegen of tow & a good bolster on that & so Continue that dressing while it is all most well & the bone hes Cast of & then finish the Cure with Arseaus his Linement; your parchment must haue a third fastened in the middle

For Cutts or Sores

Take the Scine of Salt Beefe & so Laye it to the Cutt or sore

For To Heale or Dry Vp a Sore

Take Sallet oyle and Read Lead and boyle it well together and dipe peces of Lining Cloath in it Keep them for use

For The Ague

Take the Drye shell of a Turtell beat smale & boyled in water while 2 thirds of the water be consumed & drinke of it 2 or 3 times when the Ague Cometh

[189]

Probatum Easte January the 10 1681

The Greene Oyntment that m[s] Feeld did Vse to make[189]

Jt Cureth all Spraines and Aches Cramps and Scaldings and Cutts healeth all wounds it doth suple molyfy Ripen & Disolues all Kind of tumors hot and Cold and it will heale olde Rotten Sores and bites of Venemos Beasts itch and mangenes and stench bloud it Easeth Swelling and paines of the head and throate Eyes and Eares Gout and Seattica and all outward Greefes

Take baye Leaues, Wormwood, Sage, Rue, Cammemoyle, mellelote, groundsell, Violets, Plantaine, oake buds or Leaues [ ] Suckbery Pursline, Lettuc, Red colworts, Saint Johns wort, mallows, mullin, Jsop, Sorrell and Comfrye, yarrow, and Dead Nettles, and Mint, mugwort, Rose leaues, gather them all in the heat of the Daye, pick them Cleene but wash them not, Beat them well then take Sheepe Suett three Pound Picke it Cleene and Shrid it Smale Pound them all well together, then take 2 quarts of Sallet oyle then work them all together with your hand till it be a Like then put it in an Earthen Pott and Couer it Close and Lett it Stand[190] 14 Dayes in a Coule Place then Sett it ouer a Softe fire and Lett it Boyle 14 howers Stiring it well then put into it 4 ounces of oyle of Spicke then Straine it through a Corse Cloath & put it into [ ] Pott and Couer it Cloase and Keepe it for your vse

For Ye Toothe Ache[90]

Take a Litle Pece of opium as big as a great pinnes head & put it into the hollow place of the Akeing Tooth & it will giue preasant Ease, often tryed by me apon many People & neuer fayled

Zerobabel Endecott

––––––––––––

Who would know the virtues of the herbs and simples that grew in the gardens of the Massachusetts Bay? Many herbals have been compiled and printed, none more enticing than Nicholas Culpepper's "English Herbals," more truly entitled "The English Physician Enlarged," and first published in 1653. It had an enormous sale. Since that year twenty-one different editions have served their day, the last having been printed at Exeter, N.H., as late as 1824.

Culpepper, the son of a clergyman, was born in London in 1616 and died when only thirty-eight years old. In that short time, however, he gained fame as a writer on astrology and medicine. At first apprenticed to an apothecary, he later set up for himself as a physician and acquired a high reputation among his patients.

In his catalogue of the simples he premises a few words to the reader, viz.: "Let a due time be observed (cases of necessity excepted) in gathering all Simples: for which take these few Rules. All Roots are of most virtue when the Sap is down in them, viz. towards the latter end of the summer, or beginning of the spring, for happily in Winter many of them cannot be found: you may hang up many of them a drying, by drawing a string through them, and so keep them a whole year.

"Herbs are to be gathered when they are fullest of juyce, before they run up to seeds; and if you gather them in a hot sunshine-day,[191] they will not be so subject to putrifie: the best way to dry them, is in the Sun, according to Dr. *Reason*, though not according to Dr. *Tradition*: Such Herbs as remain green all the year, or are very full of juyce, it were a folly to dry at all, but gather them only for present use, as Houseleek, Scurvy-grass, etc.

"Let flowers be gathered when they are in their prime, in a sunshine-day, and dryed in the sun. Let seeds be perfectly ripe before they be gathered.

"Let them be kept in a dry place: for any moysture though it be but a moist ayr, corrupts them, which if perceived in time, the beames of the Sun will refresh them again."

Ageratum dryes the brain, helps the green sickness, and profit such as have a cold or weak Liver: outwardly applyed, it takes away the hardnesse of the matrix, and fills hollow ulcers with flesh.

Anemone. The juyce snuffed up the nose purgeth the head, it clenseth filthy ulcers, encreaseth milk in Nurses, and outwardly by oyntments helps Leprosies.

Asphodel or Daffodil. I know no physicall use of the roots, probably there is: for I do not believe God created anything of no use.

Balm, outwardly mixed with salt and applied to the neck, helps the Kings Evil, biting of mad dogs and such as cannot hold their necks as they should do; inwardly it is an excellent remedy for a cold, cheers the heart, takes away sorrow, and produces mirth.

Basil gives speedy deliverance to women in travail.

Bedstraw. Stancheth blood: boyled in oyl is good to annoynt a weary traveller: inwardly it provokes lust.

Borrage, cheers the heart and drooping spirits, helps swooning and heart qualms.

Briony, both white and black, they purg the flegm and watry humors, but they trouble the stomack much, they are very good for dropsies: the white is most in use, and is admirable good for the fits of the mother; both of them externally used, take away Freckles, Sun-burning, and Morphew from the face, and clense[192] filthy ulcers: It is a churlish purge, and being let alone, can do no harm.

Buglosse. Continual eating of it makes the body invincible against the poyson of Serpents, Toads, Spiders, etc. The rich may make the Flowers into a conserve, and the herb into a syrup: the poor may keep it dry: both may keep it as a Jewell.

Burdoc or Clot-bur, helps such as spit blood and matter, bruised and mixed with salt and applyed to the place, helps the biting of mad dogs. It expels wind, easeth paines of the teeth, strengthens the back ... being taken inwardly.

Celondine. The root is manifestly hot and dry, clensing and scouring, proper for such as have the yellow Jaundice, it opens the obstructions of the liver, being boiled in White Wine, and if chewed in the mouth it helps the tooth-ach.

Chamomel is as gallant a medicine against the stone in the bladder as grows upon the earth. It expels wind, belchings, used in bathes it helps pains in the sides, gripings and gnawings in the belly.

Chick-weed is cold and moist without any binding, aswages swelling and comforts the sinews much, and therfore is good for such as are shrunk up, it helps mangy hands and legs, outwardly applyed in a pultis.

Cinkfoyl or Five-fingered grass. The root boyled in vinegar is good against the Shingles, and appeaseth the rage of any fretting sores.

Colts-foot. Admirable for coughs. It is often used taken in a Tobacco-pipe, being cut and mixed with a little oyl of annis seeds.

Columbines help sore throats and are of a drying, binding quality.

Comfry is excellent for all wounds both internal and externall, for spitting of blood, Ruptures or Burstness, pains in the Back and helpeth Hemorrhoyds. The way to use them is to boyle them in water and drink the decoction.

Cottonweed. Boyled in Ly, it keeps the head from Nits and Lice; being laid among Cloaths, it Keeps them safe from Moths;[193] taken in a Tobacco-pipe it helps Coughs of the Lungues, and vehement headaches.

Dill. It breeds milk in Nurses, staies vomiting, easeth hiccoughs, aswageth swellings, provoks urin, helps such as are troubled with the fits of the mother, and digests raw humors.

Dittany, brings away dead children, hastens womens travail, the very smell of it drives away venemous beasts; it's an admirable remedy against wounds made with poysoned weapons; it draws out splinters, broken bones, etc.

Fennel. Encreaseth milk in Nurses, provokes urine, easeth pains in the Reins, breaks wind, provokes the Terms.

Fleabane. Helps the bitings of venemous beasts. It being burnt, the smoke of it kills all Gnats and Fleas in the chamber. It is dangerous for women with child.

Flower-de-luce or *water flag,* binds, strengthens, stops fluxes of the belly, a drachm being taken in red wine every morning.

Fumitory helps such as are itchy and scabbed, helps Rickets, madness, and quartain agues.

Gentian, some call Bald-money, is a notable counter-poyson, it opens obstructions, helps the bitings of venemous beasts, and mad dogs, helps digestion, and cleanseth the body of raw humors.

Golden Rod clenseth the Reins, brings away the Gravel; an admirable herb for wounded people to take inwardly, stops Blood, etc.

Groundsel helps the Cholick, and pains and gripings in the belly. I hold it to be a wholsom and harmless purge. Outwardly it easeth womens breasts that are swollen & inflamed, (or as themselves say) have gotten an ague in their breasts.

Hellebore. The root of white Hellebore, or sneezwort, being grated & snuffed up the nose, causeth sneezing, Kills Rats and Mice, being mixed with their meat. Doctor Bright commends it for such as are mad through melancholly. If you use it for sneezing, let your head and neck be wrapped hot for fear of catching cold.

Henbane. Stupifies the senses and therefore not to be taken inwardly;[194] outwardly applyed to the temple it provokes sleep.

Hops. The young sprouts clense the Blood and cleer the skin, helps scabs and itch. They are usually boyled and taken as they eat Sparagus or they may be made into a conserve.

Horehound clenseth the breast and lungs, helps old coughs, easeth hard labour in child-bearing, brings away the after-birth.

Hysop. Helps Coughs, shortness of Breath, Wheezing, Kills worms in the body, helps sore throats and noise in the ears.

Knotgrasse helps spitting of blood, stops all fluxes of blood, gonorrhaea or running of Reins, and is an excellent remedy for hogs that will not eat their meat.

Lavender. The temples and forehead bathed with the juyce of it, as also the smell of the herb helps swoonings.

Lavender cotton resists poyson, kills worms.

Lettice. Cools the inflamation of the stomack commonly called heart-burning, provokes sleep, resists drunkenesse and takes away the ill effects of it, cools the blood, and breeds milk. It is far wholsommer eaten boyled than raw.

Liverwort is excellent for inflamations of the Liver and yellow jaundice.

Lovage cleers the sight, takes away redness and Freckles from the Face.

Lungwort helps infirmities of the lungs, coughs and shortness of breath.

Mallows. They are profitable in the stingings of Bees, Wasps, etc. Inwardly they resist poyson and provoke to stool....

Man Drakes. Fit for no vulgar use, but only to be used in cooling oyntments.

Marigolds. The leaves loosen the belly and the juyce held in the mouth helps the toothach.

Marshmallowes are meanly hot, of a digestion softening nature, ease pains, help bloody fluxes, the stone and gravell; being bruised and well boiled in milk, and the milk drunk is a gallant remedy for the gripings of the belly, and the bloddy flux.

[195]

Mint. Provokes hunger, is wholesome for the stomack, stays vomiting, helps sore heads in children. Hinders conception and is naught for wounded people, they say by reason of an antipathy between it and Iron.

Mugwort, an herb appropriate to the foeminine sex; it brings down the terms, brings away birth and afterbirth, easeth pains in the matrix.

Mullin. Stops fluxes and cures hoarsenesse and such as are broken winded; the leaves worn in the shooes provokes the Terms, (especially in such Virgins as never had them) but they must be worn next their feet.

Nettles. The juyce stops bleeding; they provoke lust exceedingly; help that troublesome cough that women call Chin-cough. Boyl them in white wine.

Onions, are extreamly hurtfull for cholerick people, they breed but little nourishment, and that little is naught; they are bad meat, yet good physick for flegmatick people, they are opening and provoke urine, and the terms, if cold be the cause obstructing; bruised and outwardly applyed they cure the bitings of mad dogs; roasted and applied they help Boils, and Aposthumes; raw they take the fire out of burnings; but ordinarily eaten, they cause headach, spoil the sight, dul the senses and fill the body full of wind.

Orpine for Quinsie in the throat, for which disease it is inferior to none.

Penyroyal. Strengthens women's backs, provokes the Terms, staies vomiting, strengthens the brain (yea the very smell of it), breaks wind, and helps the Vertigo.

Pimpernal, male and foemale. They are of such drawing quality that they draw thorns and splinters out of the flesh, amend the sight, and clense Ulcers.

Plantain. A little bit of the root being eaten, instantly staies pains in the head, even to admirations.

Purslain. Cools hot stomacks, admirable for one that hath his teeth on edge by eating sowr apples, helps inward inflamations.

[196]

Reubarb. It gently purgeth Choller from the stomack & liver, opens stoppings, withstands the Dropsie, and Hypocondriack Melancholly. If your body be any strong you may take two drams of it at a time being sliced thin and steeped all night in white Wine, in the morning strain it out and drink the white Wine.

Rosemary. Helps stuffings in the head, helps the memory, expels wind.

Rue, or Herb of Grace. Consumes the seed and is an enemy to generation, helps difficulty of breathing. It strengthens the heart exceedingly. There is no better herb than this in Pestilential times.

Sage. It staies abortion, it causeth fruitfullness, it is singular good for the brain, helps stitches and pains in the sides.

St. Johns Wort. It is as gallant a wound-herb as any is, either given inwardly or outwardly applied to the wound. It helps the Falling sickness. Palsie, Cramps and Aches in the joynts.

Savory. Winter savory and summer savory both expell wind gallantly, and that (they say) is the reason why they are boyled with

Pease and Beans and other such windy things; 'tis a good fashion and pitty it should be left.

Senna. It cheers the sences, opens obstructions, takes away dulness of the sight, preserves youth, helps deafness (if purging will help it), resists resolution of the Nerves, scabs, itch and falling sickness. The windiness of it is corrected with a little Ginger.

Solomon's Seal. Stamped and boyled in Wine it speedily helps (being drunk, I mean, for it will not do the deed by looking upon it) all broken bones, it is of an incredible virtue that way; it quickly takes away the black and blew marks of blows, being bruised and applyed to the place.

Sorrel cutteth tough humors, cools the brain, liver and stomack, and provokes apetite.

Southern-wood or Boy's love, is hot and dry in the third degree, resists poyson, kills worms, provokes lust; outwardly in plaisters it dissolves cold swellings, makes hair grow; take not above half a drachm at a time in powder.

Spinage. I never read any physicall virtues of it.

[197]

Spleenwort is excellent good for melancholy people, helps the stranguary and breaks the Stone in the bladder. Boyl it and drink the decoction; but because a little boyling will carry away the strength of it in vapours, let it boyl but very little, and let it stand close stopped till it be cold before you strain it out; this is the generall rule for all Simples of this nature.

Spurge. Better let alone that taken inwardly; hair anoynted with the juyce of it will fall off: it kills fish, being mixed with anything they will eat, outwardly it takes away Freckles and sunburning.

Sweet-Majorum is an excellent remedy for cold diseases in the brain, being only smelled to; it helps such as are given to much sighing, and easeth pains in the belly....

Tansie. The very smell of it staies abortion or miscarriages in women. The root eaten, is a singular remedy for the Gout; the rich may bestow the cost to preserve it.

Toad-flax clenses the Reins and Bladder, outwardly it takes away yellowness and deformity of the skin.

Toads-stools. Whether these be roots or not it matters not much; for my part I know little need of them, either in food or Physick.

Tyme. Helps coughs and shortness of breath, brings away dead children and the after birth, helps Sciatica, repels wind in any part of the Body, resisteth fearfullness and melancholy.

Valerian, white and red, comforts the heart and stirs up lust.

Vervain. A great clenser. Made into an oyntment it is a soveraign remedy for old headache. It clears the skin and causeth a lovely color.

Wake-Robins or *Cuckow-pints.* I know no great good they doe inwardly taken, unlesse to play the rogue withall, or make sport; outwardly applyed they take off Scurf, Morphew, or Freckles from the face, cleer the skin, and cease the pain of the Gout.

Water-Lilies. The roots stop lust. I never dived so deep to find any other virtue.

Wood Bettony helps the falling sickness, and all headaches comming of cold, procures apetite, helps sour belchings, helps cramps[198] and convulsions, helps the Gout, Kills worms, helps bruises, and cleanseth women after their labor.

Wormwood helps weakness of the stomack, clenses choller, kills worms, helps surfets, cleers the sight, clenses the Blood, and secures cloaths from moths.

Yarrow. An healing herb for wounds. Some say the juice snuffed up the nose, causeth it to bleed, whence it was called Nose-bleed.

[199]

CHAPTER XIV

CRIMES AND PUNISHMENTS

The men who controlled the affairs of the Massachusetts Bay Colony at the time of its founding, determined not only that the churches, but that the government of the commonwealth they were creating, should be based strictly upon the teachings of the Bible. The charter provided that the Governor, Deputy Governor and Assistants might hold courts "for the better ordering of affairs," and so for the first ten years, the Court of Assistants, as it was styled, exercised the entire judicial powers of the colony. Its members were known as the magistrates. During this period but few laws or orders were passed. When complaints were made, the court, upon a hearing, determined whether the conduct of the accused had been such as in their opinion to deserve punishment, and if it had been, then what punishment should be inflicted. This was done without any regard to English precedents. There was no defined criminal code, and what constituted a crime and what its punishment, was entirely within the discretion of the court. If in doubt as to what should be considered an offence, the Bible was looked to for guidance. The General Court itself, from time to time, when in doubt, propounded questions to the ministers or elders, which they answered in writing, much as the Attorney General or the Supreme Judicial Court at the present day may advise.

But the people soon became alarmed at the extent of personal discretion exercised by the magistrates and so, in 1635, the freemen demanded a code of written laws and a committee composed of magistrates and ministers was appointed to draw up the same. It does not appear that much was accomplished although Winthrop records that Mr. Cotton of the committee, reported "a copy of Moses his judicials, compiled in an exact method, which was taken into further consideration till the next general court." The "judicials,"[200] however, never were adopted. In 1639 another committee was directed to peruse all the "models" which had been or should be presented, "draw them up into one body," and send copies to the several towns. This was done. In October, 1641, action was taken which led to a definite and acceptable result. Rev. Nathaniel Ward of Ipswich, who had been educated for the law and had practiced in the courts of England, was requested to furnish a copy of the liberties, etc. and nineteen transcriptions were sent to the several towns in the Colony. Two months later at the session of the General Court, this body of laws was voted to stand in force.

This code, known as "the Body of Liberties," comprised about one hundred laws, civil and criminal. The civil laws were far in advance of the laws of England at that time, and in substance were incorporated in every subsequent codification of the laws of the Colony. Some of them are in force today, and others form the basis of existing laws. The criminal laws were taken principally from the Mosaic code and although many of them may seem harsh and cruel yet, as a whole, they were much milder than the criminal laws of England at that time. No reference was made to the common law of England. All legislation in regard to offences was based upon the Bible, and marginal references to book, chapter and verse were supplied to guide future action. This Code served its intended purpose well and remained in force until the arrival of the Province charter in 1692 save during the short period of the Andros administration.

The judiciary system of the Colony therefore provided for the following courts:

First, the Great and General Court which possessed legislative powers and limited appellate authority from the Court of Assistants.

Second, the Court of Assistants—a Supreme Court or Court of Appeals that had exclusive jurisdiction in all criminal cases extending "to life, limb, or banishment," jurisdiction in civil cases in which the damages amounted to more than £100., and appellate jurisdiction from the County Quarterly Courts.

[201]

Third, County or Inferior Quarterly Courts that had jurisdiction in all cases and matters not reserved to the Court of Assistants or conferred upon commissioners of small causes. These courts also laid out highways, licensed ordinarys, saw that an able ministry was supported, and had general control of probate matters, and in 1664 were authorized to admit freemen.

The juries were made judges of the law and the fact and when upon a trial there was insufficient evidence to convict, juries were authorized to find that there were strong grounds of suspicion, and accordingly sentence afterwards was given by the Court. In order to facilitate court proceedings an excellent law was passed in 1656 which authorized the fining of a person 20 shillings an hour for any time occupied in his plea in excess of one hour.

John Winthrop with his company arrived at Salem in June, 1630, and ten weeks later the first court in the Colony was held at Charlestown. The maintenance of the ministry was the first concern, to be followed by an order regulating the wages of carpenters, bricklayers, thatchers and other building trades. Thomas Morton at "Merry Mount" was not forgotten for he was to be sent for "by processe," and a memorandum is entered to obtain for the next Court an estimate "of the charges that the Governor hathe beene att in entertaineing several publique persons since his landing in Newe England."

At the second meeting of the Court of Assistants, three of the magistrates were fined a noble apiece for being late at Court and three weeks later Sir Richard Saltonstall, because of absence, was fined four bushels of malt. It was at this Court that Thomas Morton was ordered "sett into the bilbowes" and afterwards sent prisoner into England by the ship called the *Gifte*. His goods were ordered seized and his house burnt to the ground "in the sight of the Indians for their satisfaction, for many wrongs he hath done them from time to time." Several towns were christened the names by which they are still known, and those who had ventured to plant themselves at Aggawam, now Ipswich, were commanded "forthwith to come away."

[202]

Aside from Morton's offences at Mount Wollaston, nothing of a criminal nature seems to have been brought to the attention of the Court until its third session on September 28th. To be sure the Governor had been consulted by the magistrates of the Colony at Plymouth concerning the fate of one John Billington of Plymouth who had murdered his companion John New-Comin. Billington was hanged, and "so the land was purged from blood."

Unless murder may have been committed at an earlier date by a member of some crew of unruly fishermen along the coast, this was the first murder committed in the English settlements about the Massachusetts Bay. But unfortunately it was not the last. Walter Bagnell's murder in 1632 was followed by that of John Hobbey and Mary Schooley in 1637, and the next year Dorothy, the wife of John Talbie, was hanged for the "unnatural and untimely death of her daughter Difficult Talby." The daughter's christian name at once suggests unending possibilities.

In the winter of 1646 a case of infanticide was discovered in Boston. A daughter of Richard Martin had come up from Casco Bay to enter into service. She concealed her condition well and only when accused by a prying midwife was search made and the fact discovered. She was brought before a jury and caused to touch the face of the murdered infant, whereupon the blood came fresh into it. She then confessed. Governor Winthrop relates that at her death, one morning in March, "after she was turned off and had hung a space, she spake, and asked what they did mean to do. Then some stepped up, and turned the knot of the rope backward, and then she soon died."

This curious "ordeal of touch" had also been applied the previous year at Agamenticus on the Maine Coast when the wife of one Cornish, whose bruised body had been found in the river, with her suspected paramour, was subjected to this supreme test. It is recorded that the body bled freely when they approached which caused her to confess not only murder but adultery, both of which crimes were punishable by death. She was hanged.

Probably the last instance in Massachusetts when this "ordeal of[203] touch" was inflicted, occurred in a little old meetinghouse in the parish of West Boxford, in Essex County, one July day in the year 1769. The previous December, Jonathan Ames had married Ruth, the eldest daughter of the widow Ruth Perley. He took his bride to the house of his parents, some five miles distant, and lived there. As in some instances since that time, the mother-in-law soon proved to be not in full sympathy with the young bride living under her roof. In May a child was born and a few days after the young mother died under circumstances which caused suspicion in the neighborhood. The body was hastily buried, none of the neighbors were invited to be present, and soon, about the parish, were flying rumors, which a month later crystalized into a direct accusation and a coroner's inquest. It was held in the meetinghouse that formerly stood in the sandy pasture near the old cemetery. The Salem newspaper records that the building was "much thronged by a promiscuous multitude of people."

The court opened with prayer, the coroners then gave the jury "their solemn charge" and then the entire company proceeded, "with decency and good order," over the winding roadway up the hill to the burying ground, where for five weeks had lain the body of the young bride. During the exhumation the crowd surged around the grave so eagerly that they were only held in check by the promise that all should have an opportunity to inspect the remains. The autopsy at the meetinghouse resulted in a report from the jury that Ruth Ames "came to her death by Felony (that is to say by poison) given to her by a Person or Persons to us unknown which murder is against the Peace of our said Lord the King, his Crown and Dignity." When it was found that no sufficient evidence could be adduced to hold either the husband of the murdered girl, or his mother, then was demanded an exhibition of that almost forgotten "ordeal of touch." The body was laid upon a table with a sheet over it and Jonathan and his mother were invited to prove their innocence by this gruesome test. The superstition required the suspected party to touch the neck of the deceased with the index finger of the left hand. Blood would immediately follow the touch[204] of the guilty hand, the whiteness of the sheet of course making it plainly visible. Both mother and son refused to accept the ordeal. Whether or no they believed in the superstition, we never shall learn. Fear may have held them motionless before the accusing eyes. Certainly the nervous tension at such a time must have been very great.

The *Gazette* states that the examination gave great occasion to conclude that they were concerned in the poisoning, and a week after the inquest they were arrested and confined in the ancient jail in Salem where the persons accused of witchcraft were imprisoned many years before. They were indicted and brought to trial. John Adams, afterwards President of the United States, then thirty-four years of age, was counsel for the accused. Jonathan Ames turned King's evidence against his mother. It was midnight before the counsel began their arguments and two of the three judges were explicit in summing up the evidence, that there was "a violent presumption" of guilt, but at nine o'clock in the morning the jury came in and rendered a verdict of "not guilty." May the result be attributed to John Adams's eloquence and logic or to the vagaries of our jury system?

But we are a long way from the third session of the Court of Assistants held September 28, 1630. Not until this time did the law begin to reach out for its victims. John Goulworth was ordered whipped and afterwards set in the stocks for felony, not named. One other was whipped for a like offence and two Salem men, one of whom has given us an honored line of descendants, were sentenced to sit in the stocks for four hours, for being accessory thereunto. Richard Clough's stock of strong water was ordered seized upon, because of his selling a great quantity thereof to servants, thereby causing much disorder. No person was to permit any Indian to use a gun under a penalty of £10. Indian corn must not be sold or traded with Indians or sent away without the limits of the Patent. Thomas Gray was enjoined to remove himself out of the Patent before the end of March, and the oath was administered to John Woodbury, the newly elected constable from Salem.

[205]

At the next session William Clark, who had been brought to book at a previous Court for overcharging Mr. Baker for cloth, now was prohibited cohabitation and frequent keeping company with Mrs. Freeman and accordingly was placed under bonds for a future appearance. Three years later this offender became one of the twelve who went to Agawam and founded the present town of Ipswich, and ten years later still another William Clark of Ipswich was sentenced to be whipped "for spying into the chamber of his master and mistress and reporting what he saw."

November 30, 1630, Sir Richard Saltonstall was fined £5, for whipping two persons without the presence of another assistant, as required by law; while Bartholomew Hill was whipped for stealing a loaf of bread, and John Baker suffered the same penalty for shooting at wild fowl on the Sabbath Day. And so continues the record of intermingled punishment and legislation.

The struggling communities that had planted themselves along the shores of the Massachusetts Bay largely had refused to conform to the rules and ordinances of the English Church. If the records of the Quarterly Courts are studied it will be seen that the settlers also failed to obey the rules and laws laid down by the magistrates of their own choosing. To be sure there were large numbers of indentured servants and the rough fishermen along the coastline have always been unruly. Much also may be attributed to the primitive and congested life in the new settlements. Simple houses of but few rooms and accommodating large families, surely are not conducive to gentle speech or modesty of manners nor to a strict morality. The craving desire for land holding, and the poorly defined and easily removed bounds naturally led to frequent actions for trespass, assault, defamation, slander and debt. The magistrates exercised unusual care in watching over the religious welfare of the people and in providing for the ministry. It has been stated frequently that in the olden times everyone went to church. The size of the meetinghouses, the isolated location of many of the houses, the necessary care of the numerous young children, and the interesting side lights on the manners of the[206] times which appear in the court papers, all go to prove that the statement must not be taken literally. Absence from meeting, breaking the Sabbath, carrying a burden on the Lord's Day, condemning the church, condemning the ministry, scandalous falling out on the Lord's Day, slandering the church, and other misdemeanors of a similar character were frequent. A number of years before the Quakers appeared in the Colony it was no unusual matter for some one to disturb the congregation by public speeches either in opposition to the minister or to some one present. Zaccheus Gould, a very large landholder, in Topsfield, in the time of the singing the psalm one Sabbath afternoon sat himself down upon the end of the table about which the minister and the chief of the people sat, with his hat on his head and his back toward all the rest of them that sat about the table and although spoken to altered not his posture; and the following Sabbath after the congregation was dismissed he haranged the people and ended by calling goodman Cummings a "proud, probmatical, base, beggarly, pick thank fellow." Of course the matter was ventilated in the Salem Court.

At the February 29, 1648, session of the Salem Court eight cases were tried. A Gloucester man was fined for cursing, saying, "There are the brethren, the divil scald them." Four servants were fined for breaking the Sabbath by hunting and killing a raccoon in the time of the public exercise to the disturbance of the congregation. If the animal had taken to the deep woods instead of staying near the meetinghouse the servants might have had their fun without paying for it. A Marblehead man was fined for sailing his boat loaded with hay from Gloucester harbor, on the Lord's Day, when the people were going to the morning exercise. Nicholas Pinion, who worked at the Saugus Iron works, was presented for absence from meeting four Lord's Days together, spending his time drinking, and profanely; and Nicholas Russell of the same locality was fined for spending a great part of one Lord's day with Pinion in drinking strong water and cursing and swearing. He also had been spending much time with Pinion's wife, causing jealousy in the[207] family; and the lady in question, having broken her bond for good behavior, was ordered to be severely whipped. The other cases were for swearing, in which the above named lady was included; for being disguised with drink; and for living from his wife. And so the Court ended.

A curious instance of Sabbath breaking occurred at Hampton in 1646. Aquila Chase and his wife and David Wheeler were presented at Ipswich Court for gathering peas on the Sabbath. They were admonished. The family tradition has it that Aquila returned from sea that morning and his wife, wishing to supply a delicacy for dinner, fell into grave error in thus pandering to his unsanctified appetite.

While we are discussing matters relating to the Sabbath and to the church it may be well to allude to the ministry. It has been shown that the first concern of the Court of Assistants was a provision for the housing and care of the ministry. Much the larger number were godly men actuated by a sincere desire to serve their people and to preserve their souls. But many of them were men, not saints, and so possessed of men's passions and weaknesses. While all exercised more or less influence over the communities in which they lived, yet the tangible result must have been negative in some instances. Take for example the small inland town of Topsfield, settled about 1639. Rev. William Knight rendered mission service for a short time early in the 40's and a dozen years later Rev. William Perkins moved into town from Gloucester. He had been one of the twelve who settled the town of Ipswich in 1633; afterwards he lived at Weymouth where he was selectman, representative to the General Court, captain of the local military company and also a member of the Ancient and Honorable Artillery Company. He also was schoolmaster in 1650 and the next year appears at Gloucester as minister, from which place he soon drifted into Court. Cross suits for defamation and slander were soon followed by the presentment of Mrs. Holgrave for unbecoming speeches against Mr. Perkins, saying "if it were not for the law, shee would never come to the meeting, the teacher was so dead ... affirming that the[208] teacher was fitter to be a ladys chamberman, than to be in the pulpit."

Mr. Perkins removed to Topsfield in 1656. The next year he tried to collect his salary by legal process and again in 1660. Three years later a church was organized and their first minister was settled. He was a Scotchman—Rev. Thomas Gilbert. Soon Mr. Perkins was summoned to Salem Court where Edward Richards declared in court before Mr. Perkins' face, that the latter being asked whither he was going, said, to hell, for aught he knew. Of course Mr. Perkins denied the testimony. Later in the same year he was fined for excessive drinking, it appearing that he stopped at the Malden ordinary and called for sack. But goody Hill told him that he had had too much already and Master Perkins replied, "If you think I am drunk let me see if I can not goe," and he went tottering about the kitchen and said the house was so full of pots and kettles that he could hardly go.

But what of Mr. Gilbert. Three years after his settlement Mr. Perkins appeared in Court and presented a complaint in twenty-seven particulars "that in public prayers and sermons, at several times he uttered speeches of a high nature reproachful and scandalous to the King's majestie & his government." He was summoned into Court and bound over in £1000 to the next General Court where eventually he was solemnly admonished publicly in open court by the Honored Governor. With twenty-seven particulars, could a Scotchman restrain his tongue? Mr. Gilbert could not, and shortly Mr. Perkins brought two complaints of defamation of character. Mr. Gilbert also soon developed a love of wine for it appears by the court papers that one sacrament day, when the wine had been brought from the meetinghouse and poured into the golden cup, Mr. Gilbert drank most of it with the usual result, for he sank down in his chair, forgot to give thanks, and sang a Psalm with lisping utterance. He was late at the afternoon service, so that many went away before he came and Thomas Baker testified "I perceived that he was distempered in his head, for he did repeat many things many times over; in his prayer he lisped and[209] when he had done to prayer, he went to singing &

read the Psalm so that it could not be well understood and when he had done singing he went to prayer again, and when he had done he was going to sing again, but being desired to forbear used these expressions: I bless God I find a great deal of comfort in it; and coming out of the pulpit he said to the people I give you notice I will preach among you no more." His faithful wife testified that his conduct was due to a distemper that came upon him sometimes when fasting and in rainy weather. The following April he was again before the Court charged with many reproachful and reviling speeches for which he was found guilty and sharply admonished and plainly told "that if he shall find himself unable to demean himself more soberly and christianly, as became his office, they do think it more convenient for him to surcease from the exercise of any public employment." The stubborn Scot refused to submit and affixing a defiant paper to the meetinghouse door he deserted his office for three successive Sabbaths, when his exasperated people petitioned the Court to be freed from such "an intollerable burden" and so the relation ceased but not until further suits and counter suits had been tried for defamation, slander, and threatened assault.

His successor was Rev. Jeremiah Hobart, a Harvard graduate, who preached for a while at Beverly and found difficulty in collecting his salary. He remained at Topsfield eight years and during that time became a familiar figure at the County Courts, because of non-payment of salary, for cursing and swearing, and for a damaging suit for slander exhibiting much testimony discreditable to him. Even his brother ministers and the churches were not free from his reproachful and scandalous speeches so he at last was dismissed and two years later was followed by a godly man, Rev. Joseph Capen of Dorchester, who enjoyed a peaceful pastorate of nearly forty years.

The severe penalties of the English legal code were much modified in the Bay Colony but public executions continued until the middle of the nineteenth century and were usually more or less a public holiday. The condemned was taken in a cart through the streets to[210] the gallows. Not infrequently a sermon was preached by some minister on the Sunday previous to the execution and speeches from the gallows always thrilled the crowd. The execution of pirates drew many people from some distance. Several Rhode Island murderers were executed and afterwards hung in chains. The gibbeting of the bodies of executed persons does not seem to have been general.[91]

While executions by burning took place in Europe, and Salem is sometimes accused of having burned witches at the stake, there are but two instances, so far as known, when this extreme penalty was inflicted in Massachusetts. The first occurred in 1681 when Maria, the negro servant of Joshua Lamb of Roxbury willfully set fire to her master's house, and was sentenced by the Court to be burned alive. The same year Jack, a negro servant, while searching for food set fire to the house of Lieut. William Clark of Northampton. He was condemned to be hanged and then his body was burnt to ashes in the same fire with Maria, the negress. The second instance of inflicting the penalty of burning alive occurred at Cambridge in the fall of 1755, when Phillis, a negro slave of Capt. John Codman of Charlestown, was so executed. She poisoned her master to death by using arsenic. A male slave Mark, who was an accomplice was hanged and the body afterwards suspended in chains beside the Charlestown highway where it remained for nearly twenty years,[92] Why was the woman deemed more culpable than the man in such[211] instances of poisoning? The old English law so provided and at a later date, under Henry VIII, poisoners were boiled alive in oil. The last execution in Massachusetts for the crime of arson occurred on Salem Neck in 1821 when Stephen Merrill Clark, a Newburyport lad, fifteen years of age, paid the penalty. He had set fire to a barn in the night time endangering a dwelling house.

Ten years before the adoption of the "Body of Liberties," adultery became a capital crime in accordance with the Mosaic law. The first case was one John Dawe, for enticing an Indian woman. He was severely whipped, and at the next session of the General Court, the death penalty was ordered for the future. When we consider the freedom of manners of the time, the clothing worn by the women, the limited sleeping accommodations and the ignorance of the servants, it is remarkable that the penalty was inflicted in so few cases. The records are full of cases of fornication, uncleanness, wanton dalliance, unseemly behaviour, unchaste words, and living away from wife, and the more so during the earlier years. Possibly, the juries may have thought the penalty too severe and found the parties guilty only, of "adulterous behavior," which happened in Boston in 1645. This followed a case of the previous year where a young woman had married an old man out of pique and then received the attentions of a young man of eighteen. They both were hanged.

The Court Records of the County of Essex always must have a curious interest because of the witchcraft cases. But the first execution in Massachusetts for witchcraft did not take place in Salem, but in Boston, in 1648, when Margaret Jones of Charlestown was hanged. It was shown that she had a malignant touch, that she produced deafness, practiced physic, and that her harmless medicines produced violent effects. She foretold things which came to pass and lied at her trial and railed at the jury. The midwives found that mysterious excrescence upon her, and for all these crimes she was hanged, and as a proof from Heaven of the justice of her taking off there was a great tempest in Connecticut on the very hour she was executed.

[212]

But Essex County court records show several witchcraft cases during the first twenty-five years following the settlement. In September, 1650, Henry Pease of Marblehead, deposed that he heard Peter Pitford of Marblehead say that goodwife James was a witch and that he saw her in a boat at sea in the likeness of a cat, and that his garden fruits did not prosper so long as he lived near that woman, and that said Pitford often called her "Jesable." Erasmus James, her husband, promptly brought suit for slander, and at the next Court another suit for defamation by which he received 50s. damages. The court records show that this Jane James had previously made her appearance, for in June, 1639, Mr. Anthony Thatcher complained that she took things from his house. She and her husband were bound for her good behavior and "the boys to be whipped by the Governor of the Family where they had offended." Six years later, in September, 1645, John Bartoll said in open court that he could "prove Jane James a common lyer, a theif & a false forsworn woman," and a year later, in September, 1646, Thomas Bowen, and his wife, Mary, testified that Jane James spoke to William Barber in Bowen's house in Marblehead and Barber said, "get you out of doors you filthy old Baud or else I will cuttle your hide, you old filthy baggage," & he took up a firebrand but did not throw it at her. Peter Pitford's accusation was not the only one for in the following year John Gatchell said that Erasmus James's wife was an old witch and that he had seen her going in a boat on the water toward Boston, when she was in her yard at home. But Erasmus promptly brought suit in the Salem court and recovered a verdict in his favor.

There are several other cases before 1655. In October, 1650, Thomas Crauly of Hampton sued Ralph Hall for slander, for saying he had called Robert Sawyer's wife a witch.

John Bradstreet, a young man of Rowley, was presented at Court in 1652 for having familiarity with the devil, witnesses testifying that Bradstreet said that he read in a book of magic and that he heard a voice asking him what work he had for him to do, and Bradstreet answered "go make a bridge of sand over the sea, go[213] make a ladder of sand up to Heaven and go to God and come down no more." There was much palaver but the Court showed common sense and Bradstreet was ordered to be fined or whipped for telling a lie.

In 1653 Christopher Collins of Lynn brought suit against Enoch Coldan for slander, for saying that Collins' wife was a witch and calling her a witch. The judgment however was for the defendant. Another accusation was promptly squelched in the fall of the same year.

Edmond Marshall of Gloucester unwisely stated publicly that Mistress Perkins, Goodey Evans, Goodey Dutch and Goodey

Vincent were under suspicion of being witches. Their husbands at once brought suit for defamation of character and the verdict in each case was, that the defendant should make public acknowledgment within fourteen days in the meetinghouses at Salem, Ipswich and Gloucester.

To sentence a culprit to expiate his crime before the congregation in the meetinghouse was a common thing. The publicity, in theory, induced shame and thus served as a future deterrent. To sit in the stocks and then make public acknowledgment before the congregation was a favorite penalty. Sometimes the offender was ordered to stand at the church door with a paper on his hat inscribed with the crime he had committed. If for lying, a cleft stick might ornament his tongue. Whipping was the most frequent penalty, closely followed by the stocks, and after a time imprisonment became more common. The bilboes were used only in the earliest period. The use of the stocks and whipping post was discontinued in 1813 and not a single example seems to have survived in either museum or attic. The pillory was in use in State Street, Boston, as late as 1803, and two years before, John Hawkins stood one hour in the pillory in what is now Washington Street, Salem, and afterwards had one ear cropped—all for the crime of forgery. Branding the hand or cheek was also inflicted, and Hawthorne has made famous another form of branding, the wearing prominently upon the clothing, an initial letter of a contrary color, symbolizing the crime committed.[214] This penalty was inflicted upon a man at Springfield, as late as October 7, 1754, and the law remained in force until February 17, 1785. As early as 1634 a Boston drunkard was sentenced to wear a red D about his neck for a year.[93]

Massachusetts did not purge her laws from these ignominious punishments until 1813 when whipping, branding, the stocks, the pillory, cutting off ears, slitting noses, boring tongues, etc., were done away with.

There lived in Salem, nearly three centuries ago, a woman whose story is told by Governor Winthrop and the records of the Quarterly Courts. She was, in a sense, a forerunner of Anne Hutchinson and we may fancy at heart a suffragette. Her story gives you an outline picture of the manners of the times in a few details. Her name was Mary Oliver and her criminal record begins in June, 1638. Governor Winthrop relates: "Amongst the rest, there was a woman in Salem, one Oliver, his wife, who had suffered somewhat in England by refusing to bow at the name of Jesus, though otherwise she was conformable to all their orders. She was (for ability of speech, and appearance of zeal and devotion) far before Mrs.[215] Hutchinson, and so the fitter instrument to have done hurt, but that she was poor and had little acquaintance. She took offence at this, that she might not be admitted to the Lord's supper without giving public satisfaction to the church of her faith, etc., and covenanting or professing to walk with them according to the rule of the gospel; so as upon the sacrament day she openly called for it, stood to plead her right, though she were denied; and would not forbear, before the magistrate, Mr. Endecott, did threaten to send the constable to put her forth. This woman was brought to the Court for disturbing the peace in the church, etc., and there she gave such premptory answers, as she was committed till she should find surities for her good behavior. After she had been in prison three or four days, she made means to the Governor and submitted herself, and acknowledged her fault in disturbing the church; whereupon he took her husband's bond for her good behavior, and discharged her out of prison. But he found, after, that she still held her former opinions, which were very dangerous, as, (I) that the church is the head of the people, both magistrates and ministers, met together and that these have power to ordain ministers, etc. (II) That all that dwell in the same town, and will profess their faith in Christ Jesus, ought to be received to the sacraments there; and that she was persuaded that, if Paul were at Salem, he would call all the inhabitants there saints. (III) That excommunication is no other but when Christians withdraw private communion from one that hath offended." September 24, 1639, this Mary Oliver was sentenced to prison in Boston indefinitely for her speeches at the arrival of newcomers. She was to be taken by the constables of Salem and Lynn to the prison in Boston. Her husband Thomas Oliver was bound in £20 for his wife's appearance at the next court in Boston.

Governor Winthrop continues: "About five years after, this woman was adjudged to be whipped for reproaching the magistrates. She stood without tying, and bore her punishment with a masculine spirit, glorying in her suffering. But after (when she came to consider the reproach, which would stick by her, etc.) she[216] was much dejected about it. She had a cleft stick put on her tongue half an hour for reproaching the elders."

March 2, 1647-8, Mary Oliver was fined for working on the Sabbath day in time of public exercise; also for abusing Capt. Hathorne, uttering divers mutinous speeches, and denying the morality of the Sabbath. She was sentenced to sit in the stocks one hour next lecture day, if the weather be moderate; also for saying "You in New England are thieves and Robbers" and for saying to Mr. Gutch that she hoped to tear his flesh in pieces and all such as he was. For this she was bound to good behavior, and refusing to give bond was sent to Boston jail, and if she remained in the court's jurisdiction was to answer to further complaints at the next Salem Court.

It appears from depositions that she went to Robert Gutch's house in such gladness of spirit that he couldn't understand it, and she said to some there, not members, "Lift up your heads, your redemption draweth near," and when reminded what she already had been punished for, she said that she came out of that with a scarf and a ring.

November 15, 1648, Mary Oliver for living from her husband, was ordered to go to him before the next court, and in December she brought suit against John Robinson for false imprisonment, taking her in a violent manner and putting her in the stocks. She recovered a judgment of 10s. damages. The following February Mary Oliver was again presented at Court for living from her husband, and in July, having been ordered to go to her husband in England by the next ship, she was further enjoyned to go by the next opportunity on penalty of 20 li.

November 13, 1649, Mary Oliver was presented for stealing goats, and a month later she was presented for speaking against the Governor, saying that he was unjust, corrupt and a wretch, and that he made her pay for stealing two goats when there was no proof in the world of it. She was sentenced to be whipped next lecture day at Salem, if the weather be moderate, not exceeding twenty stripes. Capt. William Hathorne and Mr. Emanuel Downing[217] were to see the sentence executed. At the same court George Ropes complained that Mary Oliver kept away a spade of his and she was fined 5s.

February 28, 1649-50, Mary Oliver thus far had escaped the second whipping, for at her request Mr. Batter asked that her sentence be respited, which the Court granted "if she doe go into the Bay with Joseph Hardy this day or when he goeth next into the Bay with his vessell" otherwise she was to be called forth by Mr. Downing and Capt. Hathorne and be punished. If she returned, the punishment was to hold good.

The next day Mary Oliver's fine was remitted to the end that she use it in transporting herself and children out of this jurisdiction within three weeks. And there ended her turbulent career in the town of Salem, so far as the Court records show.

Until comparatively recent times New England shipping sailed the seas in frequent danger of attack by pirate vessels. Before the town of Boston was settled, Capt. John Smith, "the Admiral of New England," wrote: "As in all lands where there are many people, there are some theeves, so in all Seas much frequented, there are some Pyrats," and as early as the summer of 1632, one Dixey Bull was plundering small trading vessels on the Maine coast and looting the settlement at Pemaquid. Shipping, sailing to and from England, was obliged to run the gauntlet of the Dutch and French privateers and the so-called pirates sailing out of Flushing and Ostend made several captures that affected the fortunes of the Boston traders. In 1644, the Great and General Court sitting in Boston, granted a commission to Capt. Thomas Bredcake to take Turkish pirates—the Algerines—who were a constant danger to vessels trading with Spain. John Hull, the mint-master who made the "pine tree shillings," had a brother

Edward, who went a-pirating in Long Island Sound and after dividing the plunder made for England.

It was the treaty of peace between England and Spain, signed at Aix-la-Chapelle in 1668, that contributed largely to the great increase of piracy in the West Indies and along the New England[218] coast. The peace released a great many men who found themselves unable to obtain employment in merchant ships and this was particularly true in the West Indies where the colonial governors had commissioned a large number of privateers. It was but a step forward to continue that fine work without a commission after the war was over and to the mind of the needy seaman there was very little distinction between the lawfulness of one and the unlawfulness of the other. The suppression of buccaneering in the West Indies happened not long after and many of these adventurers raised a black flag and preyed upon the ships of every nation. The operation of the Navigation Acts also led to insecurity on the high seas and eventually to outright piracy; and so it came about that the pirate, the privateer, and the armed merchantman, often blended the one into the other.

The first trial and execution of pirates in Boston took place in 1672. Rev. Cotton Mather, the pastor of the North Church, Boston, in his "History of Some Criminals Executed in this Land," relates the story of the seizure of the ship *Antonio*, off the Spanish coast. She was owned in England and her crew quarrelled with the master and at last rose and turned him adrift in the ship's longboat with a small quantity of provisions. With him went some of the officers of the ship. The mutineers, or pirates as they were characterized at the time, then set sail for New England and on their arrival in Boston they were sheltered and for a time concealed by Major Nicholas Shapleigh, a merchant in Charlestown. He was also accused of aiding them in their attempt to get away. Meanwhile, "by a surprising providence of God, the Master, with his Afflicted Company in the Long-boat, also arrived; all, Except one who Dyed of the Barbarous Usage.

"The Countenance of the *Master*, who now become Terrible to the Rebellious *Men*, though they had *Escaped the Sea*, yet *Vengeance would not suffer them to Live a Shore*. At his Instance and Complaint, they were Apprehended; and the Ringleaders of this Murderous Pyracy, had sentence of Death Executed on them, in *Boston*."

---

[219]

The three men who were executed were William Forrest, Alexander Wilson, and John Smith. As for Major Shapleigh; he was fined five hundred pounds, which amount was afterwards abated to three hundred pounds because of "his estate not being able to beare it."

The extraordinary circumstances of this case probably induced the General Court to draw up the law that was enacted on October 15, 1673. By it piracy became punishable by death according to the local laws. Before then a kind of common law was in force in the Colony based upon Biblical law as construed by the leading ministers. Of course the laws of England were theoretically respected, but Massachusetts, in the wilderness, separated from England by three thousand miles of stormy water, in practice actually governed herself and made her own laws.

In 1675, the Court of Assistants found John Rhoade and certain Dutchmen guilty of piracy on the Maine coast and they were sentenced to be hanged "presently after the lecture." Just then, King Philip went on the warpath and all else, for the time, was forgotten in the fearful danger of the emergency. Before long the condemned men were released, some without conditions and others were banished from the Colony. It is fair to say, however, that politics and commercial greed were sadly mixed in this trial.

A bloody fight occurred at Tarpaulin Cove, near Woods Hole, in October, 1689, between a pirate sloop and a vessel sent out from

Boston in pursuit. The pirate was taken and after trial the leader, Capt. Thomas Pound, late pilot of the King's frigate *Rose*, then at anchor in the harbor, Thomas Hawkins, a well-connected citizen of Boston, Thomas Johnston of Boston, "a limping privateer," and one Eleazer Buck, were sentenced to be hanged. When they were on the gallows Governor Bradstreet reprieved all save Johnston—"Which gave great disgust to the People; I fear it was ill done," wrote Judge Sewall. The same day one William Coward was hanged for piracy committed on the ketch *Elinor*, while at anchor at Nantasket Road.

The capture in Boston in 1699, of William Kidd, Joseph Bradish,[220] born in Cambridge; Tee Wetherly, James Gillam, and other men concerned with the Madagascar pirates, created much excitement, but these men were tried in England and gibbetted at Hope Point on the Thames.

In June, 1704, a trial for piracy was held in the Old State House, and the testimony and proceedings were afterwards published. Captain John Quelch had sailed from Marblehead, the previous year, in command of a brigantine commissioned as a privateer. Instead of proceeding against the French off Newfoundland he had sailed south and on the coast of Brazil had captured and plundered several Portuguese vessels. While he was absent, a treaty of peace between England and Portugal had been signed and when Quelch returned to Marblehead harbor he learned that he had piratically taken various vessels belonging to subjects of "Her Majesty's good Allie," the King of Portugal. His arrest and trial followed and with six of his ship's company he was sentenced to be hanged on a gallows set up between high- and low-water mark off a point of land just below Copp's hill. The condemned were guarded by forty musketeers and the constables of the town and were preceded by the Provost Marshal and his officers. Great crowds gathered to see the execution. Judge Sewall in his diary comments on the great number of people on Broughton's hill, as Copp's hill was called at that time.

"But when I came to see how the River was cover'd with People, I was amazed: Some say there were 100 Boats. 150 Boats and Canoes, saith Cousin Moodey of York. Mr. Cotton Mather came with Capt.

Quelch and six others for Execution from the Prison to Scarlet's Wharf, and from thence in the Boat to the place of Execution about midway between Hanson's [*sic*] point and Broughton's Warehouse. When the scaffold was hoisted to a due height, the seven Malefactors went up: Mr. Mather pray'd for them standing upon the Boat. Ropes were all fasten'd to the Gallows (save King, who was Repriev'd). When the scaffold was let to sink, there was such a Screech of the Women that my wife heard it sitting in our Entry next the Orchard, and was much surprised at it;[221] yet the wind was sou-west. Our house is a full mile from the place."

Capt. Samuel Bellamy, in the pirate ship *Whydah*, was wrecked on Cape Cod near Wellfleet, the spring of 1717, and 142 men were drowned. Six pirates who reached shore were tried in Boston and sentenced to be hanged "at Charlestown Ferry within the flux and reflux of the Sea." After the condemned were removed from the courtroom the ministers of the town took them in hand and "bestowed all possible *'Instructions* upon the Condemned Criminals; often *Pray'd* with them; often *Preached* to them; often *Examined* them; and *Exhorted* them; and presented them with Books of Piety.'" At the place of execution, Baker and Hoof appeared penitent and the latter joined with Van Vorst in singing a Dutch psalm. John Brown, on the contrary, broke out into furious expressions with many oaths and then fell to reading prayers, "not very pertinently chosen," remarks the Rev. Cotton Mather. He then made a short speech, at which many in the assembled crowd trembled, in which he advised sailors to beware of wicked living and if they fell into the hands of pirates, to have a care what countries they came into. Then the scaffold fell and six twitching bodies, outlined against the sky, ended the spectacle.

In 1724 the head of Capt. John Phillips, the pirate, was brought into Boston in pickle. He had been killed by "forced men" who had risen and taken the pirate ship. Only two of his company lived to reach Boston for trial and execution, and one of them, John Rose Archer, the quartermaster, was sentenced to be "hung up in Irons, to be a spectacle, and so a Warning to others." The gibbet was erected on

Bird Island which was located about half-way between Governor's Island and East Boston. In the Marshal's bill for expenses in connection with the execution appears the following item:

"To Expenses for Victuals and Drink for the Sherifs, Officers and Constables after the Executions att Mrs. Mary Gilberts her Bill £3.15.8."

The enforcement of the English statute relating to piracy was variously interpreted in the Colonial courts, and local enactments sometimes superseded it in actual practice. Previous to 1700, the[222] statute required that men accused of piracy should be sent to England to be tried before a High Court of Admiralty. Pound, Hawkins, Bradish, Kidd, and other known pirates were accordingly sent in irons to London for trial. But the difficulties and delays, to say nothing of the expense, induced Parliament by an Act of 11 and 12 William III, to confer authority by which trials for piracy might be held by Courts of Admiralty sitting in the Colonies. On the other hand, the Massachusetts Court of Assistants in 1675 found John Rhoades and others, guilty of piracy. This was in accordance with an order adopted by the Great and General Court on October 15, 1673. When Robert Munday was tried at Newport, R. I., in 1703, it was by a jury in the ordinary criminal court, in open disregard of the King's commission.

The Courts of Admiralty held in the Colonies were composed of certain officials designated in the Royal commission, including the Governor, Lieutenant-Governor, the Judge of the Vice-Admiralty for the Province, the Chief Justice, the Secretary, Members of the Council, and the Collector of Customs. Counsel was assigned to the accused to advise and to address the Court "upon any matter of law," but the practice at that time was different from the present. Accused persons in criminal cases were obliged to conduct their own defence and their counsel were not permitted to cross-examine witnesses, the legal theory at the time being that the facts in the case would appear without the necessity of counsel; that the judge could be trusted to see this properly done; and the jury would give the prisoner the benefit of any reasonable doubt.

Trials occupied but a short time and executions generally took place within a few days after the sentence of the Court was pronounced. During the interval the local clergy labored with the condemned to induce repentance, and all the terrors of hell were pictured early and late. Usually, the prisoners were made the principal figures in a Sunday spectacle and taken through the streets to the meetinghouse of some prominent minister, there to be gazed at by a congregation that crowded the building, while the reverend divine preached a sermon suited to the occasion. This discourse was[223] invariably printed and avidly read by the townsfolk, so that few copies have survived the wear and tear of the years. From these worn pamphlets may be learned something of the lives and future of the prisoners as reflected by the mental attitude of the attending ministers.

The day of execution having arrived, the condemned prisoners were marched in procession through the crowded streets safely guarded by musketeers and constables. The procession included prominent officials and ministers and was preceded by the Marshal of the Admiralty Court carrying "the Silver Oar," his emblem of authority. This was usually about three feet long and during the trial was also carried by him in the procession of judges to the courtroom where it was placed on the table before the Court during the proceedings.

Time-honored custom, and the Act of Parliament as well, required that the gallows should be erected "in such place upon the sea, or within the ebbing or flowing thereof, as the President of the Court ... shall appoint," and this necessitated the construction of a scaffold or platform suspended from the framework of the gallows by means of ropes and blocks. When an execution took place on land, that is to say, on solid ground easily approached, it was the custom at that time to carry the condemned in a cart under the crossarm of the gallows and after the hangman's rope had been adjusted around the neck and the signal had been given, the cart would be driven away and the condemned person left dangling in the air. In theory, the proper adjustment of the knot in the rope and the short fall from the body of the cart when it was driven away, would be sufficient to break the bones of the neck and also cause strangulation; but in practice this did not always occur.

When pirates were executed on a gallows placed between "the ebb and flow of the tide," the scaffold on which they stood was allowed to fall by releasing the ropes holding it suspended in mid-air. This was always the climax of the spectacle for which thousands of spectators had gathered from far and near.

Not infrequently the judges of a Court of Admiralty had[224] brought before them for trial a pirate whose career had been more infamous than the rest. A cruel and bloody-minded fellow fit only for a halter,—and then the sentence to be hanged by the neck until dead would be followed by another judgment, dooming the lifeless body of the pirate to be hanged in chains from a gibbet placed on some island or jutting point near a ship channel, there to hang "a sun drying" as a warning to other sailormen of evil intent. In Boston harbor there were formerly two islands—Bird Island and Nix's Mate—on which pirates were gibbeted.[94] Bird Island long since disappeared and ships now anchor where the gibbet formerly stood. Nix's Mate was of such size that early in the eighteenth century the selectmen of Boston advertised its rental for the pasturage of cattle. Today every foot of its soil has been washed away and the point of a granite monument alone marks the site of the island where formerly a pirate hung in chains beside the swiftly flowing tides.

What constitutes a crime? It all depends upon the minds of the people and oftentimes upon the judges. Manners and crimes vary with the centuries as do dress and speech. Here are some of the crimes penalized by Essex County Courts before the year 1655, viz.: eavesdropping, meddling, neglecting work, taking tobacco, scolding, naughty speeches, profane dancing, kissing, making love without consent of friends, uncharitableness to a poor man in distress, bad grinding at mill, carelessness about fire, wearing great boots, wearing broad bone lace and ribbons. Between 1656 and 1662 we find others, viz.: abusing your mother-in-law, wicked speeches against a son-in-law, confessing himself a Quaker, cruelty to animals, drinking tobacco, *i.e.*, smoking, kicking another in the street, leaving children alone in the house, opprobrious speeches, pulling hair, pushing his wife, riding behind two fellows at night[225] (this was a girl, Lydia by name), selling dear, and sleeping in meeting. The next five years reveal the following, viz.: breaking the ninth commandment, dangerous well, digging up the grave of the Sagamore of Agawam, going naked into the meetinghouse, playing cards, rebellious speeches to parents, reporting a scandalous lie, reproaching the minister, selling strong water by small measure, and dissenting from the rest of the jury.

With such minute supervision of the daily life of the colonists it can readily be appreciated that it was an age for gossiping, meddlesome interference with individual life and liberty and that in the course of time nearly every one came before the courts as complainant, defendant or witness. There were few amusements or intellectual diversions and they could only dwell on the gossip and small doings of their immediate surroundings. But all the while there was underlying respect for law, religion and the rights of others. The fundamental principles of human life were much the same as at the present day, and men and women lived together then as now and as they always will—with respect and love.

Are the Times Improving?

Edward Johnson's estimate in his *Wonder-working Providence* supposes in 1643, a population in Massachusetts of about 15,000. There were then 31 towns in the Bay Colony, of which 10 were within the limits of the present Essex County. The population of these 10 towns was probably about 6,000. They were located for the most part along the shore line. The same geographical area in 1915 had a population of about 360,000, or exactly 60 times as great as the population in 1643, 272 years before.

164
3

1915

	6,000	360,000
Population		
Increase in 272 years—60 times as great.		
In 1643, 1 person in 60 was a criminal.		
In 1915, 1 person in 600 was a criminal.		
10 times more crime in 1643 according to population.		
Murder (4), manslaughter (6), assault to murder (2)	0	12
Arson	0	7

[226]Robbery, breaking and entering, etc.	8	165
Assault of various kinds	10	86
Drunkenness	7	70
Illegal sale of liquor	0	74
Sexual crimes, including bastardy, streetwalking, etc.	6	71
Living from wife	14	0
Non-support and desertion	0	48
Profanity, reproachful speeches,	13	2

evil speeches, etc.		
Extortion, oppression, shortweight, etc.	7	5
Idle and disorderly	3	22
Slander and libel	1	3
Forgery	0	3
Lying and perjury	2	0
Breaking the Sabbath	5	1
Misc. Putting oxen in field, absence from watch, neglect of a servant, etc.	25	—

Delinquency, cruelty to horse, adulterating drugs, automobile cases, junk dealers fines, etc.	—	39
	— —	— —
Total	101	607

In 1643—7 were servants.

In 1915—251 were South European names and a large part of the remainder were Irish.

ILLUSTRATIONS

SECTION
OF
ILLUSTRATIONS

THE GOVERNOR'S "FAYRE HOUSE" IN THE 1630 COLONIAL VILLAGE AT SALEM

Plate 1

ENGLISH MERCHANT VESSEL AT THE BEGINNING OF THE SEVENTEENTH CENTURY

From the model of an "English Merchantman of the size and date of the *Mayflower*", built by R. C. Anderson for the Pilgrim Society, Plymouth, Mass. Courtesy of the Marine Research Society

Plate 2

AN ENGLISH MERCHANTMAN OF 1655

Showing the Rigging Plan. From Miller's *Complete Modellist*. Courtesy of the Marine Research Society

Plate 3

A DUTCH SHIP OF ABOUT 1620

From Furttenbach's *Architectura Navalis*, 1629. Courtesy of the Marine Research Society

Plate 4

GOVERNOR JOHN ENDECOTT 1558-1665
From the original painting in the possession of William C. Endicott, jr.

Plate 5

THE COLONIAL VILLAGE ERECTED IN 1930 AT SALEM, MASSACHUSETTS

Plate 6

ENGLISH WIGWAMS, FIRST TWO COVERED WITH BARK 1630
Colonial Village, Salem, Massachusetts

FRAMEWORK OF THE ENGLISH WIGWAMS 1630 Colonial Village, Salem, Massachusetts

Plate 7

THATCH-ROOFED, ONE-ROOM COTTAGES; THE SQUARE OF THE 1630 COLONIAL VILLAGE SHOWING THE PILLORY AND STOCKS

INTERIOR OF AN ENGLISH WIGWAM 1630 Colonial Village, Salem, Massachusetts

Plate 8

FRONT ENTRY AND STAIRS IN THE GOVERNOR'S "FAYRE HOUSE" 1630 Colonial Village, Salem, Massachusetts

Plate 9

THE "HALL" IN THE GOVERNOR'S "FAYRE HOUSE" IN THE 1630 COLONIAL VILLAGE AT SALEM

Plate 10

REAR VIEW OF WILLIAM DAMME GARRISON HOUSE, DOVER, N. H.

Built before 1698 and now preserved on the grounds of the Woodman Institute, Dover

Plate 11

CORNER OF THE MCINTYRE GARRISON HOUSE, NEAR YORK, ME.

Built in 1640 to 1645, therefore contemporary with the earliest possible Swedish buildings in the Delaware Valley, and possibly the oldest log structure standing in the United States.

Courtesy of the Bucks County Historical Society.

DOVETAILED LOGS AT THE CORNER OF THE BUNKER GARRISON HOUSE DURHAM, N. H.

Built *ca.* 1690. From a photograph made in 1911

Plate 12

THE FAIRBANKS HOUSE, DEDHAM, MASSACHUSETTS
Built *ca.* 1637. Courtesy of the Walpole Society

Plate 13

THE FRAME OF THE FAIRBANKS HOUSE
Dedham, Mass. Built *ca.* 1637
From Isham, *Early American Houses*, 1928. Courtesy of the Walpole Society

Plate 14

THE FRAME OF AN ORIGINAL LEANTO HOUSE—THE WHIPPLE-MATTHEWS HOUSE, HAMILTON, MASS. BUILT *CA.* 1690
From Isham, *Early American Houses*, 1928. Courtesy of the Walpole Society

Plate 15

WATTLE AND DAUB IN ENGLAND
From Oliver, *Old Houses and Villages in East Anglia.*
Courtesy of the Walpole Society

THE CORWIN-"WITCH HOUSE," SALEM. BUILT BEFORE 1678

From an old watercolor at the Essex Institute

Plate 16

THE SPENCER-PIERCE HOUSE, NEWBURY, MASS.

Built about 1651. This house of the smaller English manor house type, has the only original two-story porch and porch chamber now existing in New England. Courtesy of the Essex Institute

Plate 17

PARSON CAPEN HOUSE, TOPSFIELD, MASS.

Built in 1683

Plate 18

PARSON CAPEN HOUSE, TOPSFIELD, MASS.

Front Door

Plate 19

PARSON CAPEN HOUSE, TOPSFIELD, MASS.

Front entry and stairs

Plate 20

PARSON CAPEN HOUSE, TOPSFIELD, MASS.

Overhang and one of the "drops"

Plate 21

THE JOHN WARD HOUSE, SALEM. BUILT IN 1684

Showing overhanging second story, gable windows and casement sash

JOHN WARD HOUSE, SALEM, MASS.

The kitchen showing roasting jack, settle, birch broom, hands of seed corn, etc.

Plate 22

THE JETHRO COFFIN HOUSE, NANTUCKET, MASSACHUSETTS

Built in 1686. From a photograph made about 1880

Plate 23

REAR OF THE SAXTON HOUSE, DEERFIELD, MASS.

Showing unpainted weatherboarding

Plate 24

PROSPECT OF THE COLLEGES IN CAMBRIDGE IN 1726

From an engraving, after a drawing by William Burgis

Plate 25

DIAMOND-PANE, LEADED GLASS, DOUBLE SASH

Period of 1675-1700; in museum of the Society for the Preservation of New England Antiquities, Boston

CROWN GLASS WINDOW SASH

Period of 1725-1750; in museum of the Society for the Preservation of New England Antiquities, Boston

Plate 26

FRAMING DETAILS OF THE MOULTHROP HOUSE, EAST HAVEN, CONN.

Built before 1700. Showing methods of construction to be found everywhere in New England

Drawing by J. Frederick Kelley

Plate 27

WOODEN LATCH OF ABOUT 1710

Found in the French-Andrews House, Topsfield

KNOCKER, LATCH AND BOLT ON THE DOOR OF THE "OLD INDIAN HOUSE"

Built in 1698 at Deerfield, Mass.

Plate 28

TYPES OF WROUGHT-IRON DOOR LATCHES

FIG. A   FIG. B   FIG. C

Figure A. An inner door, wrought-iron latch that may have been made by a local blacksmith. Outer door latches were of similar type but larger. The lifts were made straight until about 1800 and the thumb-press was not saucered until about the same time. There is great individuality in the ornamentation, varying with the fancy of the smith.

Figure B. This latch was imported from England. It was cheap and in common use between 1750 and 1820. The cusp, resembling the outline of a lima bean, and the grasp, thumb piece and lift are always flat.

Figure C. The Norfolk latch appeared about 1800 and until about 1810 was made with a straight lift. The grasp is riveted to the plate of sheet iron as is the end of the bar and after about 1825, the catch. This latch was commonly used in the 1830's. After 1840 the cast-iron latch was generally adopted.

Plate 29

JOHN WARD HOUSE, SALEM, MASS.

The Parlor

JOHN WARD HOUSE, SALEM, MASS.

Corner of the kitchen showing dresser with its "dress of pewter," wash bench, meal chest, wooden ware, etc.

Plate 30

PARLOR IN PARSON CAPEN HOUSE, TOPSFIELD, MASS.

Built 1683

DRESSER IN THE KITCHEN OF THE PARSON CAPEN HOUSE, TOPSFIELD, MASS.

Plate 31

THE DASH CHURN

From a photograph by Miss Emma L. Coleman

Plate 32

AMERICAN COURT CUPBOARD. ABOUT 1660

**Owned by Gregory Stone of Watertown and Cambridge
Courtesy Concord Antiquarian Society**

Plate 33

**RECESSED COURT CUPBOARD OF AMERICAN OAK About 1680.
From the Dwight M. Prouty collection**

Plate 34

A SEVENTEENTH-CENTURY OAKEN CHEST ON FRAME

**Probably made about 1651-1655 for Samuel and Hannah
Appleton of Ipswich, Mass.**

Plate 35

CANE-BACK ARM CHAIR, 1680-1690

From the family of Hon. Peter Bulkley

Courtesy Concord Antiquarian Society

Plate 36

BANISTER-BACK CHAIR, ABOUT 1720

Courtesy Concord Antiquarian Society

Plate 37

A QUILTING BEE IN THE OLDEN TIME

From a drawing by H. W. Pierce

Plate 38

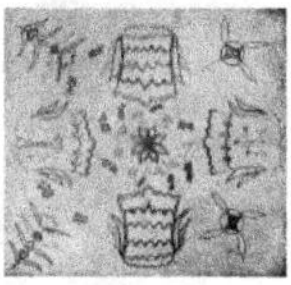

COUNTERPANE MADE FROM A BLANKET SHEET

Embroidered in blue, greenish blue, red and yellow

Plate 39

QUILTED COUNTERPANE MADE IN BEVERLY, MASS., BEFORE THE REVOLUTION

Plate 40

COUNTERPANE WITH PATTERN WORKED IN INDIGO BLUE ON A HOMESPUN LINEN SHEET

Plate 41

JOHN WINTHROP THE YOUNGER

1606-1676

Founder of Ipswich and Governor of Connecticut

From the original portrait in possession of Mrs. Robert Winthrop

Plate 42

REV. RICHARD MATHER

1596-1669

From a wood engraving by John Foster made in 1669

Plate 43

DOCTOR JOHN CLARKE

1601-1664

Practiced in Newbury, Ipswich and Boston

Courtesy of Massachusetts Historical Society

Plate 44

MRS. ELIZABETH (PADDY) WENSLEY

Painted in Boston about 1670-1675

Courtesy of the Pilgrim Society, Plymouth

Plate 45

MRS. ELIZABETH (CLARKE) FREAKE AND DAUGHTER MARY

Painted in Boston in 1674

Courtesy of Mrs. William B. Scofield

Plate 46

MARGARET GIBBS

Daughter of Robert and Elizabeth (Sheaffe) Gibbs of Boston

Dated 1670. Courtesy of Mrs. Alexander Quarrier Smith

Plate 47

ALICE MASON

Painted in 1670, aged two years

Daughter of Arthur and Joanna (Parker) Mason of Boston

Courtesy of the Adams Memorial

Plate 48

DAVID, JOANNA AND ABIGAIL MASON

Children of Arthur and Joanna (Parker) Mason of Boston

Painted in 1670. Courtesy of Mr. Paul M. Hamlen

Plate 49

CAPTAIN THOMAS SMITH

A self portrait

May have painted the portraits of Major Savage and Capt. George Corwin

Courtesy of the American Antiquarian Society

Plate 50

MAJOR THOMAS SAVAGE

1640-1705

Born and died in Boston

Courtesy of Mr. Henry L. Shattuck

Plate 51

EDWARD RAWSON

1615-1693

Secretary of the Massachusetts Bay Colony. From the painting by an unknown artist, now owned by the New England Historic Genealogical Society

Plate 52

REBECCA RAWSON

1656-1692

From the painting by an unknown artist, now owned by the New England Historic Genealogical Society

Plate 53

SAMUEL SEWALL

1652-1730

Chief Justice of the Superior Court in Massachusetts, 1718-1728

From an original painting in possession of the Massachusetts Historical Society

Plate 54

REV. COTTON MATHER

1663-1728

Pastor of the Second (North) Church, Boston, 1685-1728

From a mezzotint by Peter Pelham after a portrait painted in 1728

Plate 55

NATHAN FESSENDEN AND HIS SISTER CAROLINE

From a photograph taken about 1885 in Lexington, Mass.

Showing costume of a much earlier date

Plate 56

WELLCURB AT THE JOHN WARD HOUSE, SALEM, MASS.

Showing wellsweep, wooden bucket and girl dressed in the costume of the late seventeenth century

Plate 57

THE SOWER

From a photograph by Miss Emma L. Coleman

Plate 58

TRACING SEED CORN IN A FARMER'S BARN

From a photograph by Miss Emma L. Coleman

Plate 59

A FARMYARD SCENE AT DEERFIELD, MASSACHUSETTS

From a photograph by Miss Emma L. Coleman

Plate 60

HORSES AND A RAIL FENCE

From a photograph by Miss Emma L. Coleman

Plate 61

LOADING HAY ON AN OXCART

From a photograph by Miss Emma L. Coleman

Plate 62

GUNDALOW LOADED WITH SALT HAY

From a photograph made by Miss Emma L. Coleman, about 1880, on Parker River, Newbury, Mass.

Similar craft were early used in Boston harbor and with a stump mast and lateen sail carried cargo up the Merrimack River

Plate 63

BRUSHING UP THE HEARTH. NIMS HOUSE, DEERFIELD, MASSACHUSETTS

From a photograph by Miss Emma L. Coleman

Plate 64

THE OLD HAND LOOM

Used a hundred years ago by Mrs. Jane Morrill Cummings

The harness and reeds are modern

Plate 65

A BACK DOOR SCENE

From a photograph by Miss Emma L. Coleman

Plate 66

TITLE-PAGE OF "THE DAY OF DOOM"

From the original owned by the late John W. Farwell

Plate 67

REV. GRINDALL RAWSON

Minister at Mendon, Mass. Born 1659, died 1715

Portrait cut on his gravestone

GRAVESTONE OF MRS. MARY ROUS

CHARLESTOWN, MASS., 1715

Plate 68

GRAVESTONE OF WILLIAM DICKSON, CAMBRIDGE, MASS., 1692

GRAVESTONE OF CAPT. JOHN CARTER, WOBURN, MASS., 1692

Plate 69

FIRE BACK CAST AT THE SAUGUS IRON WORKS IN 1660 FOR THE PICKERING HOUSE, SALEM

The letters I A P stand for John Pickering and Alice his wife

Plate 70

PRICE SHEET OF JOSEPH PALMER & CO., CHANDLERS

Engraved by Nathaniel Hurd

Plate 71

WEIGHTS AND VALUES OF COINS

A table engraved by Nathaniel Hurd of Boston

Original engravings are owned by the American Antiquarian Society, Worcester, and the Pocumtuck Valley Museum, Deerfield

Plate 72

SHINGLE HORSE ON WHICH WERE SHAVED SHINGLES, CLAPBOARDS AND BARREL STAVES

From a photograph by Miss Emma L. Coleman

Plate 73

AN OLD BASKET MAKER

Dried apples hang on strings against the wall

Plate 74

CHARCOAL BURNERS PREPARING A KILN

From a photograph made in 1884 by Miss Emma L. Coleman

Plate 75

SPINNING WITH THE WOOL WHEEL

Photograph by Miss Emma L. Coleman

Plate 76

AN OLD-TIME NEW ENGLAND LOOM

Now in the museum of the Society for the Preservation of New England Antiquities

Plate 77

PROSPECT OF THE HARBOR AND TOWN OF BOSTON IN 1723

From an engraving (central part only) after a drawing by William Burgis

Plate 78

A VIEW OF CASTLE WILLIAM, BOSTON, ABOUT 1729

Showing a ship of war of the period, probably after a drawing by William Burgis

Plate 79

VIEW OF BOSTON LIGHT IN 1729 AND AN ARMED SLOOP

From the only known example of a mezzotint engraved in 1729 after a drawing by William Burgis

Plate 80

SHIP "BETHEL" OF BOSTON

Owned by Josiah Quincy and Edward Jackson

From an oil painting made about 1748, showing the vessel in two positions

The earliest known painting of a New England ship. Now owned by the Massachusetts Historical Society

Plate 81

NEW ENGLAND SHILLING

Minted in 1650-1652. Obverse and reverse. From a coin in the cabinet of the Massachusetts Historical Society

PINE TREE SHILLING

Minted in 1652. Obverse and reverse. From a coin in the cabinet of the Massachusetts Historical Society

WILLOW TREE SHILLING   OAK TREE SHILLING

Minted in 1662 and soon after. From coins in the cabinet of the Massachusetts Historical Society

Plate 82

MASSACHUSETTS PAPER MONEY OF 1690

The first paper money issued by any colony

From an original in the cabinet of the Massachusetts Historical Society

Plate 83

MASSACHUSETTS PAPER MONEY PRINTED ON PARCHMENT IN 1722

From originals in the cabinet of the Massachusetts Historical Society

Plate 84

A MASSACHUSETTS MANUFACTORY BILL OF 1740

From an original in the cabinet of the Massachusetts Historical Society

Plate 85

MASSACHUSETTS PAPER MONEY OF 1744

From an original in the cabinet of the Massachusetts Historical Society

Plate 86

AN EARLY EXECUTION BY HANGING

The cart which brought to the gallows the condemned man and his coffin is in the foreground, and behind it, on horseback, is the sheriff

Plate 87

SETH HUDSON'S SPEECH FROM THE PILLORY

Caricature engraved by Nathaniel Hurd

Plate 88

Plate 89

Plate 90

[227]

APPENDIX A

BUILDING AGREEMENTS IN SEVENTEENTH-CENTURY MASSACHUSETTS

Few seventeenth-century agreements to erect buildings in Massachusetts have been preserved. The following, with two exceptions, have been gleaned from court records where originally they were submitted as evidence in suits at law. They are of the greatest interest in connection with present day restoration work as they preserve detailed information of indisputable authority in relation to early building construction in the Bay Colony. The gable window, the second story jet, the stool window and casement sash, the catted chimney and the treatment of the inner and outer walls of the house have much curious interest at the present time. These architectural features long since fell into disuse and only here and there has a fragment survived. Two centuries ago the towns in New England must have presented an appearance most picturesque to our twentieth-century eyes. The dwellings seem to have been studies in projecting angles, strangely embellished with pinnacles, pendants and carved work. The unpainted and time-stained walls, the small windows and elaborate chimney tops, the narrow and curiously fenced ways, winding among the irregularly placed buildings, all contributed to the quaintness of the picture. The following agreements between builder and owner should help to solve some of the debated problems of this bygone construction that now confront those interested in the preservation and restoration of our early New England dwellings.

CONTRACT TO BUILD THE FIRST MEETINGHOUSE IN MALDEN, NOVEMBER 11, 1658

Articles of agreement made and concluded ye 11th day of ye ninth mo., 1658, betweene Job Lane of Malden, on the one partie,[228] carpenter, and William Brakenbury, Lieut. John Wayte, Ensigne J.

Sprague, and Thomas Green, Senior, Selectmen of Malden, on the behalf of the towne on the other partie, as followeth:

Imprimis: The said Job Lane doth hereby covenant, promiss and agree to build, erect and finish upp a good strong, Artificial meeting House, of Thirty-three foot Square, sixteen foot stud between joints, with dores, windows, pullpitt, seats, and all other things whatsoever in all respects belonging thereto as hereafter is expressed.

1. That all the sills, girts, mayne posts, plates, Beames and all other principal Timbers shall be of good and sound white or Black oake.

2. That all the walls be made upp on the outside with good clapboards, well dressed, lapped and nayled. And the Inside to be lathed all over and well struck with clay, and uppon it with lime and hard up to the wall plate, and also the beame fellings as need shalbe.

3. The roofe to be covered with boards and short shinglings with a territt on the topp about six foot squar, to hang the bell in with rayles about it: the floor to be made tite with planks.

4. The bell to be fitted upp in all respects and Hanged therein fitt for use.

5. Thre dores in such places as the sayd Selectmen shal direct, viz: east, west and south.

6. Six windows below the girt on thre sids, namely: east, west and south; to contayne sixteen foot of glass in a window, with Leaves, and two windows on the south side above the girt on each side of the deske, to contayne six foot of glass A piece, and two windows under each plate on the east, west and north sides fitt [to] conteine eight foote of glass a peece.

7. The pullpitt and cover to be of wainscott to conteyne ffive or six persons.

8. The deacon's seat allso of wainscott with door, and a table joyned to it to fall downe, for the Lord's Supper.

[229]

9. The ffloor to be of strong Boards throughout and well nayled.

10. The House to be fitted with seats throughout, made with good planks, with rayles on the topps, boards at the Backs, and timbers at the ends.

11. The underpining to be of stone or brick, and pointed with lyme on the outside.

12. The Allyes to be one from the deacon's seat, through the middle of the house to the north end, and another cross the house ffrom east to west sides, and one before the deacon's seat; as is drawne on the back side of this paper.

13. And the said Job to provide all boards, Timber, nayles, Iron work, glass, shingles, lime, hayre, laths, clapboards, bolts, locks and all other things whatsoever needful and belonging to the finyshing of the said house and to rayse and finish it up in all respects before the twentie of September next ensuing, they allowing help to rayse it.

And the sd Selectmen for themselves on behalfe of the town in Consideracon of the said meeting house so finished, doe hereby covenant, promise and agre to pay unto the sd Job Lane or his Assigns the sume of one hundred and ffiffty pounds in corne, cordwood and provisions, sound and merchantable att price currant and fatt catle, on valuacon by Indifferent men unless themselves agree the prices.

In manner following, that is to say, ffifftie pound befor ye first of ye second mo. next ensuing, And ffifftie pounds befor the first of ye last mo. which shall be in the year sixteen hundred 59, and other ffifftie pounds before the first of ye second mo. which shall be in the year one thousand six hundred and sixtie. And it is further Agreed that when the sd. house is finished in case the sd. Job shall find and judgeth to be woth ten pounds more, that it shall be referred to Indifferent workmen to determine unless the sayd Selectmen shall se just cause to pay the sd. ten pounds without such valuacon.

[230]

In witness whereof the partys to these presents have Interchangeably put their hands the day and year above written.

WILLIAM BRACKENBURY,
JOHN SPRAGUE,
JOH. WAYTE.

Witness,
JOSEPH   HILLS,
GERSHOM HILLS.

NOTE. This contract for building the first meetinghouse in Malden is copied from the *Bi-Centennial Book of Malden*, 1850, pages 123-125. The original document then in existence has since disappeared. The contract provides for the construction of a building of the type almost universal in New England at that time, of which an example still exists at Hingham—the "Ship Meeting House," so-called. The square meetinghouse with hip roof surmounted by a "territ," and at a somewhat later date supplied with "lucomb" (dormer) windows in the roof, was the type of public building in the Massachusetts Bay Colony that prevailed well into the eighteenth century, especially in the country towns. The "territ" or belfry seems to have been common, but only the larger towns were supplied with a bell. The bell was rung from the central aisle, the bell rope coming down in the center of the auditorium.

In the Malden meetinghouse, the "territ" was built as provided in the contract, but for some now unknown reason the bell was not hung in it but placed in a framework erected nearby, below a large rock which thereby obtained its name—"Bell Rock," a name that has continued until the present time.

Malden was able to afford the luxury of plastered walls surfaced with lime, but the ceiling showed the joists and boarding. In shingling the roof a distinction was made between long and short shingles. The lower windows were made up with "leaves," *i.e.*, they were double casements, and each opening contained sixteen feet of glass, thereby indicating sash about twenty-eight by forty inches in size. The single casement windows placed high, just[231] under the coving, also were about the same size and undoubtedly were fixed sash, *i.e.*, were not hinged. Two smaller windows on the south side, placed just above the girth, supplied additional light on either side of the pulpit. The deacons' seat at that time was located in front of the pulpit and faced the congregation. The possible use of brick for the underpinning is a surprising feature, especially in a country town. In fact, the use of underpinning at that time seems to have been uncommon.

CONTRACT TO BUILD A MINISTER'S HOUSE AT MARLBOROUGH, MASS., IN 1661

This indenture made the fifth day of Aprill one thousand six hundred and sixty one and between obadias Ward, Christopher Banyster and Richard Barnes of the Towne of Marlborough on ye one party; And the Inhabitants and all the Proprietors of the same Towne on ye other party Witnesseth That ye said obadias Waed, Christopher Banyster and Rich'd Barnes hath covenanted, promised and bargained to build a fframe for the minister's house, every way like to ye fframe yt Jno Ruddock hath built for himselfe in ye afores'd Town of Marlborough, the house or fframe is to bee a Girt house thirty-seven foote Long, eighteen foote wide and twelve foote (between Joynts) and a halfe, the studs standing at such distance that A foure foote and a halfe Claboard may reach three studs; and two ffloores of juice [*sic*] and foure windows on the foreside and two windows at the west end and two Gables on the foreside of ten foote wide; and eight foote Sparr, with two small windows on the foreside of the Gables and they are to ffell all the tinber and bring it in place and do all yt belongs to the fframe only the Towne is to helpe raise the affores'd fframe and all this worke is to bee done and ye fframe raised within a ffortnight after Michll tyde; And this being done the Town of Marlborough doth promise and engage to pay unto them the sd obadias Ward, Christopher Banyster and Rich'rd Barnes the sume of ffifteene Pounds in Corne within fourteen daies after the house is raised the one halfe of it and the other halfe some time in March; the whole paye[232] is to be one third in Wheat and one third in Rie and the other third in Indian Corn, the halfe in Wheat and Rie to be paid fourteen daies after the house is up in Wheat and Rie and the other halfe in Rie and Indian some time in March; wheat at four shillings and sixe pence a bushell and is to be pd at Sudbury betweene Petter King's and Serient Woods house in the streete.—*Marlborough, Mass., Town Records.*

CONTRACT FOR THE FRAME OF A BOSTON HOUSE, AUGUST 20, 1679

Articles of Agreement indented made and Concluded the twentieth day of August Ano Domi One thousand six hundred Seventy and nine. And in the thirty first yeare of the Reigne of King Charles the Second over &c. Betweene Robert Taft of Brantery, in New England housewright on the one part and John Bateman of Boston in New England aforesd shopkeeper on the other part are as followeth—

HOUSE BUILT FOR JOHN BATEMAN, IN 1679, AT WHAT IS NOW THE CORNER OF NORTH AND BLACKSTONE STREETS, BOSTON

From a drawing by Lawrence Park

Imps The sd Robert Taft for himselfe heires Execrs and Admrs doth hereby covenant promiss and grant to and with the sd John Bateman his Execr and assignees in manner and forme following (that is to Say) that the sd Robert Taft his Execror assignees shal and will erect set up and finish for the sd John Bateman his Execrs or Assignes the frame of a new Tenemt or dwelling house to contain thirty foot in length and twenty Seven foot or thereabout in breadth according to the dimentions of the Cellar frame of the sd house two Storey high besides the garrett and each roome seven foote high betweene the Sumer and floare and to make the sd house to jet at the first storey in the front Eighteen inches and to make and place frame for the Cellar according to the present dimentions thereof and place the same and to build three floares of Sumers and joise and to make and place in the front of the sd house two gable ends to range even with the Roof of the sd house and also two gable ends on the backside to range as aforesd and to make and place in the front of ye Second Storey two large casement windows and two windows in the garett and in the end next the Mill[233] Creeke three windows Vizt one large Casement window in the low[er] Roome and one large Casement window in the Second Storey and one window in the garrett and on the backside one large Casement window in the low[er] Roome two large Casement windows in the second Storey and two windows in the garrett and to make & send to Boston the frame of the Cellar within Six weeks next after the date hereof and to rayse the same in place within one week then next following (provided the cills of the sd Cellar be cleare) and to finish the frame of the sd house on or before the first day of march next and rayse the same with all possible Speed after it is brought to Boston. In Consideration whereof the sd John Bateman for himself his 3 heires execr and Admrs doth hereby covenant promis and grant to and with the sd Robert Taft his[234] Execr and assignes to pay for the transportation of the frame of the sd cellar and house from Brantery the place where it is to be framed to Boston and also to pay or cause to bee paid unto the sd Robert Taft his Execr Admrs or Assignes the full and just sum of thirty pounds Vizt one halfe part thereof in lawfull money of New England and the other halfe part thereof in English goods at money price and to pay the same in manner and forme following (that is to Say) five pounds in money and five pounds in goods at the time of Ensealing hereof and five pounds in money and five pounds in goods when the frame of the Cellar is laid down and the floare of the cellar is laid and five pounds in money and five pounds in goods when the whole worke is compleated and in every respect finished in matter and forme aforesd. And for the true performance hereof the sd partys binde themselves their heires Execr and Admrs each unto the other his Execr and Assignes in the penall Sume of fifty pounds of lawfull money of New England well and truly to be paid by virtue of these presents. In witness whereof the partys above-named to these present Articles interchangeably have Set their hands and Seals the day and yeare first above written.

JOHN BATEMAN. [Seal]

Signed	Sealed	&	Delivd	in	presence	of
John			Hayward			scr
Eliezer			Moody			Servt

Owned in Court p Bateman 27 April 1680 p Is Addington Cler Vera Copia Attestd Is Addington Cler

—Suffolk County Judicial Court Files, No. 1916.

NOTE. This contract provides for the frame of a house and not for a complete building. But it is of unusual interest for it supplies proof of the existence in Boston of a house having two gables on each side of the roof, *i.e.*, six gables on a rectangular building twenty-seven by thirty feet in size.

Robert Taft, of Braintree, an ancestor of ex-President Taft, delivered the frame, but before he had completed the work Bateman entered into possession and set his carpenters at work to finish[235] the building. Taft brought suit to recover payment for the frame and the Court gave a verdict in his favor, from which Bateman appealed. From the testimony it appears that on the ground floor there were two rooms, one of which was eleven by twenty-four feet, and a space nine by eight feet had been left in which to build the chimney. The "articles of agreement" required that Taft provide for fourteen windows but he put up "six more than my Couanant was." Bateman, on the other hand, claimed that the frame was "the weakest slenderest and most dozed timber that hath been Seen ... most of the timber Wany & on many of the Sumers the Bark left on to make it square and wch Indeed was the Occasion of all this Trouble."

This house was built for a "shop keeper" and probably the long front room on the ground floor was to be used for a shop. It was located at what is now the southeasterly corner of North and Blackstone streets, the canal to the mill pond being on the northerly end of the house and the harbor behind it.

CONTRACT TO BUILD THE FIRST KING'S CHAPEL, BOSTON JULY 21, 1688

Memorandum it is agreed by and between John Holebrook of Weymouth in the county of Suffolk, housewright, Stephen French of the same place, housewright—and Jacob Nash of the same place housewright of the one part and Anthony Hayward Esq of the other part as followeth (that is to say) Imprimis the said John Holebrooke, Stephen French & Jacob Nash doe Covenant pmise and agree to and with the said Anthony Heywood his heires Admrs and Assins and Also in the consideracion herein after mencioned that they the said John Holebrooke Stephen French and Jacob Nash or some or one of them shall & will by or before the last day of November now next ensueing Erect sett up and build on such spott of Ground as the sd Anthony Heywood shall for that end assigne of good sound timber well & workmanlike wrought one frame of building of the Dimensions following (that is to say) in length fifty four feet in breadth thirty six feet studd twenty feet[236] with five windows in the front five windows in the rear and two windows at each end of such dimensions as are sett downe in a platt of the same made by Mr. P. Wells Surveyor and the same frame shall clapboard fill with brick & seale with lime and hair & white washing and the roofe thereof with board & shingles make tight & stanch and shall & will on the west end of the sd frame Erect, build & sett up One Belfry of ten feet square twenty feet above ye roofe of the sd frame and of sufficient strength for a bell of five hundred weight and the said entire frame shall finish & complete with Masons and smiths worke and sufficiently glaze all the sd windows with good square glasse & iron casemts and the same building see completed and finished as above is Covenanted & locked with sufficient locks to the doors thereof shall deliver with the keys thereof in to the sd Anthony Haywood In Consideracion whereof the said Anthony Haywood doth cove't pmise & agree to pay or Cause to be paid unto the said

John Holebrooke Stephen French Jacob Nash the sume of two hundred & Sixty pounds (that is to say) One hundred & thirty pounds thereof in Goods & merchandize at the price for which same shall be then sold for money Sixty five pounds in money & sixty five pounds in goods perform'd as the said frame shall be raised and remaining Sixty five pounds in money & sixty five pounds in Goods when the sd building shall be finished as above is Covenanted. In witness whereof all the sd partyes have hereunto to sett their hands and seales and Consent that the same shall remaine in the hands ye sd Anthony Haywood this one & twentieth day of June Anno Dme 1688.

JOHN HOLEBROOK
STEPH FRENCH
JACOB NASH
ANTHONY HAYWOOD

Sealed   &   delivered   in   the   presence   of

Benja   Bullivant
Will   White
Thaddeus Mackarty

—*Suffolk County Judicial Court Files, No. 2598.*

[237]

NOTE. The foundations for the first Episcopal Chapel in America were laid in Boston in October, 1688, following a long controversy between the local authorities and the representatives of the King and their followers. Little has been known as to the details of the construction of this building. Judge Sewell records in his Diary, under date of Oct. 16, 1688, "The ground-sills of ye Chh are laid ye stone-foundation being finished." The records of the Church preserve no information and any contemporaneous documents seem to have disappeared with the exception of this contract for the construction of the building which is now printed for the first time. The exact size of the building heretofore has not been known. Rev. Henry Wilder Foote in his *Annals of King's Chapel*, Boston, 1882, supplies no information although he states that the Chapel was built at a cost of £284.16.0, an amount that probably represents the total cost including furnishings. In the *Annual Report of the Boston Cemetery Commissioners* for 1902-3, an attempt is made to show by a plan, partly based upon grants of land by the town, the several enlargements of the Chapel made at various times. Here, the size of the first building is shown to have been forty-six by sixty-four feet, proportions quite at variance with the correct size—thirty-six by fifty-four feet, as shown in the contract here printed.

The windows, probably of generous proportions for the time, were to be supplied with iron casements filled with "square glasse." Iron casement sash probably were rare in Massachusetts at that time. One is mentioned in the inventory of the estate of Edward Wharton, of Salem, in 1678, valued at six shillings. Square glass is most unusual. It probably was cut to size at special order as diamond-shaped glass was in common use. In January, 1752, and probably much later, "Diamond Glass, and 6 by 4" were still sold in the shops in Boston. These glass windows were a source of constant expense to the church wardens because of the popular dislike of the townspeople and the antagonism of the Puritan small boy. The first service was held in the Chapel, June 30, 1689. Four moths later the church records show a payment of £5.10.0. "for[238] mending church windows." On November 5, 1691, was taken "A Colecktion for mendin ye church winders" and a few days later £7.0.0. was paid out for the work. The next March, six shillings was paid for "24 Squ: glas."

OLD THREE-LIGHT CASEMENT WINDOW FRAME IN GABLE, *ca.* 1690 From Isham, *Early American Houses*, 1928. Courtesy of the Walpole Society

[239]

APPENDIX B

REV. SAMUEL SKELTON'S ACCOMPTE (1629-1630)

Rev. Samuel Skelton, the rector at Sempringham, England, came over under appointment of the Massachusetts Bay Company to minister to the spiritual needs of the little colony at Naumkeag, afterwards named Salem. He sailed in the ship *George* arriving in the summer of 1629. During the voyage and until the end of the following year the minister and his family were furnished with the following supplies from the Massachusetts Bay Company storehouse.

Coppie of An Accompte of monies Mr. Skelton is Creditor viz.[95]

		li. s. d.
Ano. 1629	Imprimis p. so much wch. should haue bene paid him in England towards fitting him for ye voyadg.	20-00-00
	Item for Charges att Tillbury, Cowes, & Plimoth,	02-10-00

being wind
bound

Item p. Twenty li. p. Annum for 3 years is ye some of	60- 00- 00
Item for on bushell of wheat flower	00- 15- 00
Ite. for one bushell of oatmeale	00- 10- 00
Ite. for one holland & 2 ordenary Cheess	00- 10- 00
Ite. for xx li. of powder sugar att	01- 03- 09
Ite. for one Loafe Cont 7li. att 1s. 6d.	00- 10- 06

Ite. for one sugar Loafe Cont 5li. att 1s. 7d. p. li.	00-07-11
Ite. 6li. of pepper	00-12-00
Ite. Nutmeggs 4 oz.	00-01-08
Ite. one oz. of Clovs, & one oz. of mace	00-02-00
Ite. iij li. of starch	00-01-03
Ite. xij li. of Rice	00-06-00
Ite. vj li. of Vntryed suett	00-03-00
Ite. one gall. of aquavite	00-03-08

Ite. for one flitch of Bacon		00-14-00
Ite. Castle soape ix li. att 8d. p. li.		00-06-00
Ite. frute viz Rasons Corrants & pruens		00-14-00
Ite. Safron ij oz.		00-05-00
[240]	Ite. five qu. of stronge water	00-08-00
Ite. Almonds ij li. at 1s. 2d.		00-02-04
Ite. xv li. of tryed suett at 8d. p. li.		00-10-00
Ite. one gall. of Sallert oyle		00-06-00

	Ite. vj li. of Candles	00-03-00
	Ite. v geese & ix ducks	00-08-00
Ano. 1630	Ite. xij li. of Butter att	00-08-00
	Ite. vj potts of Butter Cont. vij li. p. pott	01-08-00
	Ite. ij Cheeses about x li. a pc.	00-11-08
	Ite. half a firkin of butter of Mr. Gibbs	00-17-06
	Ite. one Third prt. of a barrell of wt. biskett	00-10-00

Ite. one pott of honey vij li. wat. att	00-07-10
Ite. one pott of butter att	00-03-00
Ite. x li. of Corrants att	00-05-00
Ite. [ ] Bacon	00-10-00
Ite. one doz. of Candles	00-08-00
Ite. ij Cheeses att vj d. p. li.	00-11-03
Ite. iij Cheeses att vij p. li.	00-17-09
Ite. one porkett	01-05-00

Ite. xij li. of tryed suett	00-08-00
Ite. vj. gees & xij ducks	00-14-00
Ite. vj. po: of powder suger about 20d.	00-10-00
Ite. v po: of powder suger 18d.	00-07-06
Ite. x li. of Loaf suger	01-00-00
Ite. Cloves & mace	00-01-00
Ite. ij oz. of Nutmeggs j s. & Sinamo. 16d.	00-02-04
Ite. workmens wadges for	03-00-00

Cutting &
bringing
home wood
against
winter
about

— —
— —

Suma to lis.   105-
18-
11

Mr.   Skeltons   account   wth.   the   Companie
Mr. Skelton is D. pr. viz.

li. s.
d.

[Per] 14
yards of
Dutch   02-
serge   05-09
Reed. att

It. 17 yards
of ffustian   01-
att   07-00

It. 11 yards
of wt.   00-
English   13-09
ieans

It. 12 yards
of Red p.
petuana

01-
16-00

It. 12 yards
of Greene
say

01-
13-00

It. 12 yards
of yellow
say

01-
13-00

It. 12 elns
of lin
[torn] men

00-
14-00

It. 14 elns
Nouess
[torn] llain

01-
17-04

It. 20 elns
o[floc]
krum

01-
05-10

It. 20 elns
stript
[linsey]
woolsye

01-
09-04

It. [ ] yards
[torn]
buckrum

00-
05-03

[241
]

It. one peece of Noridg serg		00-15-00
It. 20 elns of Lockerum		01-05-10
It. 15 yards of wt. fflannell		00-15-00
It. 20 elns of Course Canvas		01-04 [torn]
It. one pound of whalbone		0[torn]
		——
		——
		20-11-00

Item [per] so much pd. [per] Mr. Renell prt. of Mr.		08-00-00

Pearce his
bill, the
some of

Item [per] 9 li. of Iron att 3d. is	00-02-03
It. [per] one syth	00-03-00
It. [per] one fishing line	00-03-00
It. [per] 30 pound ocum	00-07-06
It. [per] 2000 Nails 6d. p. C.	00-10-00
It. [per] 600 Nails 10d. p. C.	00-05-05
It. [per] 1 Reame of paper	00-10-00
Item. borrowed of Cp.	00-17-06

Endicot of
ye Comp.
7 yrds. of
bays att
2s. 6d.
[per] yd. is

halfe a elne of ffustian att	00-00-10
It. 2 yards & half of yellow Carsey 3s. 4d.	00-08-04
	—— ——
Suma Totalis St.	031-19-05
Ite. 2 gall. of Metheglen	00-08-00
It. one Lether Jack	00-01-06
It. two Tubbs}	

It. one
wooden   00-
hand   03-06
boule}

Ite.
vinegar}

It. 3 peuter
botles
quarts}

It. one
pinte   00-
peuter   00-10
botle

Ite. one   00-
hatt   10-00

                          ——
                          ——

                          33-
                          03-03

rec. of Mr.
Winthrop
Governr.

Ite.   3 yrds. of
            Cambrick

6 yrds. & a
h: of
Loomewor
ke

2 Drinking
hornes

8 pr. of
shoes for
men

6 pr. of
gray
stockings
for men

6 pr. of
stockings
for women

6 pr. of
stockings
for
children

10 yrds. of
Carsey

Thred

2000 of
pinnes

6 Alls

one webb
of blew
gartering

2 knots of
Tape

---

[242]

APPENDIX C

AN ABSTRACT OF THE INVENTORY OF CONTENTS OF THE SHOP OF CAPT. JOSEPH WELD OF ROXBURY, MADE FEBRUARY 4, 1646-7

48	yds.	greene	cotton	at	22d.
85	yds.	red	cotton	at	2/1.
1¾	yds.		kersey	at	5s.
11	yds.		do	at	3/2.
52	yds.	yellow	cotton	at	22d.
8	yds.	white	cotton	at	20d.
21	yds.	red	cloth	at	7/9.
39	yds.	broad	cloth	at	8/8.
21	yds.	broad	cloth	at	9/7.
8	yds.	do	do	at	15/4.
42	yds.	greene	tamie	at	2/1.
5	yds.	red	do	at	2/1.
3	yds.		flannel	at	2/2.
12	yds.	scarlet	broad	cloth at	16/6.
41	yds.		course	at	3/2½.
24	yds.		frize	at	4/7.
31	yds.		penniston	at	2/7.
38	yds.		do	at	2/11.
44	yds.	grey	Kersey	at	5/6.
66	yds.		fustian	at	1s.
15	yds.		Holland	at	5/9.
7	yds.		do	at	4/1½.
7	yds.	Slezie	lawne	at	4/.
8	yds.	blue	linen	at	1/4.
29	yds.		lane	at	6/9.
3	pr.		bodies	at	3/2.
11		belts		@	3/2.
15		do		@	3/.
23		bandeliers		at	2/.
14	pr.		Stockings	at	1/6.
41	pr.		do	at	1/3.
15	pr.		Jecs	at	2/9.

10	doz.	points	at	2/.
61	combs		at	3½d.
14	doz.	thimbles	at	1/9.
18	pr.	pads	at	6d.
1	spectacle	case		1/.
26	gro.	thread buttons	at	9d.
29	primers		at	2d.
8	lb.	thread	at	12/3.
10	pces.	tape	at	1/1.
5	gro.	buttons	at	2/.
5	gro.	do	at	1/.
6	doz.	great buttons	at	1/2.
17	silk	buttons	at	2/.
14	yds.	lace	at	2d.
64	yds.	lace	at	3½d.
3	pces.	binding	at	1/2.
80	yds.	ribboning	at	2½d.
21	doz.	tape	at	1/.
43	lb.	ginger	at	1/.
6	pr.	slippers	at	2/.
20	1b.	whalebone	at	10¾d.
17	1b.	pepper	at	2/1.
2	1b.	worm seed	at	8/.
5	1b.	cinnamon	at	8/4.
7	hat	bands	at	4d.
2	1b.	nutmegs	at	1/9.
½	lb.	blue starch	at	1/8.
Cloves,				10d.
3	yds.	buckram	at	1/2.
Pack	needles	and tainter	hooks,	15/.
40	lb.	sugar	at	10d.
3	lb.	powder	at	2/2.
26	lb.	raisins	at	4d.
A	barrell	of	fruit,	£5.11.3.
4	lb.	starch	at	4d.
1	counter,			£1.

4		pr.		scales,		8s.
48		lb.		Lead	weights,	9s.
1	file	of		brass	weights,	5s.
[243]12		lb.		yarn,		£1.13.0.
A	net	24		yards	[no	value].

2 sconces, a melting ladle, a hitchell, 8/.

—*Suffolk County Probate Records*, Vol. II, p. 52

Robert Turner of Boston, shoemaker, died in 1651. In his shop were children's shoes at 9d. per pair, No. 7 shoes were valued at 3s., No. 10 at 4s., No. 11 at 4/4, No. 12 at 4/8, No. 13 at 4/10. Boots were 14s. per pair, and wooden heels were 8d. per doz. He also sold hats. Black hats were valued from 5 to 14 shillings, each; colored hats from 5 to 10 shillings; black castors were 14s. each, black coarse felts, 3s. each, children's colored, 3/6, and children's black castor with band, 4s.—*Suffolk County Probate Records*, Vol. II.

[244]

APPENDIX D

ABSTRACT OF AN INVENTORY OF THE GOODS OF CAPT. BOZONE ALLEN, SHOPKEEPER, OF BOSTON, DECEASED, MADE SEPT. 22, 1652, BY EDWARD HUTCHINSON AND JOSEPH ROCK

Broadcloth	at	18s.		per	yard.
Red	broadcloth		at		15s.
Red	ditto		at		15s.
Tammy		at			20d.
Grogram		at			3s.
Silk	mohair		at		3/6.
Blue	grogram	or	cheney	at	3s.
Blue	paragon		at		3s.
Black	satinisco	(½		ell)	2s.
Calico		at			15d.
Buckram		at			14d.
Bengal	tafety		at		3s.
Silk	grogram		at		7/6.
Satinisco		at			3/4.
Noridge	stuff		at		2/10.
Hair	color	satinisco		at	3/3.
Colchester	serge		at		2/8.
Cotton	cloth		at		2/10.
3	Couerlids		at		15s.
Packitt	Lawn		at		6/6.
4	papers	Manchester		at	5s.
1	pr.	stockings		at	4s.
10	pr.	cotton	gloves	at	22d.
5	pr.	ditto		at	14d.
Tapes	white	&	colored,		11s.
5	gr.	briches	clasps	at	2/2.
2	packetts	pins		at	2s.
Small		clasps,			3/8.

Dutch thread (per lb.) at 6s.
Feathers (per doz.) at 3s.
2 doz. Collars & belly pieces at 2/3
Stomachers at 12d.
7 gr. thread buttons at 7s.
8 masks at 8d.
7 gr. Chaine & other silk buttons at 34s.
7½ gr. flatt cassacke at 6s.
4 gr. small coat at 6/6.
4 gr. large cloak at 14s.
3 gr. silver buttons at 9s.
2 doz. gold cloake buttons at 3s.
7 doz. Jacks at 2s.
25 oz. Silver & silver & gold lace at 5/10.
34 yds. silver lace at 16d.
37 yds. silk & silver lace at 5d.
9 doz. silk lace at 20d.
Green ribbon (per doz.) at 9s.
22 yds. ditto at 3/4.
Silk & gold fringe (per yd.) at 15s.
344 yds. looped lace at 18d.
Colored silk (per oz.) at 2s.
30 yds. loom lace at 14d.
12 yds. ditto at 2/4.
10 yds. ditto at 22d.
17 yds. black galloon at 2½d.
Band strings (per lot) £2.0.0.
2 pr. eastailes (*sic*) at 5d.
1 doz. side hinges (per doz.) at 7s.
1 doz. lamb heads (per doz.) at 7s.
23 sm. Key rings & 10 large 4/10.
Latches (per doz.) at 8s.
1 smoothing iron, 2/8.
1 doz. steeles, 2/3.
8 padlocks at 5d.
Cupboard locks (per doz.) at 12s.

4		gimletts	at	2d.
[245]2		handsaws	at	18d.
4		files	at	6d.
22	hour	glasses (per doz.)	at	7/6.
4		bells	at	13½d.
57		scales (per doz.)	at	16d.
1	doz. wire	candlesticks and 5 bigger,		6/4.
6	doz.	taylor's thimbles	at	8d.
5½	doz.	waistband clasps	at	20d.
14	pr.	snuffers	at	11d.
12	doz.	neck buttons	at	6/8.
Little	glasses &	twists & small ribbon,		1.02.06.
8	doz.	sissers	at	3/4.
13	pr.	tobacco tongs (per doz.)	at	3s.
4	doz.	combs	at	2/6.
A		parcell paper,		11.0.0.
10	bush.	pease	at	4s.

Weights, scales & Counters & the graite, 3.5.0.

—Suffolk (Co.) Judicial Court Files, No. 1389.

---

[246]

APPENDIX E

MANUFACTURES AND OTHER PRODUCTS LISTED IN THE RATES ON IMPORTS AND EXPORTS ESTABLISHED BY THE HOUSE OF PARLIAMENT, JUNE 24, 1660[96]

IMPORTS OF MERCHANDISE

Andirons   or   Creepers   of   Lattin,   of   Iron
Anvills
Apples,   the   barrell   conteyning   3   bushell
Aquavitæ
Argall,   white   &   red,   or   powder
Arrows   for   trunkes
Aule   blades
Auglers   for   carpenters
Axes   or   hatchets
Babies   or   Puppets   for   children
Babyes   heads   of   earth
Toys   for   children
Baggs, with locks, and with steel rings without locks
Ballances,   gold   Ballances,   ounce   Ballances
Balls.   Tennis   balls,   Washing   balls
Bands.   Flanders   bands   of   bone   lace
Cut   worke   of   Flaunders
Barbers aprons of checkes, the piece not above tenn yards
Barlings,   the   hundred
Baskets,   hand   baskets   or   sports
Basons   of   Lattin
Bast,   or   straw   hats   knotted   and   plain
Bast   ropes
Battry   Bashrones   or   Kettles
Bayes   of   Florence
Beades, of Amber, Bone, Box, Corrall, Christal, Glass & Wood,
Jasper   square

Beaupers, the peece conteyning xxv yards
Bells. Hawkes bells French making, Norembrough making, Horse bells, Doggs bells, Morrice bells, Clapper bells
Bellows
Bitts   for   Bridles
Blacking   or   Lamp   black
Blankets. Paris mantles coloured, and un-coloured
Boards. Barrell bords, Clapbords, Past boords for books, Pipe bords or pipe holt, White boords for shoemakers
Bodkins
Boratoes or Bumbazines, narrow, broad, or of Silke
Bookes, unbound, the basket or maund
Bosses   for   Bridles
Botanoes,   per   piece
Bottles, of Earth or Stone, of Glass covered with Wicker, of Glass with vices covered with leather, of Glass uncovered, of Wood, sucking   bottles
[247]Boultell, Raines, and the baile
Bowe   staves
Boxes.   Fire   or   Tinder   Boxes
Nest   Boxes
Pepper   Boxes
Spice   Boxes
Round Boxes or French Boxes for Marmalade or Jelly
Sand   Boxes
Sope   Boxes
Touch   Boxes   covered   with   leather
do   covered   with   velvet
do of Iron or other Metall guilt
Tobacco   Boxes
Braceletts or Necklaces, Red or of Glass
Brass, Laver Cockes, Pile weights, Trumpets, Lamps
Bridles
Brouches, of Lattin or Copper
Brushes.   Bearde   brushes
of   Heath   course

of   Heath   fine   or   head   brushes
of   Hair,   called   head   brushes
of   Heath,   called   rubbing   brushes
of   Hair,   called   comb   brushes
of   hayre,   called   weavers'   brushes
of   hair,   called   rubbing   brushes
Brimstone
Buckrams, of Germany, fine, of the East countrey, of French making,   Carricke   buckrams
Buckles,   for   Girdles,   for   Girths
Buffins, Mocadoes & Lille Grograms, narrow and broad
Bugasines   or   Callico   Buckrams
Bugle.   Great,   small   or   seed   Bugle,   Lace
Bullions   for   purses
Bulrushes
Burr   for   Milstones
Buskins   of   Leather
Bustians
Buttons,   of   Brasse,   Steel,   Copper,   or Lattin, of Crystall, of Glass, of Thred, of silke, of fine damaske, of
Bugle,   for   Handkirchers,   of   Hair
Cabinets   or   Countores,   large   and   small
Caddus   or   Cruel   Ribbon
Camaletto,   half   silk,   half   haire
Candles   of   Tallow
Candle   plates   or   Wallers   of   Brasse   or   Lattin
Candlesticks,   of   Brasse   or   Lattin   or   of   wyre
Candleweeke
Callicoes,   fine   or   course
Canes   of   wood
Capers
Capravens
Capp   hookes   or   hooke   ends
Capps,   double   turfed   or   Cockered   Capps
for   Children
Night   Caps   of   Sattin,   Velvet

Night   Caps   of   Silke   Knitt
Night   Caps   of   Woollen
Night   Caps   of   Linnen
Cards.   Playing   Cards,   Wool   cards
Carpetts, of Tonny, of Scotland, of Cornix, Brunswicke Carpets,
China of Cotten, course, Gentish, Turkey or Ventice, of Persia
Carrells
Cases   for   looking   glasses   guilt
for   spectacles   guilt
do   unguilt
for   Needles   or   Pin   cases
for   Needles   French   guilt
Casketts,   of   Iron,   of   Steele
Caveare
Cawles   of   Linnen   for   women,   of   Silke
Cesternes   of   Lattin
Chafing   dishes   of   Brasse,   Lattin,   or   Iron
[248]Chaines   for   Keys   or   Purses,   for   Doggs
Chairs   of   Walnutt   tree
Chamblett, unwatered or Mohaire, watered, half silke halfe haire
Cheese
Cherries
Chesse   boards
Chess-men
Chests,   of   Iron,   large   &   small
of   Cipresse   wood,   the   nest   of   3
of   Spruce   or   Danske,   the   nest   of   3
painted
Chimney   backs,   small   and   large
China   Pease
Chizells   for   Joyners
Citternes
Clapboord,   the   small,   the   great   &   the   Ring
Claricords,   the   payre
Clokes   of   Felt
Cochaneile,   Silvester   or   Campeache

Coles of Scotland
Coffers, covered with gilt Leather
covered with Velvett
with Iron barrs, the nest of 3
plaine, the nest
painted, the nest
Comashes out of Turkey
Combes, for wool, of bone, of box, lightwood combes, of horne for
Barbers, of Ivory, Horse Combes
Comfetts
Compasses, of Iron for Carpenters, of brasse for Ships
Copper, unwrought brickes or plates, round or square, chaines,
purles or plate
Copras, green
Cordage, tard or untard
Corke tackles, of Iron and Steele
Cork for Shoemakers
Corne, wheat, rye, beanes, barly, mault
Coverlets of Scotland
Counters of Lattin
Crosbows, of Lathes, Thred and Rackes
Cruses of Stone, without covers, & with
Cushons of Scotland
Cushon cloths, course, and of Tapestry
Cuttle bones
Daggs with fire lockes or Snap-lances
Daggers. Blades, for children, of bone for children, blacke with
velvet sheathes, gilt, with velvett sheathes
Deales, Meabro, Norway, Burgendorp, Spruce
Desks or stayes for bookes
for women to worke upon covered with wollen
Dialls of wood and bone
Dimitty
Doggs of earth
Dornix, with caddas, silke, woll, thred, and French making
Dudgeon

Durance or Duretty, with thred or silk

Druggs—a great variety listed including Bezor Stone of the East India, Holliworsles, white and red Corall, Fox lungs, Guiny pepper, Hornes of Harts or Staggs, Lapis Lazuli, mummia, Musk Codds, Nutmegs, oyle of Scorpions, oyle Petrolium, Red Lead, Sanguis draconis, Scorpions

Earthen Ware, Brickstones, Flaunders Tile to scower with, Gally Tiles, Paving Tiles, Pann Tiles etc.

[249]Elephants teeth

Emery stones

Fanns, for Corne, of Paper, for Women and Children, French making

Feathers for bedds, also Ostridge Feathers

Felt for Cloakes, French making

Fiddles for Children

Fire shovells

Figuretto, the yard

Files

Fish, Codd, Cole, Eeles, Haddockes, Herrings, Lamprells, Linge, Newland, Salmon, Scale fish, Stock fish, cropling, lubfish and titling, Whiting

Flannele

Flaskes, of horne, covered with leather, with velvett

Flax, Spruce Moscovy, undrest and wrought

Fleams to let blood

Flockes

Flutes, course

Freeze of Ireland

Frizado, the yard

Furrs, Armins the Timber, Badger, Bare skins, Beaver, Budge, Calaber, Catts, Dokerers the Timber, Fitches the Timber, Foxes, Foynes, Grays, Jennets, Letwis, Leopard, Lewzernes, Martrones, Miniver, Minkes, Mole skins, Otter, Ounce, Sables, Weazell, Wolfe, Wolverings

Fustians, Amsterdam Holland or Dutch Barmillions

Cullen   fustians
Holmes   and   Bevernex
Jeane
Millian
Naples,   tript   or   velure   plain
Wrought   or   Sparta   velvett
Osbro   or   Augusta   fustians
with   silk
of   Weazell
Gadza, without gold or silver, the yard stript with gold or silver
Gally   dishes
Gantletts,   the   pair
Garters   of   silk,   French
Gaules
Gimlets   for   vinters
Girdles, of cruell, or leather, of silk, of velvett, of woollen, of
counterfeite   gold   &   silver
Glasse   for   Windows,   Burgundy   white   and   coloured
Normandy   white   and   coloured
Renish,   the   weigh   or   webb
Muscovy   glasse   or   slude
Drinking Glasses, of Venice, Flanders, Scotch and French, course
drinking glasses, Burning glasses, Balme glasses, Vialls, Water
glasses
Looking Glasses, Halfe penny ware, Penny ware, of Steele, small
and   large,   of   Christall,   small   and   Middle
Hower Glasses, of Flaunders making, course, of Venice making
Glass   stone   plates   for   spectacles,   rough
Glass   plates   or   sights   for   looking   glasses   unfiled
Glass   pipes
Glew
Globes,   small   and   large
Gloves, of Bridges or French making, of Canary, Millane or Venice
unwrought,   of   Vaudon,   of   silke   knit,   of   Spanish   plaine
Gold   and   Silver   thred   counterfeite
Bridges,   gold   &   silver

[250]Cap, gold & silver
Copper gold & silver upon quills & rolls or in skaine
Cullen gold & silver
French copper gold & silver
Lyons copper gold & silver double gilt
Gold & Silver thred right
Venice, Florence or Millane gold & silver
French and Paris gold & silver
Gold foile
Gold paper
Granies, French or Guiny
Graines or scarlet powder of Sevill in berries & granies of Portugall
or Rotta
Grindle stones
Grocery wares: Almonds, Anniseeds, Cloves, Currans, Dates, Ginger, Licoras, Maces, Nutmegs, Pepper, Cinomom, Raisins (great, and of the Sun), Raisins of Smirna, Figgs, Prunes, Sugar (candy brown, candy white, Muscovadoes refined double & single in loves, St. Thome & Panneils, white)
Grogrames, Turkey
Guns. Calervers, Muskets
Gunpowder. Serpentine, Corne powder
Halberds, guilt & unguilt
Hammers, with and without wooden handles, Horsemens hamers
Hankirchirs
Harness Roses
Harness, Corslets complete, Curatts, Morians or headpeeces graven, ditto plaine
Harp strings or Catlings
Hatbands
Hatts, of beaver, wool or hair, of Bridges, Dutch felts or hatts made of wool, Spanish or Portugall felts, of silke French making, of straw, see Bast, of Venice, of wool or worsted trimd
Hawkes, Falcons, Goshawkes, Jerfalcons, Jerkins, Lanners, Lannarets, Tassels of all Sorts
Hawkes hoods

Hair   bottomes   for   sives
Haire,   Camells,   Elkes   haire   for   saddles,   Goates
Heath   for   brushes
Hemp, short drest, cullen & steel hemp, Spruce, Muscovia & all
rough   hemp
Hides. Buffe hides, Cow hides of Barbary & Muscovia, Cow or
horse hides, India hides, Losh hides, Red or Muscovia tanned,
coloured   &   uncoloured
Hilts   for   swords   or   daggers
Honey
Hoopes   of   Iron   for   pipes   or   hogsheads,   for   Coopers
Hops
Horses   or   mares
Hose   of   Cruel   made   in   Mantua
Jett
Jews   Trumps
Inke   for   Printers
Imperlings   blew   or   red
Ink   horns
Incle,   unwrought   and   wrought   Rowles   (36   yards)
Indico,   of   Turkey,   of   the   West   Indyes   or   rich   Indico
[251]Instruments for Barbers & chirurgeons, Bullet scrues, Incision
sheeres, Setts (the bundle), Paices or Tooth drawers, Plulicanes,
Trepans
Iron,   Amis   Spanish   Spruce   and   Swedish
Backes   for   chimneys,   small   and   large,
Bands   for   Kettles
Fire   irons
Hoopes
Stones
Juice   of   Lemons   (the   pipe)
Ivory
Key   knops
Knives, Almanie, Bohemia & other course knives, Butchers,
Carving, Collen knives, French knives, Glover's knives, Penknives,
Sker   knives,   Stock   knives   (gilt   and   ungilt)

Lace, bone lace of thred, Brittaine lace, Cruell lace, Gold & Silver,
Pomet,   Purle   or   antlet,   Silke   bone
Ladles,   Melting
Lapis   magnata
Lattin,   black   &   shaven
Leade   oare
Leomons,   Pickled
Lemon   water
Leather, Bazill, Spanish or Cordivant, Hangings, Spruce or Dansk
leather, Leather for Maskes, Turkey & East India Cordivant
Leaves   of   Gold
Lewers   for   Hawkes
Lime   for   Dyers
Lines   of   Hambrough   for   ships
Lin-seed
Linnes   blew   or   red
Linnen   Cloth
Callicoes,   fine   or   course
Cambricks,   fine   or   course
Canvas, Dutch Barras & Hessens, French or Normandy & lyne
narrow   browne   or   white,
French & line broad for tabling, Packing canvas guttings & spruce
canvas, poledavies, Spruce Elbing or Quinsbrow, Stript or tufted
canvas with thred, stript tufted or quilted canvas with silke, stript
canvas with copper, Vaudolose or Vittry canvas, working canvas for
cushions   (narrow   and   broad)
Damask, Tabling of Holland, Towelling & napkening of Holland,
Tabling   or   Silesia
Diaper,   Tabling   of   Holland   and   Silesia
Lawnes,   Callico   lawnes,   French   &   Silesia   lawnes
Flaunders, Holland cloth:—Flemish, Gentish, Islingham, Overisils,
Rowse, Brabrant, Embden, Freeze, Bag Holland, Browne Holland
Cowsseild   cloth   or   platts
Drilling   &   pack   duck
Elbing   or   Danske   cloth   double   ploy
Hambrough   &   Silesia   cloth   broade   &   narrow

Hinderlands, Headlake & Muscovia linnen narrow
Irish cloth
Lockrums, Treager (great & narrow) or common dowlace, Broad
dowlace
Ministers, the roll
Ozenbrigs, the roll
Soulthwitch
Polonia Ulsters, Hanovers, Lubecke, narrow Silesia, narrow
Westphalia, narrow Harford, plain napkening & narrow cloth from
high Dutchland & the East Countrey (brown and white)
Strawsbrough or Hambrough
[252]Twill & Ticking of Scotland
Lockers or Chapes for Daggers
Lockes, Budgets or hanging lockes, small & large
Lutes, Cullen & Venice making
Lute strings, Catlings & Minikins
Litmus
Madder, Crop and all bale Madder, Fatt & Mull madder
Magnus
Maskes, of velvett & sattin
Match for Gunns
Matts of Russia
Medlers (the baskett)
Mallasses of Rameales
Messelanes (30 yds. to piece)
Metheglin
Methredate
Mocado ends
Morters & Pestells, brass
Muster seed
Mittens of Wadmul
Nailes. Chaire nailes, copper nailes, rose nailes, Sadlers nailes, Head
nailes, Harness nailes, spring nailes, Tenter hookes
Napkins of French making
Neats tongues, of Russia
Neckerchirs of Flanders making

Needles,	Pack	&	sale	needles
Nutmegs,				pickled
Nutts,	small	&		walnutts
Okeham				
Oaker				
Oares				
Oyle,	Rape	&		Linseed
Sivile, Marjorca,	Minorca,	Apuglia	Province, and	Portugall
Sallat				oyle
Traine	oyle	of		Greenland
Traine	oyle	of		Newfoundland
Fish				oyle
Ollives				
Onions				
Orchall				
Oranges	&	Lemons	(the	hogshead)
Orsdew				
Packthred				
Panns,	Dripping &	frying	pans, warming	pans
Paper.	Blew,	Browne,	Cap,	Demy
Ordinary	printing	&	copy	paper
Painted	paper		(the	ream)
Pressing	paper, Rochell	paper,	Royall	paper
Parchment				
Past		of		Jeane
Peares	or	apples,		dryed
Pease				
Petticoates		of		silke
Penners				
Percer				bitts
Pike				heads
Pikes,	with	and	without	heads
Pinns		(the		thousand)
Pincers		&		plyers
Pintadoes	or	Callecoe	cubbard	clothes
Pipe				staves

Pipes, for Tabors, and for children
Pitch Pipes, small band, great band
Plaister of Paris
Plaine irons
Plankes of Ireland
Plate, silver white or ungilt, of silver parcell gilt, of silver gilt
Plates, single & double white or blacke, Harnesse plates or iron doubles
Playing Tables of walnut tree (the paire)
Pointe, of thread, of Capiton and of fine silke
Pomistones
Pomegarnets
Potatoes (the hundred weight)
Potts, of Earth or Stone, covered and uncovered
[253]Gally pots
Melting potts for Goldsmiths
Of Iron, French, or Flemish making
Pullies, of Iron, of Brasse, of Wood
Punsons & Gravers for Goldsmiths
Quills, Goose
Quilts, of French making, of Callico, of Sattin or other Silke
Rackets
Rape of Grapes
Rape seed
Rashes, Bridges or Leyden Rashes, single & double, Cloth Rashes
Rattles for Children, and with Bells
Razers
Recorders (the set)
Ribbon, of Silke
Rice
Rosen
Rugs, Irish and Polish
Rims for Sives
Rings, for Keyes, for Curtaines, of Wyre, of Brass, Copper or St.
Martins gilt, of Haire
Sackcloth

Saddles   of   Steele

Safflora

Saffron

Salt, white or Spanish Salt, Bay or French Salt, Salt peter

Saws. Hand sawes, Tenant sawes, Whip sawes, Legg sawes

Says.   Double   Sayes   or   Flaunders   Serges

Double   Say   or   Serge

Mild   sayes

Honnscot   say

Scamoty   (the   yard)

Scissers

Sea   holly   rootes

Sea   morse   [horse]   teeth

Serge,   of   Athens,   of   Florence

Sheares, for Shearmen, for glovers, for Seamesters, for Taylers, Forceps,

Sheets   of   Callaber

Shumacke

Shruff   or   old   Brass

Syder

Silke. Bridges silke, Ferret or Floret silke, Fillozell or Paris silke

Granado.   Silke   black   &   colours

Naples.   Silke,   black   &   colours

Orgazine, Pole & Spanish, Raw China, Raw Silke, short and long, Raw Morea, Satin Silke, Sleave Silke, Silke Nubbs or Husks, Throwne   silke

Skins. Buckskins (in the Haire & drest), Calves (of Ireland), Cordivant (of Turkey, East Indies, or Scotland), Dog fish skins for Fletchers, Fox skins, Gold skins, Goate skins, of Barbary or the East Country,   of   Scotland   or   Ireland

Husse   skins   for   Fletchers

Kidd skins, Portugall skins, Seale skins, Shamway skins, Sheep skins, Spanish Civill or Cordivant skins, Spruce skins

Skeets   for   Whitsters

Slip   (the   Barrell)

Smalts

Snuffers

Soape, Castle or Venice, also Flemish

Spangles of Copper

Spectacles without cases

Spoones of Horne

Standishes, of wood, Brasse & covered with Leather, also Pocket Standishes

Steele. Long steel, Wisp steel & gad steele

Stockings of Wadmol

Stone birds or Whistles

[254]Stones. Blood stones, Cane stones, Dogg stones, Mill stones, Querne stones (small and large), Slick stones

Sturgeon

Stuff of all sorts made or mixed with Wool

Succade wet or dry

Sword blades, of Venice, Turkey or other fine blades, Course blades of Flaunders

Table bookes, course and fine

Tables, playing Tables of Wainscott

Tackes of Iron

Tallow

Tannets of Cruell

Tapistry, with Haire, Caddas, Silke, Gold or Silver & Wool

Tarras (the Barrell)

Tarr (small & great Band)

Tazells

Thimbles

Thred, Bridges, Crosbow, Lyons or Paris, Outnall, Peecing, Sisters, whited browne

Thrums, of linnen or Fustian, also of Woolen

Tikes. Brizel Tikes & Turnall Tikes, also of Stoade

Tiking of the East countrey

Tincall

Tinfoyle

Tinglasse

Tinsell, copper, right Gold & silver

Tinshore
Tobacco, Spanish & Brazill in pudding or role
St. Christophers, Barbadoes, Virginia & Somer Islands
Tooles. Carving Tooles
Tow
Trayes of wood (the shocke)
Triacle, of Flaunders, of Jeane
Trenchers, white (commen sort)
and red or painted
Treene nailes
Trunnells
Tweezes of France
Twine of Hambrough
Twist for bandstrings
Vallances of Scotland
Verditer
Verders of Tapistry
Vellum for Table bookes
Violls
Vice harps
Vice tongues or hand vices
Viniger
Vizards
Wadmoll
Wainscott
Wax
Whale fins
Whetstones
Whipcorde
Whistles Cockes or Bellows
Whistles, Cockes or Birds of Stone
Woad, Islands or green woad, also Tholose
Worme seeds
Worsted, St. Omers narrow ½ worsted
Russells worsted or broad worsted
Wood. Boxwood for Combs, also Brazill or Farnumbuck wood

Braziletto	or	Gemeaco	wood
Ebony			
Fusticke			
Lignum			vitae
Plankes		of	Ireland
Red	or	Guiny	wood
Speckled			wood
Sweet	wood	of	West	India

Wool. Beaver wool, Cotton wool, Estridge wool, Irish wool, Lambs wool, Polonia wool, Spanish wool, Spanish felt wool, Red wool
[255]Wrests for Virginalls
Wyer. Dagger and quarter wyer, Iron wyer, Lattin wire, Steel wyre, Strawsbrough wyre, Virginall wyre
Yarne, Cable, Camell or Mohaire, Cotton, Grograine, Irish, Raw Linnen, Saile, Spruce or Muscovia, Scotch wollen or bay yarne

EXPORTS OF MERCHANDISE

Allabaster			
Allom,			English
Apothecary	and	Confectionary	wares
Anvills			
Apples			
Apples		called	Pippins
Aquavitae			
Ashes	of	English	wood
Bacon			
Baggs			
Bandaleirs			
Beefe			
Beere			
Beere			Egar
Bell			metall
Bellowes			
Billetts			
Birding			pieces

Bird   lime
Bodyes,   stitched   with   Silke,   also   with   Whalebone
Bridles
Brushes,   English,   of   Heath
Buckweed
Buttons   of   Haire
Bays. Barnstaple course, Manchester or Barnstaple fine and other
single   bayes,   Double   bayes,   Minikin   bayes
Cambodium
Candles
Canvas,   English   tufted,   also   Shropshire
Capps, Monmouth plain and trimmed, buttoned English, of wool
blacke
Cards,   Stocke,   Tow,   Woll
Playinge   Cards
Cardboard
Carpets,   Northern
Catlings   or   English   Hatt   makers   strings
Cloke   baggs
Coaches   and   Chariots
Coals. Sea Coles, the Chalder, New Castle measure, Sea Coles of
Wales   or   the   West   Country
Combes   of   wood,   bone,   or   horn
Cobwebb   Lawnes
Comfets
Cony   haire   or   wool,   blacke   or   white
Cordage,   tard   or   untard
Coverletts,   of   wool   &   haire,   of   Caddice
Curricombes
Cushons   of   Yorkshire
Cottons, Northerne, Manchester, Tanton and Welch, also Welsh
plaines
Corne, Barley, Mault, Beanes, Oates, Pease, Wheate, Rye, Buck
wheate
Darnix,   of   English   making,   also   Coverlets
Dice

Dimitty
Doublets   of   Leather
Dust   of   Cloves   and   other   Spices
Emery   stones
Earthen Ware, Brickes & Tiles and also sorts of Earthen & Stone
ware   made   in   England
[256]Fennell   seed
Figuretto,   with   silke   or   copper,   narrow   and   broade
Filozelles,   broad   of   silke
Fire   lockes
Flannell
Flasks   of   Horne
Flax
Freezes
Fustians
Gartering   of   cruell
Garters   of   worsted
Girdles   of   Leather   for   men,   &   for   children,   of   Norwich
Glasse   for   windowes,   and   bottles   &   other   sorts
Glew
Gloves,   plaine   of   Sheepe   Kidd   or   Lambes   leather
fringed   &   stitched   with   silke
furd   with   Cony   wool
of   Buckes   leather
Goose   quills
Grindlestones
Gunpowder
Haberdashers ware—Packthred, Inkle, Tape, Filleting, Buttons,
Hookes   &   Eyes,   etc.
Haire,   Harts   haire,   Horse   haire,   Oxe   or   Cowe   haire
Hairecloth
Harts   horne
Hatbands   of   Cruel
Hatchets
Hatts,   Beavers   &   Demicasters,   Felts,   etc.
Hawkes   hoods

Hempseed

Herrings

Holsters

Hops

Hornes, Blowing hornes (small), of Buckes, Inkhornes, Hornes with Lanthornes, Oxe hornes, Powder hornes, of Rames, of Sheepe, Shooing hornes, Stags hornes, Tips of hornes

Horselitters & Sedans

Horse tailes with haire

Horse collers

Hoopes for barrells

Iron wrought, viz., Axes, Adzes, Hoes, Armour, Bitts, Knives, Lockes, fowling peeces, Muskets, Pistolls, Cissors, Stirrops, Carpenters & Gravers tooles, Jack work, clock work, & Ironmongers wares

Old Iron

Iron Ordnance

Irish Mantles

Knives, Shoemakers, paring knives, Sheffield knives, Cutting knives, London knives

Lace of gold & silver, of velvet, Statute lace

Letherage or Lead

Lamprills

Loome work

Lime

Linnen, made of Hemp or Flax

Linseed

Linsey woolsey

Lists of cloth

Lead, cast and uncast

Musterd seed

Malasses or Rameales

Nailes

Nutts

Oatmeale

Oyle, Traine oyle

Oysters
Oker,   yellow   and   red
Parchment
Paste   board
Pilchers
Points   of   Leather
Purles   of   Broadcloth
[257]Rape   cakes
Rape   seed
Rugs,   Irish   Ruggs   for   beds,   and   by   the   yard
Russetting   for   painters
Rashes,   silk   Rashes,   broad   and   narrow
Ribbon
Saddles,   and   saddle   trees
Sack   cloth
Saffron
Salt   peter
Sea   morse   [horse]   teeth
Scabbords   for   swords
Shag,   with   thred
Shovells,   shod   and   unshod
Shoes,   Bootes   and   Slippers
Skins, Cony, Kid, Lambe, Otter, Sheepe & Lamb, Rabbit, Hare,
Cats, Fox, Swans, Dogs, Elke, Wolfe, Badgers, Squirrell
Soape
Spanish   sattins,   English   making
Starch
Steel,   Gad   steele
Stockings, Irish, Kersey long & short, Leather, Silk, Wollen men &
children
Stones,   Hilling   stone,   Slate
Stuffs,   Perpetuanoes   &   Serges
Sugars,   refined   &   made   into   loaves   in   this   kingdom
Tapistry   or   Dornix   Hangings   made   in   England
Thred,   Black,   Brown,   Blew
Thrums

Tiking
Tiffany,   made   of   thred
Tobacco   pipes
Tuff   Taffates,   broad   and   narrow,   with   thred
Tynn,   unwrought   and   wrought,   i.e.   Pewter
Velure,   single   and   double
Vingiger   of   wine
Virginalls,   the   payre
Watches
Wadmoll
Wast Coates, of Wadmoll, Cotton, Kerseys of Flannell, Worsted
knit   and   Wollen   knit
Wax
Weld
Whalebone   cut   or   wrought
Whale   finns
Woad
Woad   nets
Wood,   Redwood,   Gambray,   Boxwood
Worsted,   narrow   and   broade
Yarne,   Grograine   yarne
Wollen   Cloths
Dorset   &   Somerset   dozens   rudge   washed
Cardinalls, Pinwhites, Strayts, Statutes, Stockbridges, Tavestocks
Tauntons,   Bridgewaters   &   Dunsters,   Deven   dozens
Ordinary Pennistons or Forrest Whites, Sorting Pennistones
Narrow Yorkshire Kerseys whites & reds, Hampshire ordinary
Kersies, Newbery whites and other Kersies, sorting Hampshire
Kersies
Northern   Dozens   single   sorting   Pennistons
The   new   sort   of   Cloth   called   Spanish   Cloth
Cloth Rashes, alias Cloth Serges

[258]

APPENDIX F

COPY OF THE INVENTORY OF THE ESTATE OF WM.
PAINE OF
BOSTON, MERCHANT, APPRAISED BY HEN. SHRIMPTON,
JOSHUA SCOTTOW AND JOHN RICHARDS, AND ALLOWED
IN COURT AT BOSTON, NOV. 14, 1660, UPON
OATH OF MR. JOHN PAINE, HIS SON

IN THE WAREHOUSE CHAMBER:

4 peeces white Trading cloath, 42li.;

39 yrds. blew trading cloath, 9li. 15s.;

5¼ ⅛ yrds. white trading cloath, 1li. 4s. 2d.;

4 Bales nowells, 2 Bales pantozells, 1 Bale fine sheeting, 2½ Bales of broad, 4 peeces Kentings, half Bale napkening, 232li. 16s. 2d.;

2 Bales nowells Cont. 6 poanles, 43li. 6s. 8d.;

5 ps. villaranes cont., 70½, 35¼, 23, 11½ and 21¾ yrds. in all 162 yrds. at 21d. p., 14li. 3s. 6d.;

5 peeces Kenting, 44¼ yrds. at 2s. 3d. p., 4li. 19s. 6d.;

120 yrds. Humains, 123 yrds. Humanes, 123 yrds. Humanes, 99¼ Humanes, 342½ yrds. at 18d., 25li. 13s. 4½d.;

3 Ruggs, 6li. 15s.;

2 Barrells bate, 12li. powder, 9li.;

4 peeces searge, 16li.;

1 ps. carsey, 2O½ yrds., 4li. 2s.;

1 ps. more, No. 2, 5li.;

11 yrds. ⅝ of carsy at 5s. 6d. 3li. 4s.;

6¾ of carsey at 7s., 2li. 7s. 3d.;

6¾ of carsey at 4s., 15s.;

8 peeces wt. calleco at 14s., 5li. 12s.;

50½ yrds. broad dowlas at 2s., 5li. 1s.;

23½ dowlas at 21d. 2li. 1s.;

3⅛ of locrum at 16d., 4s. 2d.;

12 of blew calleco at 18d., 18s.;

1 ps. blew calleco at 20s., 1li.;

4½ yrds. searge at 4s., 18s.;

4½ yrds. red broad cloth at 8s., 1li. 16s.;

3 yrds., 3 nailes broad cloath at 16s., 2li. 11s.;

8 yrds. ¾ red carsey at 6s., 2li. 10s. 3d.;

2¼ red at 3s. 6d., 7s. 10d.;

9¾ ⅛ peneston at 2s. 10d., 1li. 8s.;

12⅜ Role cotton at 2s. 3d., 1li. 19s.;

8 pr. Irish stockens at 18d., 12s.;

8½ narrow blew linen at 13d. 9s. 2d.;

3¼ broade blew linen at 20d., 5s. 5d.;

23½ broad blew linen at 2s., 2li., 7s.;

2 pr. Stockens, 5s. 6d.;

5 pr. bodeys at 4s. 1li.;

1 groace of silver coat & other buttens with Riboning & lace, 30li. 16s. 11d.;

2 yrds. holland at 6s., 12s.;

17½ of east cloath, 8s.;

31 halfe linds at 14d., 1li. 16s. 2d.;

5 ham bourough linds at 2s., 10s.;

5 knottes of housing at 4d., 1s.;

[259]

5¼ vittery at 14d., 6s. 1d.;

10 parchmen skins, 1 trunk, 2O bookes,—of wax candle, 1li. 10s.;

58 reame of paper at 7s., 20li. 6s.;

4 baggs cotten wooll, 550li. at 5d., 11li. 9s. 2d.;

71li. hopps at 4d., 1li. 3s. 8d.;

200 hhs. salt at 11s., 110li.;

Remant Ratling, 2s.;

pcell bookes, 2li.

IN THE LOWER ROOME:

2 Bailes nowells, 43li. 6s. 8d.;

1 bagg hopps, 1li. 13s. 4d.;

6li. rod Iron at 2s., 8li. 8s.;

2 Bushells wheat, 19s. 6d.;

silkware in 2 boxes, 31li. 14s.;

3 bate naile of Turky Gregrum, 10s.;

2 yrds. broad cheny & remnant of Satten, 7s.;

2li. 11 silk, 3li.;

1li. ½ fringe & muccado ends, 7s.;

2¾ soft wax, 2s.;

5½ Butts thread, 14s.;

13 yrds. old fashion lace, 2s.;

20 yrds. wt. callico, 22 laces, 2½ doz. poynts, 1li. 1s.;

8 doz. short laces, 2 doz. ¾ long, 18s.;

13 oz. coventry thred, 4s.;

1li. cource wt. thred, 6s.;

½li. whited Browne, 2s.;

3li. colloured thred, 9s.;

4li. black & browne, 2li. 2s.;

12 Hatts, 10 bands, 3li.;

20 browne holland, 2li. 10s.;

18½ yrds. Humanes, 18d., 1li. 7s. 9d.;

83¾ pantolanes, 4li. 3s. 9d.;

41¼ yrds. vittery at 14d., 2li. 10s. 6d.;

26½ poledavy at 18d., 1li. 19s. 9d.;

30¾ nowells at 16d., 2li. 1s.;

5¾ locrum at 18d., 8s. 7d.

36 locrum at 18d., 1li. 19s.;

8¾ ⅛ blew linen at 14d., 10s. 1d.;

30 yrds. sacking at 9d., 1li. 2s.;

221¼ yrds. Cotten cloath at 2s., 4d., 25li. 16s. 3d.;

8 yrds. greene Cotten at 14d., 9s. 4d.;

18 of wt. cotten at 1s., 18s.;

24 Irish, 12s.;

3 Remnants boulting, 2s.;

3li. suger, 3li. 15s.;

1 Tire for wheeles & old Iron, 3li.;

13 cart boxes & 3li. in Iron waite, 2li, 10s.;

Basketts, Rubstones, 15s.;

pcell of wt. salt, 12s. 6d.;

pcell of cards & old hops, 15s.;

a screw & 9 mose skins, 2li. 10s.;

pll. of old rope & line, 10s.;

pcell of Cotten wooll, 5s.;

Barrell of Oatmeale, 1li. 5s.;

2 Kettles, 3 spades, 1 pan & nailes, 2li. 5s.;

1 cutting saw, 6s.

IN THE CELLAR:

30 hhds. mallasses at 3li., 90li.;

5 barrells macrell, 1 halfe barrell, 7li. 5s.;

2 Iron bound hhds., 10s.

IN THE OTHER CELLAR:

3 hhds. Rum, 30li.;

pcells of sower wine, 3li.;

old cask, 10s.;

beaver, 49li., 22li. 1s.;

beaver, 160li. at 18d., 12li.

IN THE LENTOO HOUSE END:

30 tunn salt at 40s., 60li.;

4 sawes, 2li.;

boulting mill, beam board, 2li.

IN THE IRON HOUSE:

77½li. barr Iron at 20s., 47li. 10s.;

[260]

5¾li. cast backs at 15s., 4li. 6s. 3d.;

11½li. Andirons at 15s., 8li. 12s. 6d.;

9¾li. potts & Kettles, 12li. 3s. 9d.;

5 Iron skilletts, 13s. 6d.;

beames & scales, 1li. 10s.;

39½li. cast waites, 29li. 12s. 6d.;

857li. cotten wooll at 5d., 17li. 7s. 1d.;

377 of hopps at 4d., 6li. 5s. 3d.;

7 hhd. 3 butts suger, 65li.;

2 qt. fish, 1li. 4s.;

1 firkin butter, 1 soape, 2li.;

5 li. bate, 8li. barr Iron, 4li. 18s.

IN THE YARD:

28 tun. pact casks, 9li. 16s.;

7½ hhds. lime, 1li. 13s. 9d.;

6000 pipestaves at 4li., 24li.;

1400 boards, 5s. 6d., 3li. 17s.;

12000 Rotlin, 4li.

IN THE DWELLING HOUSE:

10½ yrds. sacking & canvas, 7s. 10d.;

2¼ cloth rash at 6, 13s. 6d.;

9 bate naile of dowlas at 2s., 17s. 10d.;

yrd. narrow taffety, 6s.;

4½ liver colloured searge, 18s.;

1 groace 4½ doz. hookes & eyes, 2s. 6d.;

2 yrds. blew Trads cloath, 10s.

AT MR. SCOTTOWES:

2 Bales nowalls, 43li. 6s. 8d.;

1 ps. pantossam, 5li.;

1 ps. sheeting, 6li. 2s. 6d.

AT MR. BROUGHTON'S:

3 butts 1 hhd. suger at 25s., 35li.;

140¼ hhd. salt at Ils Shoales, 70li. 2s. 6d.;

20 hhds. at Mr. Parker's, at 10s., 10li.;

1 hhd. Rum at Mr. Handsons, 10li.;

at Linn workes, 1 horse, 10li.;

at Capt. Johnsons, leather, 00;

at Mr. Buttolls, leather, 00;

at Capt. Clearkes, an Anchor, 1li. 10s.;

ADVENTURE in Thrumboll to England, 49 hhds. oyle, 5 M. 8 C. 81li.

Cotten neate, 12 qt. fish, 289li. 7s. 5d.;

TO JAMACO & p left in Jamaco before p Adam Westgage, 52li. 12s.

THE HOUSE MORE:

3 Satten dobletts, 1 taffety cloak, 4li.;

money, 5li. 11s. 9d.;

2 gold rings, 2li.;

1½ C. wt. suger at 4, 6li.;

¾ of cast ware at workes, 100li.;

¾ stock of sow Iron & coals, 450li.;

¾ of ye workes at hamersmith & Brantree, 800li.;

DWELLING HOUSE, warehouses & appurtenances at Bostone, 400li.;

watertowne mill house, land & apprtenances, 150li.;

½ mill at exeter & halfe of the prvilidge of mill & land, 40li.

HOUSEHOLD STUFF & IS IN THE CELLAR UNDER YE HALL:

1 Iron Trivett & Tramell, 1 barr & 2 Cobbe Irons, 1 fire shovell, 1 Ketle, 2 brass pans, 1 Copper Kettle, 1 brass skillett, 1 flagon, 20 old dishes, 1 Iron pott, 1 spitt, 1 pr. bellowes, skimer, 3li. 19s. 6d.

IN THE HALL:

1 pr. Iron Andirons, 1 pr. tonges, 11s. 6d. more;

[261]

one Cubord, 15s.;

1 Tabell & carpett, 2s., 4 leather, 2 other chairs, 1li. 5s., 1 setle, 4 stooles, a cushion, 14s., 1 clock, 2li., 7li. 5s. 6d.

IN THE LITTLE ROOM:

1 Bedsteed & curtaine, one bed, one boulster, 1 rugg, 3 blanketts, 1 pr. sheets, 4 table cloath, 8 naptkins, 1 pewter dish & one bason, one salt, 2 brass candlestickes, 1 ladle, 1 warming pan, fire pan, 20s., 1 basket, 1 chaire, 1 cushion, 7li. 4s.

IN THE OTHER LITTLE ROOME:

One bedsteed, curtaines, fether bed, 3 blanketts, 1 coverled, 2 bolsters, 3 pillowes, a trundle bedsteed, a fether bed, pr. of sheets, coverled, bolster, Tables & chaires, 8 Cushions, 1 Joint stoole, 3 pewter dishes, 1 salt, 1 Brass skillett, 1 skimmer, 1 pan, 1 seive, 1 Bible, 11li. 7s. 6d.

One silver Candlestick, 1 Tankard, one beere boale, 2 wine cupps, one dram cupp, 6 spoones, 17li.;

1 brass scillett, 1 pewter dish & bason, 2 brass Candlesticks, Joynt stooles, one Tramell, 1 Ketle, 1 sive, shovell, 1 back, 2 Cob Irons & dripping pan, 1li. 15s.

IN THE CLOSETT:

13 pewter platters, 2 py plates, 6 smale plates, 5 saucers, 1 pewter & 2 brass candlesticks, 1 urin botle & 1 bed pan, 12 earthern dishes, 2 pudden pans, 5li. 10s. 6d.

IN THE HALL CHAMBER:

One bedsteed, Curtaines & vallens of red searge, 1 fether bed, 2 bolsters, 2 pillowes, 3 blanketts, 1 tapestry Cuverled, 10li.;

2 Cubberts, 2 Cubbert cloathes, 1 table, 4 red stooles, 2 red cloath chaires with fringe, 3 leather chaires, 2li. 15s.;

1 great chaire, 7 pichers, 10s., one pr. brass Andirons, one back, 3s., 8li. 5s.;

6 cushions & 1 pc. of carpeting & old vallens at 1li. 4s.;

one Trunk, 8s.;

one chest, 8s., 2li.

WITHIN THE TRUNK & CHEST & IN THE HALL CHAMBER:

7 pr. sheetes, 4 diapr. table cloathes, 2 plaine, 9 pillow beers, 4 Cubbert cloathes, 2 napkins, 1 tapestry coverled, 2 darnick carpetts, 2 pr. sheets, 7 damask naptkins, 2 short diaper table cloathes, 3 pillow beers, 26 diaper naptkins, 14 plaine naptkins, one red rugg, 21li. 18s.

IN THE GARRETT:

One Rugg, three blanketts, one flock bed, 1 Coverlett, one bolster, one blankett, 3li. 7s.;

money, 123li. 14s.;

IN VESSELLS, 200li.;

total, 4,239li. 11s. 5d.

DUE TO THE ESTATE:

In debts accotd. as certaine, 1,500li.;

as doubtfull, 700li.;

stand in the book yett acttd. of as utterly lost & desperatt, 836li. 6s. 2d.

DEBTS due from the estate, 1500li.

—*Essex County Quarterly Court Records*, Vol. II, pp. 271-274.

———————————

[262]

APPENDIX G

INVENTORY OF THE ESTATE OF EDWARD WHARTON OF SALEM, DECEASED, AND WHAT GOODS WERE IN HIS POSSESSION, CONSIGNED TO HIM BY SEVERAL, TAKEN 12:1:1677-8, BY HILLIARD VEREN, SR., JOHN HATHORNE AND JOHN HIGGINSON, JR.

VALUED IN ENGLAND AS BY INVOYCE,—

1 plaine cloath cloake, 1li. 8s.;

1 boyes worsted cloake, 1li. 5s.;

1 heare camlett cloake, 2li. 18s.;

5 cloath cloakes, 28s. p., 7li.;

1 cloath cloake, 1li. 8s.;

1 fine cloath cloake, 1li. 15s.;

1 cloath cloake, 1li. 12s.;

6 cloath cloake, 28s. p., 8li. 8s.;

3 childs stuff coates at 9s., 1li. 7s.;

1 yeolow Tamy, 10s.;

1 ditto, 13s.;

1 boyes coate, 13s.;

1 doz. home made wooll hose, 1li. 14s.;

1 doz. ditto, 1li. 10s.;

8 pr. of youths ditto, 14s.;

10 pr. of woemens home made wooll stockens, 1li. 2s.;

7 pr. of sale wooll hoase, 10s. 6d.;

17 pr. of woemens & youths stockens, 14s. 10d.;

7 pr. of home made woemens 4 thrid, 3s. 2d. p., 4 pr. ditto sale 4 thrid, 3s. 4d. p., 1li. 10s. 10d.;

4 pr. youthes 4 thrid ditto, 3s. 4d. p., 3 pr. youthes ditto, 3s., 1li. 2s. 4d.;

4 pr. of wooll home made hose, 14s.;

1 pr. mens worsted home made stockens 5s.;

8 pr. of home made worsted; 4 thrid, 1li. 14s.;

6 pr. sale ditto, 18s.;

2 pr. of fine home made, 10s.;

1 childs coate, 7s.;

1 greene say frock, 5s.;

9 childs wascoates, 5d. p., 3s. 9d.;

6 Ditto, 7d. p., 3s. 6d.;

5 Ditto, 9d. p., 3s. 9d.;

4 Ditto, 10d. p., 3s. 4d.;

2 Keasy ditto, 2s. 6d., 5s.;

1 ditto, 2s. 8d.;

2 ditto, 3s. p., 6s.;

6 childrens, 12d. p., 6s.;

4 woemens yeolow wascoate, 22d. p., 7s. 4d.;

1 Cloake of lite collrd. haire camlett, 3li. 7s.;

4 coates of the same camlett, 36s., p., 7li. 4s.;

1 cloath collrd. haire camlett cloake, 35s.;

2 worsted camlett cloakes, 34s., 3li., 8s.;

1 fine haire camlet cloake, 5li.;

2 trunks, 16s.;

3 ditto, 1li. 1s.;

1 ditto, 6s.;

2 dittoes, 5s. p., 10s.;

2 boxes or little red trunks, s. 2d. p., 6s. 4d.;

1 ditto, 2s. 8d.;

[263]

3 silk say under pettecoates lite collrd, at 12s. 6d. p., 1li. 17s. 6d.;

2 Ditto, 1li. 8s.;

cloath woemans wascoats, 8s.;

7 ditto, worth each 8s., 10s., 8s., 10s., 6s., 13s., 15s.;

1 cheny sad. Collrd. uper woemans coate, 7s.;

1 sad collrd. woemans searge coate, 17s., 6d.;

1 black fine searge upper pettecoate, 19s.;

1 stuff cloake for woeman, 10s.;

1 ditto for a girle, 7s.;

1 large worsted Rugg lite collrd, 1li. 14s.;

1 large sad collrd. ditto, worsted, 18s.;

1 ditto worsted sad colld, 1li.;

6 greene & blew plaine Rugge, 8s. p., 2li. 8s.;

1 sad callrd thrum Rugg, 11s. 6d.;

1 cabbin Rugg, 4s. 8d.;

1 Cource 8-4 Rugg, 10s.;

3 coverleds, ordinary, 6s., p., 18s.;

2 ditto at 5s., 10s.;

2 coverleds, large at 7s. 6d., p., 15s.;

1 smale one, 6s. 6d.;

1 red plaine rugg, 8s.;

1 peece wt. cotton, 19s.;

1 darnex carpett, 5s. 6d.;

1 ditto greene, 6s. 6d.;

4 pr. wt. drawers, 10s.;

6 peeces of searge at 40s., 12li.;

7 peeces narrow searge at 25s., 8li. 15s.;

1 peece padaway searge, 2li. 15s.;

13 yds. clarett collrd. Tamy at 19d. p., 1li. 1s. 1d.;

1 large draft lite collrd, 14s.;

1 2d sort, 12s.;

1 small ditto, 10s.;

1 doble 10 qtr. coverled, 1li. 4s.;

1 ditto, 9 qrts. 1li.;

2 dittos, 8 qrts., 15s. 6d., p. 1li. 11s.;

8 yrds. ¾ striped Tamarene at 18d. p, 13s. 1½d.;

12 yrds. ¾ Turky mohaire, 2s. 10d. p., 1li. 16s. 1½d.;

6 yrds. ¼ of striped stuffe at 22d. p, 11s. 5½d.;

9 yrds. striped camlett, 2s. 4d. p, 1li. 1s.;

1 peece oringe collrd worsted draft, 2li. 5s.;

4 yrds. Haire camlett, 3s. p, 2li. 2s.;

10 yrds. of ash collrd, silk moheare, 4s. p, 2li.;

6 yrds. ½ of ash collrd silk farrendine, 4s. 6d. p, 1li. 9s. 3d.;

12 yrds. ash collrd. haire camlett at 3s. p, 1li, 16s.;

1 peece sad collrd. stuff, mixt with Gold collrd, 2li. 10s.;

24 yrds. flowered silk draft, 2s. 2li. 8s.;

13 yrds. striped vest at 22d. p, 1li. 3s., 10d.;

18 yrds. Scotch Tabby at 16d. p, 1li. 4s.;

16 yrds., Scotch Tabby at 16s. p, 1li. 1s. 4d.;

10 yrds. Tiking at 15d. p, 12s., 6d.;

8 yrds. padaway at 2s. 6d. p, 1li.;

7 yrds. of Linsy at 12d. ½p, 7s. 6d.;

2 pr. boyes cotten drawers, at 2s. p, 4s.;

3 cotten wascoate at 2s. 10d. p, 8s. 6d.;

2 pr. blew drawers, 2s. 5d. p., 4s. 10d.;

1 boyes haire sad coll. camlett cloake, 2li. 15s.;

1 large flanders tike & bolster, 1li. 9s. 6d.;

[264]

30 yrds. of upper Tiking, at 18d. p, 2li. 5s.;

42 yrds. diaper at 15d. p, 2li. 12s. 6d.;

12 yrds. of Tabling, 2s. 6d. p, 1li. 10s.;

21 yrds. of diaper for napkins, 18d., p, 1li. 11s. 6d.;

2 pillow Tikins, at 2s. 2d., 4s. 4d.;

1 light coll. boyes cloake, 1li. 12s.;

2 yrds. ¼ of plush at 8s. p., 6s. 9d.;

20 tobaco boxes at 1d. ½ p, 2s. 6d.;

3 ditto at 20d. p. doz., 3¾d.;

4 brass roles for chalk lines, 5s. 6d. p. doz., 1s. 10d.;

8 ditto large at 6s. 6d., p. doz. 4s. 4d.;

8 chalk lines at 18d. p. doz., 1s.;

tinware, 4 Cullenders, 5s. 4d.;

6 ditto, 5s. 6d.;

2 doz. wood savealls, 3d. ½p, 7d.;

1 large kettle, 2s. 3d.;

1 next size, 2s.;

8 6 qrt. Ketles, 14d. p., 9s. 4d.;

3 gallon Kettles, 12d. p, 3s.;

5 3 qrt. Kettles, 9d. p., 3s. 9d.;

2 3 pt. Kittles, 7d. p. 1s. 9d.;

5 best savealls, 2s. 4d. p. doz., 11½d.;

11 second sort at 8d. p. doz., 7¼d.;

3 extinguishers, 8d. per doz., 2¾d.;

3 doble plate pans, 18d., p., 4s. 6d.;

a doble puden pan, 9d.;

2 midle sised lanthornes, 18d. p., 3s.;

4 band candlesticks, 5d. ½ p, 1s. 10d.;

5 tinder boxes & steele, 7d. p., 2s. 11d.;

4 writing candlesticks, 2d ½ p, 10d.;

2 pt. sace pans, 3s. 8d. p doz., 7d.;

3 bread or flower boxes, 3d. ½dp., 10½d.;

4 Casters, 2d p., 8d.;

1 peper box, 2d., 1 fish plate, 8d., 10d.;

6 smale bread graters, 8d. p doz., 4d.;

2 pts. at 3d. ¾ p., 1 funell, 4d., 2 covers, 8d. p., 2s. 3½d.;

3 brass savealls, 7d. p., 3 larger graters, 3d. ½ p., 2s. 7d.;

2 egg slices, 2d. ½ p., 5d.;

3 whip sawes & tillers, 5s. 6d. p., 16s. 6d.;

2 marking irons, 2s., 1 cloase stoole & pan, 8s. 9d., 10s. 9d.;

2 steele handsawes with screws, 3s. p., 6s.;

1 large steele hand saw, 2s. 2d.;

8 hand sawes at 14d. p., 9s. 4d.;

1 handsaw, 10d.;

2 faling Axes, 1s. 5d., 2s. 10d.;

8 bright smale Hamers, 6d. p. 4s.;

9 Rivited hamars at 10d. p., 7s. 6d.;

2 hamers, 4d. p, 8d.;

5 hamers, steele heads, 10s. p. doz., 4s. 2d.;

4 choppers at 15s. p. doz., 3s. 8d.;

2 mincing knives, 12d. p., 2s.;

7 small ditto, 13s. p doz., 7s. 7d.;

9 hatchetts, 12d. p., 9s.;

7 smale mincing knives, 9s. p doz., 5s. 9d.;

3 steele sawes & screwes, 3s. p., 9s.;

5 doz. 8 gimletts at 12d. p doz., 5s. 8d.;

27 pensills at 8d. p doz., 1s. 6d.;

10 percer bitts at 2d. p. 1s. 8d.;

1 large pincers to shooe horses, 1s.;

3 curry combs, 10d.;

2 large ditto, 6d. p, 1s.;

1 pr. spincers for shoomakers, 1s.;

5 pr. nippers, 4d. p, 1s. 8d.;

2 bundles of files, 20d. p. bundles, 3s. 4d.;

12 doz. of straite all blades, 5d. p. doz., 5s.;

7 doz. crooked blades at 5d. p doz., 2s. 11d.;

[265]

14 doz. of fire steeles at 6s. p grosse, 7s.;

21 pr. of spurrs at 7s. p doz., 12s. 3d.;

8 pr. dove tails at 2½d. p, 1s. 8d.;

22 pr. sid hinges, 3d. p., 5s. 6d.;

6 pr. Esses at 8d. p, 4s.;

1 smooth Iron, 1s. 4d.;

3 doble spring lockes at 20d. p, 5s.;

1 single ditto, 9d.;

2 doz. trunk lockes at 6s. p doz., 12s.;

1 doz. of single ditto, 3s. p, 3s.;

½ doz. large ditto, 4s.;

2 ship scrapers, 2s.;

6 pr. Coll. yarne mens hose, 12s.;

6 pr. worsted ditto at 3s. 4d., 1li.;

12 pr. stockens, 7d. p. 7s.;

7 pr. ditto, 9d. p, 5s. 3d.;

6 pr. ditto 8d. p., 4s.;

6 pr. ditto at 5d. p., 2s., 6d.;

10 pr. ditto at 6d. p, 5s.;

6 pr. ditto at 13d. p., 6s. 6d., 5 pr. ditto at 18d. p, 7s. 6d.;

1 pr. fine woemens red worsted, 3s.;

2 pr. mens worsted, 3s.;

2 pr. mens worsted black & colld, & 1 pr. white, 7s. 6d.

VALUED HEARE AS MONEY IN N. ENGLAND:

2 linsy woolsey pettecoates, 6s. p., 12s.;

1 little boyes coate of camlett worsted, 6s.;

2 linsey woolsey & 1 pr. of fustian draws, 9s.;

1 pr. linen drawers, more, 3s.;

1 boyes coat, 4s.;

2 red childs blanketts bound wth. feret, 4s. p, 8s.;

1 smale childs camlet pettecoat, 3s.;

9 sashes at 12d., 9s.;

50 yrds. of Irish searge at 2s. 2d. p, 5li. 8s. 4d.;

10 yrds. ½ broad worsted camlett duble, 2s. 6d. p, 1li. 6s. 3d.;

16¼ yrds. narrow camlett, 1li. 12s. 6d.;

20¼ yrds. mixt stuff, very bad, 12d. p, 1li. 3d.;

14 yrds. new Coll. Stuff at 2s. p, 1li. 8s.;

1 ell of farrindine, 2s. 4d. p yd., 2s. 11d.;

6 yrds. coll. fustian, 14d. p. 7s.;

3 yrds. red perpetuana at 2s. 6d. p, 7s. 6d.;

6 yrds. ¼ greene say at 5s. p, 1li. 11s. 3d.;

42 mens & woemens shifts, 4s. 9d. p, 9li. 19s. 6d.;

12 youth & girls ditto, 3s. 6d. p. 2li. 2s.;

8 finer mens, woemens ditto, 6s. 6d. p, 2li. 12s.;

5 white dimity wascoates, 3s. 6d. p, 17s. 6d.;

1 yrd. ½ cambrick, 4s. 6d. p, 6s. 9d.;

2 ends of fine wt. callico, 20s. p, 2li.;

2 peeces broade white calico, 40s. p. 4li.;

2 peeces cource holland, cont. 69 yrds. 30d. p, 8li. 12s. 6d.;

5¼ yrds. fine dowlas at 2s. 6d. p, 13s. 1½d.;

7 yrds. cource dowlas at 20d. p, 12s. 6d.;

1 ell cource holland at 2s. 6d. p, 3s. 1½d.;

9 yrds. scimity, 6s., 2 peeces of dimity, 6s. p, 18s.;

1 callico table cloath, 7s. 6d.;

2 callico shirts, 6s. p, 12s.;

2 calico painted table cloathes, 8s. p, 16s.;

1 large ditto, 14s.;

in English money, 2li. 7s.;

[266]

New England money, 99li. 4s;

Spanish money, 1li. 16s,;

1 peece of gold, 20s., 3 rings, about 25s., 2li. 5s.;

a dram cupp, 6s.;

3 yds. fine greene say at 6s. p., 18s.;

3 cloath coates at 20s. p, 3li.;

1 cource gray youth coats, 10s.;

7 yrds. ½ of striped linen 16d. p, yrd., 10s.;

1 silk thrum Rugg, 2li.;

28 pr. plaine shooes, 4li. 4s.;

15 pr. fale shoes & 2 pr. woemens, 3s. 6d. p. 2li. 19s. 6d.;

9 straw hats, 2s. p, 18s.;

2 pr. fishing bootes at 14s. p., 1li. 8s.;

6li. of combed worsted at 2s. 6d. p, 15s.;

knives, 5s., 2 spoones, 6d.;

6¼li wt. suger at 8d. p, 4s. 4d.;

6 brushes, 18d., 1 pr. smale stilliards, 4s., 5s. 6d.;

8½ oz. pins, 10d., p. 7s. 1d.;

2 peeces ½ ferret, black Ribbond, 12d., p. 1li. 10s.;

5 gross & ½ thrid, buttens, 15d. p, 6s. 10½d.;

about 2 gross thrid laces at 9s. p, 18s.;

1 gross great buttens upon cards, 3s.;

2 doz. ½ tweezers, 3s. 6d. p doz. 8s. 9d.;

3 childs swathes, 8d. p., 2s.;

tape & filliting, 2s.;

10 oz. fine thred, 12d p., 10s.;

a little pcell of thrid of severall coll., 1s. 6d.;

13 pr. scissers, 4s., 1 gross thrid, wt. buttens, 18d., 5s 6d.;

19 yds. red Ferrett, 4d. p. yrd., 6s. 4d.;

blew tape, 4d., green cotten ribbon, 4d., silk, 18d., 1s. 8d.;

1 pr. bodies, 3s. 6d., 1 woemens worsted cap, 12d.;

6 pr. childs yarne gloves, 3s.;

11 yrds. green ferrett, 4d. p., 3s. 8d.;

6 doz. pack needles, 5s.;

soweing needles, 6d.;

4 oz. peper, 6d., 3 pr. spectacles, & 5 cases, 22d.;

16 yrds. yellow taffaty Ribbond, 3d. p. 4s.;

6 boxes of Lockeers pills & papers, 24 yrds. ½ silk galoone, 2s. p. doz. 4s.;

16 country Ruggs & 2 cradle ditto waying 223li, at 14s. p. li, 13li.;

8 Bushells of pease at 3s. p, 1li. 4s.;

1 old sheete of cource canvas, 2s.;

1 old table, 6s., 1 brasse yoare, 20s.;

1 perpetuance under pettecoate, 9s.;

1 woemans Shamare lined, 16s.;

a womans Jerkin, 6s.;

1 pr. wooll cards, 1s.;

8 hand basketts, 12d. p. 8s.;

60 li. of sheeps woll., 6d. p bagg, 2s., 1li. 12s.;

2 sadles & stirrops, 1li. 4s.;

4 Iron plates or fenders, 3s. p., 12s.;

125li. of sheeps wooll at 6d. p, 3li. 2s. 6d.;

4 baggs, 2s. p, 8s.;

hops & bagg, 2s.;

3 smale skins, 8d. p. 2s.;

79 narrow brimd. hats, 2s. p., 7li, 18s.;

1 new, 10s.;

4 bands, 4s.;

1 boyes wt. caster, 3s.;

a large chest, 7s.;

2 tray makers adses, 3s.;

1 square & a broaken one, 1s. 6d.;

2 coop. axes, 30d. p, 5s.;

1 bill, 12d., 3 hollow shaves, 12d., p, 4s.;

2 cooper adzes, 2s. p, 1 pr. sheers, 12d.;

3 doz. 9 curtaine rings, 1s.;

[267]

4 large, 6 smale shaves, 6s.;

7 shooe punches, 6d. p., 3s. 6d.;

9 pr. Hinges, 5d. p, 3s. 9d.;

2 gouges, 2 chessell, 4d. p, 1s. 4d.;

1 tinder box & pump nailes, 1s. 6d.;

1 coopers knife, 10d.;

5 staples, 12d.;

4 bolts, 2s.;

1 auger, 12d.;

a rasp & smale auger, 1s.;

5 pr. sissers, 12d.;

a pewter salt, 12d.;

3 pr. snuffers, 18d.;

a standish, 2s. 6d.;

6 cod hoockes, 12d.;

1 bed quilt, 10s.;

1 thousand & ½ of pins, 1s. 1½d.;

21 doz. of wt. thrid buttens, 18d. p. grosse, 2s. 7d.;

pewter Bottle, 9d.;

pcell of beaver stones, 2li. 10s.;

2 pr. small scalls & some waites, 6s.;

a glasiers vice & moulds, 4li.;

a pcell of glass, drawne lead, sodering to mak up about 200 or 300 foot of glass, 4li.;

29 li. cheese at 3½d. p li., 8s. 5d.;

1 B. ½ wheat, 3s. 6d., p. 3 bagges, 3s., 8s. 3d.;

6 old shirts, 7s., 5 very old sheets, 15s., 1li. 2s.;

2 old drawers, 2s.;

3 wascoates, 8s.;

4 pillow beeres, 6s.;

1 table cloath & 4 napkins, 6s.;

1 chest, 5s.;

1 sash, 12d.;

1 carpett, 18d.;

1 bed pan, 5s.;

1 brass chafindish, 3s.;

a fether bed & bolster, 2 blanketts, 7 pillowes, a rugg & bedsteed, 7li.;

a pcell of pack cloath, 7s., a hamer, 18d., 8s. 6d.;

his woolen wearing apparell, 5li.;

1 chest, a smale table & 2 old cushions, 12s.;

2 old seives, 10d.;

1 bed, bolster, 1 pillow, 2 Ruggs, bedsteed & blankett, 4li. 10s.;

1 old trunk marked E. W., 3s.;

some odd trifling lumber, 2s.;

2 tables, 4 Joyn stools, 18s., tinn ware, 14s., 1li. 12s.;

brasse ware, 1li.;

pewter, 35s., 2 spitts, 2 fire pans, 8s., 2li. 3s.;

2 Iron potts & skillett, 12s.;

4 rasors, 1 pr. sissers & a hoand, 9s.;

some Indian dishes & other lumber, 8s.

FURRS:

49 Racoone skins, 12d. p, 2li. 9s.;

38 fox skins, 2s. 6d. p. 4li. 15s.;

2 woolves skins, 12d. p. 2s.;

a cub beare skin, 1s.;

31 Otter skins, 6s. p., 9li. 6s.;

4 wood chuck skins, 21d. p, 7s.;

21 martins & sables at 15d., 1li. 8s. 3d.;

7 muskquash, 6d. p, 3s. 6d.;

about 50li. beaver, 6s. p., 15li. 13 B. mault, 3s. p, 1li. 19s.;

150li. oacum, 25s., 3 pecks wt. salt, 1li. 6s. 9d.;

36 gall. Rume, 2s. p. 3li. 12s.;

2 new chests with ticks, 6s. p, 12s.;

4 new barrells, 8s.;

2 shovells, 18d., 301li. sheeps woole, 15s., 16s., 6d.;

1 bagg, 18d., 200 foot of board, 8s. 9s. 6d.;

2 B. wheate, 3s. 6d. p. 3 b. Ry. 3s. p. B., 9s. 3d.;

6 B. pease, 3s. p., ½ B. Beanes, 19s. 6d.;

11 hides, 5s. p., about 600 foot bord, 3li. 19s.;

[268]

16 B. Indian corne, 2s. p, 1 barrell, 2s., 1li. 14s.;

6 chests, 6s. p, about 13 C. spanish Iron, 2s. p., C, 14li. 16s.;

2 barrells of porke, 50s., 5li.;

almost 2 barrells of tarr, 7s. 6d. p, 15s.;

100li. tobbacco at 3d p, 1li. 5s.;

11 moose skins, 5li. 8d.;

2 Racoones, 12d. p, 2 sealls at 12d. p, 4s.;

1 hhd. ½ passader wine much decaid, 4li.;

pt. of 5 barrell very much decaid & pricked madera, ——;

2 hhd. mallasses nott full, 5li. 10s.;

an old small catch exceeding out of repaire almost worne out, both Hull & all appurtenances, valued by Mr. Bar. Gedney & John Norman, ship carpenters, 15li.;

a dwelling house & land neere the meeting house & apprtenances, 80li.;

a smale peece of land part of a frame for a warehouse & wharf, not finished & stones upon the ground, 14li. 10s.;

a small pcell of timber & old board, 10s.;

an old smale cannoe, 10s.;

a horse runing in the woods if alive ——;

a remant of stuff, 2s.;

a pcell of land at New Jerzey but doe not know the quantity yett & some goods at som other places not yett knowne what they are ——— ; total, 630li. 6s. 5¾d.

Samll. Shattock's account of the debts: To several in England above, 300li.;

to several in New England which cannot yet be known how much, nor Justly what yt is in England, but as himselfe said when he was sick & I ptly finde it by Invoys of Goods.

APPRAISED SINCE THE FOREGOING, GOODS BROUGHT FROM THE EASTWARD AS COST PER INVOICE:

2 coates, 19s. p. coate, 1li. 18s.;

2 coats, 16s., p, 1li. 12s.;

3 white childs coates, 1 at 11s. & 2 at 14s., 1li. 19s.;

2 coates, 19s. p, 6 or 7 yeare old, 1li. 18s.;

1 Coat tamet, 16s.;

1 boyes coate, 13s.;

a flanders Tick & bolster, 1li. 9s. 6d.;

a draft, 8 qrts., 14s.

VALUED AS COST HERE IN NEW ENGLAND:

2 silke barateene under coates, 1li. 6s.;

1 large silk Rugg, 3li.;

1 calico India carpett, 4s.;

7 bushell & ½ malt, 1li. 2s. 6d.;

3 B. & ½ of Indian, 7s.;

1 B. wheate, 3s. 6d.;

a speckled pillow beere, 1s.;

to sugar sold at 5s. 3d.;

a gold ring, 7s. 6d.;

an Iron Casement, 5s.;

460 feet of board, 3s. p, 13s. 8d.;

8 narrow brimed hats, 2s. p, 16s.;

3 old rusty curry combs, 1s.;

2 old sawes, 2s. 6d.;

4 pr. sissers, 1 twissers, 1 gimlet, punch, som ales & steeles, 4s. 6d;

3 firkins of old butter, 3li.;

decayed wine, 1li. 15s.;

an old pr. of hand screws, 1li. 10s.;

debt of 12s.;

suposed 3 acres of land at merimake, to a silver seale, 2s.;

[269]

bookes, 12s.;

mincing knife, 6d., 2 curry combes, 2s.;

Glass redy made & som lead, 1li. 10s.;

2 chests & 1 trunke, 15s.;

8 & 2 yd. of narrow serge, at 2s. p, 17s.;

Debts, 40 li.;

total 69li. 6s. 11d.

Allowed in Salem court 27: 4: 1678, Samuell Shattuck, sr., being a Friend affirming, and Samuell Shattock, jr. making oath to the truth of the inventory.

—*Essex County Probate Records*, Vol. III, pp. 203-208.

[270]

APPENDIX H

INVENTORY OF THE ESTATE OF CAPT. GEORGE CORWIN OF SALEM, TAKEN BY BARTHL. GEDNEY, BENJA. BROWNE, JOHN HIGGINSON JUNR. AND TIMO. LINDALL ON JAN. 30 AND THE BEGINNING OF FEB., 1684-5

Dwelling house & land wheron it stands & adjoyneing to it wth. the out houseing & fence, &c., 400li.;

the pastor, qt.[97] about 3 acres ½, considering a buriall place ther apointed, 90li.;

the lower warhouse & wharfe, 110li.;

the upper warhouse & land adjoyning, 50li.;

about 8 acres Medow & upland by Ely Geoules, 45li.;

the farme on the plaines goeing to Lin bought of Trask, Pickering, Adams, &c., qt. about 200 acres, 25p., 250li.;

the Farme now Reding bought of Burnap, qt. about 800 acres, aprized by Tho. Flint & Jos. Pope, 250li.;

the Farme bought of John Gold, qt. about 500 acres, 50li.;

60 acres of Land bought of Goodman Dutton, 20li.;

15 acres of medow bought of Lt. Smith, 25li.;

the houses & Land adjoyneing that was Wm. Godsoes & wharfe, 45li.;

a pc. of land at the point nere Jer. Neales yt was — —, 10li.;

the Katch Swallow wth. her apurtenances, 130li.;

the Katch George with her apurtenances, 65li.;

620 oz. ⅞ plate at 6s. 8d. [per], 206li. 19s. 2d.;

in New England mony, 47li. 1s.;

in English mony, 37li. 15s., advance, 7li. 11s., 45li. 6s.;

in peices of Eight, 1519li. 1s. 8d;

72oz. ¼ Gold at 5li. [per] oz., 361li. 5s.;

1 Silver hat band & 6 Spones, qt. 4 oz. %₁₆, 1li. 10s. 4d.;

1 watch wth. a stard case, 1 watch wth. a Silver case, 5li.;

1 Silver case & doctors Instruments, 5li.;

more in New England mony, 2li. 18s. 6d.;

1 Plate hilt rapier, 4li. 10s.;

1 Two edged Sword, 1li.;

1 Silver headed cane, 5s.

IN THE SHOPE.

2 yd. broadcl[oth] at 8s., 16s.;

1 yd. ¾ ditto at 8s., 14s.;

16 yd. ⅜ Redcloth Rash at 6s. 6d., 5li. 6s. 5¼d.;

2 yd. ¾ serge at 3s. 6d.; 9s. 7½d.;

6 yd. perpcheana at 18d., 9s.;

7 yd. ¼ perpcheana at 18d., 10s. 10½d.;

11 yd. ditto at 18d., 16s. 6d.;

[271]

20 yd. ½ ell french Stufe at 2s., 2li. 1s. 3d.;

36 yd. ½ ditto at 2s., 3li. 13s.;

25 yd. Red Cotten at 2s., 2li. 10s.;

1 Sad colerd Ruge, 18s.;

1 Grene ditto, 18s.;

9 yd. ½ Stript Stufe at 18d., 14s. 8d.;

1 yd. ¼ Grene Say, damaged, 2s.;

19 yd. ¾ Grene tamey at 10d., 16s. 25½d.;

1 yd. ¾ bl. calico at 18d., 2s. 7½d.;

4 yd. ½ crape at 18d., 6s. 9d.;

11 yd. ¾ Crape at 18d., 17s. 7½d.;

2 yd. ½ Stript Stufe at 18d., 3s. 9d.;

2 yd ½ ell Curle deroy at 18d., 3s. 11d.;

4 yd. ¾ prunella at 22d., 8s. 8½d.;

10 yd. ¼ Silk barronet at 2s. 6d., 1li. 5s. 7½d.;

7 yd. buckrom at 18d., 10s. 6d.;

10 yd. bla. Cloth rash at 6s., 3li. 4s. 6d.;

6 yd. ¾ Sad colerd ditto at 6s., 2li. 6s.;

14 yd. ½ Gr. Tamey at 10d., 12s. 1d.;

6 yd. flanell at 18d., 9s. 4½d.;

2 pr. white blanketts, 14s.;

[2]1 yd. ¾ Red cotten at 20d., 1li. 16s. 3d.;

14 yd. peniston ——, 1li. 8s.;

11 yd. ½ Carsy in Remnts. at 4s., 2li; 6s.;

1 yd. ½ Red buckrom at 18d., 2s. 3d.;

2 Sutes Curtains & valients at 4li., 8li.;

2 yd. ¼ Flanell at 18d., 3s. 4½d.;

28 yd. ½ ell persian Silke at 5s. 6d., 7li. 17s. 5d.;

6yd. ¾ wosted Farenden at 20d., 11s. 3d.;

5 yd. ¾ camlet at 20d., 9s. 7d.;

16 yd. ¾ ticking at 20d., 1li. 7s. 11d.;

20 yd. ½ ditto, at 20d., 1li. 14s. 2d.;

19 yd. ¼ ditto at 20d., 1li. 12s. 1d.;

3 yd. ¼ ditto at 20d., 5s. 5d.;

11 yd. ½ ditto at 17d., 16s. 3½d.;

17 yd. bengall at 18d., 1li. 5s. 6d.;

24 yd. ½ St. Petters canvis at 16d., 1li. 12s. 8d.;

10 yd. ¼ hall cloth at 15d., 12s. 9¾d.;

5 yd. ½ canvis at 16d., 7s. 4d.;

14 yds. ditto damaged at 14d., 16s. 4d.;

29 yds. ditto damaged at 12d., 1li. 9s.;

12 yd. ½ fugeres at 15d., 15s. 7½d.;

22 yd. ¾ Vittery at 13d., 1li. 4s. 7¾d.;

19 yd. ¾ ditto at 13d., 1li. 1s. 4¾d.;

24 yd. ¼ fine canvis at 18d., 1li. 16s. 4½d.;

3 pcs. broad linon, qt. 309 yd., at 20d., 25li. 15s.;

32 yd. ¾ blu linon at 9d., 1li. 4s. 6¾d.;

10 yd. ¾ pillow Ticking at 18d., 16s. 1⅔d.;

5 yd. wte. Fustian at 15d., 6s. 3d.;

18 yd. course holland at 2s., 1li. 16s.;

7 yd. Slesy holland at 21d., 12s. 3d.;

10 yd. ½ Scotch cloth at 16d., 14s.;

25 yd. ¾ lockrom at 15d., 1li. 12s. 2¼d.;

61 yd. ⅔ doulas at 16d., 4li. 2s. 4d.;

2 halfe peces of ⅔ doulas, 9li.;

26 yd. browne diaper at 14d., 1li. 10s. 4d.;

55 yd. Vittery at 12d., 2li. 15s.;

12 yd. high Brene at 22d., 1li. 2s.;

1 bolt Noyles, qt. 140 yd., at 16d., 9li. 6s. 8d., 2 pcs. Course ticking at 35d., 3li. 10s.;

[272]

12 pr. weo. hose, 18s.;

12 pr. mixed Stockrs. Smll. & Great, 14s.;

13 pr. bodys at 4s., 2li. 12s.;

4 pr. parogon bodys & Stomachers at 8s., 1li. 12s.;

11 pr. Small bodys at 20d., 18s. 4d.;

1 doz. large Combes, 4s. 6d.;

3 doz. ditto at 3s. [per] dz., 9s.;

5 doz. ditto at 2s. [per] dz., 10s.;

8 combes at 3d.½, 2s. 4d.;

23 wte. haft knives at 8d., 15s. 4d.;

3 thousd. pins, 2s. 6d.;

17 long bla. haft knives wthout sheaths at 3d., 4s. 3d.;

2 dz. bl. haft knives at 2s. 6d., 5s.;

3 papers manchrs. & pt. of a peice, 12s., 49 pcs. colerd tapes at 12d., 2li. 9s.;

3 papers colerd Filiting, 9s.;

40 pcs. wte. Tape at 12d., 2li.;

23 pcs. nar tape at 8d., 17s. 4d.;

17 doz. thred laces, 4s. 11d.;

a percell of broken tape, 5s.;

4 pcs. ½ diaper Filiting, 6s.;

41 Smll. pcs. Colerd tape at 3d.½, 11s. 11½d.;

a percell of broken colerd tape, 1s. 6d.;

21 cards old fasioned silke lace & 5 cards Gimp Lace, 4li.;

1li. 2 oz. fine thred at 10s., 11s. 3d.;

5 pr. Gloves, 2s.;

6 doz. ½ Sisers at 2s., 13s.;

½ doz. barbers Sisers at 6d., 3s.;

a box nedles, qt. about 3 thousand, 1li. 10s.;

44 doz. yds. flowerd & Plain Ribin at 12s., 26li. 8s.;

20 yd. flowred Ribin at 5d., 8s. 4d.;

22 yd. ¾ ferit Ribin at 4d., 7s. 7d.;

1 pc. ½ Cotten Ribin, 4s. 6d.;

2 yd. ¼ Ribin at 6d., 1s. 1d.;

12li. kniting nedles at 12d., 12s.;

1 pr. fishing boots, 12s.;

4 pr. fr. held shouse & 2 pr. Galotias, 1li.;

6 flower boxes, 4 tin poringers, 1 candle box, 1 Tinder box, 1 Calender, 4 Candlesticks, 7 driping pans, 4 fish plates, 1li.;

1 brase Skilit, 4s.;

27 m. 4d. Nayles at 2s. 6d., 3li. 7s. 6d.;

4 m. 6d. nayles at 3s. 8d., 14s. 8d.;

226 mackerell lines at 9d., 8li. 9s. 6d.;

Erthen ware & wooden ware 3s.;

4 m., 2ct. 12d. Nayles at 10s. [per] m., 2li. 2s.;

5ct: 1: 14li. Shot at 20s. [per] ct. 5li. 7s. 6d.;

147li. French lines at 10d., 6li. 2s. 6d.;

8 yd. ½ yellow Ribin at 6d., 4s. 3d.;

15 yd. bone lace at 4d., 5s.;

a percell of hat bands, 1li. 15s.;

24m. ½ hobs at 21d. [per] m., 2li. 2s. 10½d.;

11 Grose buttens at 21d., a percell loose buttons, 1li. 3s. 3d.;

1 ct. Suger, 1li.;

1li. ¼ Silke at 22s., 1li. 7s. 6d.;

3 Iron morters & 2 Iron pots, qt. 95li. at 3d., 1li. 3s. 9d.;

a parcell of Ginger in a Caske, 6s.;

1 brase morter, 9s.;

9 Cow bells at 8d., 2 pr. pattens at 12d., 8s.;

10 Chalke lines, 1s. 8d.;

7 doz. ½ Capl. hooks at 18d., 11s. 3d.;

2 Reme paper, 8s.;

a percell of white beades, 1s.;

34li. pouder blue at 14d., 1li. 19s. 8d.;

114li. alspice at 21d., 9li. 19s. 6d.;

1 pr. cards, 1s. 6d.;

[273]

33li. shott, 6s.;

4 large, 3 Smll. Salt Sellers, 8d.;

a bundle of Galome, 15s.;

3 Combs, 2s.;

10 Catticises at 12d., 3s.;

2 pr. blu Stockins, 2s. 6d.;

a percell of Red filit & tape, 2s.;

1 qt. pot, 1 pt. pot, 1 Gill pott, 4s.;

4 pr. Seales & waites, 37s., 1 pr. Stiliards, 3s., 2li.;

Cloves, mace, Cinomon & Nutmegs, 10s.;

3 black Silk Caps for men, 3s.

IN THE SHOP CHAMBER.

21 Stock locks at 8d.¼, 14s. 5¼d.;

30 ditto at 11d.¼, 1li. 8s. 1¼d.;

42 ditto at 15d.¾, 2li. 15s. 1½d.;

9 ditto at 6d.½, 14s. 7½d.;

11 ditto at 22d.½, 1li. 7½d.;

14 ditto at 25d.½, 1li. 9s. 9d.;

6 ditto at 31d.½, 15s. 9d.;

45 Smll. lines at 6d., 1li. 2s. 6d.;

5 M. brase nayles at 9s. 9d., 2li. 8s. 9d.;

5 Candlesticks at 10d.½, 4s. 4½d.;

2 doz. augers at 7s. 6d., 15s.;

13 carveing Tooles at 3d., 3s. 3d.;

5 paring Chisells at 6d.¾, 2s. 9¾d.;

19 Gouges & Chisells at 7d.½, 11s. 10½d.;

6 doz & 3 plaining Irons at 5s. [per] doz., 1li. 11s. 3d.;

Oct: 2: 5li. hooks & Twists at 48s., 1li. 6s. 2d.;

18 Spring locks at 2s. 3d., 2li. 6d.;

3 Spring locks wth. Screws at 2s. 9d., 8s. 3d.;

3 best ditto at 3s. 6d., 10s. 6d.;

6 Single Spr. Locks at 13d., 6s. 6d.;

12 warded outside chist lockes, 15s. 9d.;

155li. Frying panes at 6d., 3li. 17s. 6d.;

23 outsid box locks at 6d., 11s. 6d.;

17 Reape hooks at 9d., 12s. 9d.;

10 ward cuberd locks at 9d. ¾, 8s. 1½d.;

1 doz. latches & katches, 6s. 6d.;

26 plaine cuberd locks at 6s., 13s.;

3 pr. pinchers at 11d., 2s. 9d.;

8 pr. nipers at 4d.½, 3s.;

10 pr. marking Irons at 15d., 12s. 6d.;

2 doz. & 3 tacks at 4d. [per] dz., 9d.;

½ doz. shepe sheres at 19d.½, 9s. 9d.;

1 doz. shepe sheres, 16s. 6d.;

13 doz. ½ all Blades at 6d. [per] doz., 6s. 9d.;

3 best box Irons at 3s. 6d., 10s. 6d.;

2 plaine box Irons at 18d., 3s.;

6 Stell Sawes at 3s. 3d., 19s. 6d.;

20 Sawes at 18d., 1li. 10s.;

7 doz. & 2 wte. haft knives at 8s., 2li. 17s. 4d.;

1 pr. Tongs & fire pan, 5s. 6d.;

2 doz. ½ horne haft knives at 4s., 10s.;

5 tilers hamers at 22d.½, 9s. 4½d.;

7 pr. barbers Sisers at 6d., 3s. 6d.;

4 doz. & 5 pr. Large Sisers at 3s., 13s. 3d.;

2 doz. 11 Glass bottles at 3s., 8s. 9d.;

4 doz. 3 Sorted hamers at 12s., 2li. 11s.;

3 doz. Speke Gimlets at 4s. 3d., 12s. 9d.;

6 doz. 9 Small Gimlets at 2s., 13s. 6d.;

15 pr. buttons at 19d. ½, 1li. 4s. 4½d.;

4 Stared bridles at 3s. 3d., 13s.;

7 chafeing dishes at 12d., 7s.;

1 doz. best wte. bridles 14s., 3d.;

½ doz. ordinary ditto, 6s.;

11 bolls, 6d.¾, 6s. 2¼d.;

[274]

5 bl. plaine bridles at 14d.¼, 5s. 11¼d.;

11 dutch bridles at 25d.½, 1li. 3s. 4½d.;

2 French ditto at 22d.½, 3s. 9d.;

1 doz. best Stirop leathers at 18s., 18s.;

8 Stirop leathers at l0d.½, 7s.;

1 Grose of diaper Girt web, 1li. 2s. 6d.;

1 Grose fine plaine ditto, 1li. 3s. 3d.;

1 Grose ¼ ditto at 15s., 18s. 9d.;

7 pr. Swevell Stirop Irons at 16d.½, 9s. 7½d.;

1 doz. boxhorse combes, 5s.;

11 horse combes at 2s. 9d. [per] doz., 2s. 6¼d.;

3 pr. plaine Stirop Irons at 10d.½, 2s, 7½d.;

11 horse brushes at 12d.½, 11s. 5½d.;

2 Grose Girt buckles at 8s. 3d., 16s. 6d.;

4 Papers wte. buckles at 18d., 6s.;

11 curry combes at 5d.½, 5s., ½d.;

4 best wte. Cury combs at 18d. 6s.;

5 wte. ditto at 15d., 6s. 3d.;

14 Files at 8d.¼, 9s. 7½d.;

4 horse locks at 14d.½, 4s. 10d.;

6 Twisted Snafells at 7d.½, 3s. 9d.;

5 large plaine ditto at 6d., 2s. 6d.;

4 small ditto at 4d.½, 1s. 6d.;

8 Smll. padlocks at 9d., 6s.;

3 large ditto at 12d.¾, 3s. 2¼d.;

4 tiling trowells at 12d., 4s.;

2 pointing trowells at 12d., 2s.;

45 pr. plaine Spures at 6d.¼, 1li. 3s. 5¼d.;

3 pr. Joynted Spures at 7d.½, 1s. 10½d.;

287 Curtaine rings at 18d. [per] ct., 4s. 4d.;

10 Curr Bitts at 22d.½, 18s. 9d.;

12 pr. bosses, 8s. 3d.;

2 drawing knives at 14d., 2s., 4d.;

3 doz. 1 Shoue Spurs at 2s. 6d., 7s. 8½d.;

3 shoue knives at 2d.½, 7d.½;

4 wimble bits & 1 Gimlet, 1s.;

1 brick Joynter, 4d.;

4 outside Chist lock at 10d. [per], 3s. 4d.;

1 Chist lock, 10d.;

12 li. pack thred at 12d. [per], 14s.;

1 Cutting Knife, 6d.;

2 X Garnels at 8d., 1s. 4d.;

1 cow bell, 8d.;

1 halfe pt. pott, 1s.;

14 yd. ¾ Carsy at 3s. 6d., 2li. 11s. 7½d.;

8 pcs. blu linon, qt. 233 yd. ¾, at 9d., 8li. 15s. 3¾d.;

37 yd. ticking at 2d., 3li. 14s.;

25 yd. ¾ yellow flanell at 18d., 1li. 18s. 7½d.;

61 yd. ¾ fine doulas, and ½ pc. fine Doulas, 13li.;

1 pc. Course Ticking, qt. 35 yds., at 12d., 1li. 15s.;

171 yd. Genting in 20 pls. & Severll. Remnts. at 18d., 12li. 16s. 6d.;

4 yd. ¾ peniston at 2s., 9s. 6d.;

45 yd. ¾ St. Petters linon at 15d., 2li. 17s. 2¼d.;

16 yd. ¼ Red flannell at 20d., 1li. 7s. 1d.;

½ doz. chusians at 2s., 12s.;

35 yd. Small Noyles at 9d., 1li. 6s. 3d.;

18 yd. ¼ medrinix damaged at 4d., 6s. 1d.;

1 pc. Red Cotten, qt. 72 yd., at 21d., 6li. 6s.;

1 pc. ditto, qt. 76 yd., at 21d., 6li. 13s.;

42 yd. medrinix at 9d., 1li. 11s. 6d.;

33 yd. St. Petters Linon at 14d., 1li. 18s. 6d.;

[275]

59 yd. ½ medrinix at 9d., 2li. 4s. 7½d.;

45 yd. ¾ broad linon at 18d., 3li. 8s. 7½d.;

26 yd. broad Linon at 15d., 1li. 12s. 6d.;

94 yd. Narow Brene at 15d., 5li. 17s. 6d.;

32 yd. ¾ Longloses at 16d., 2 li. 3s. 8d.;

115 yd. Vittery at 13d., 6li. 4s. 7d.;

107 yds. ditto damaged at 8d., 3li. 11s. 4d.;

1 Ruge Eaten, 20s., 1li.;

1 ditto, 1li. 4s.;

1 ditto, 16s.;

1 ditto, 1li. 2s.;

1 ditto, 1li. 3s.;

70 yd. Smll. Noyles at 9d., 2li. 12s. 6d.;

35 yd ½ Red Cotten at 2s., 3li. 11s.;

45 yd ½ St. Petters linon at 16d., 3li. 8d.;

1 bolt Ranletts, qt. 70 yd., at 12d., 3li. 10s.;

62 yd. Lockrom at 12d., 3li. 2s.;

1 pc. course Ticking, qt. 35 yd., at 12d., 1li. 15s.;

16 yd. ½ Medrinix at 9d., 12s. 4½d.;

59 yd. Vittery damaged at 6d., 1li. 9s. 6d.;

63 yd. fine hall cloth at 16d., 4li. 4s.;

13 doz. & 8 pr. large Sisers at 3s., 2li. 1s.;

4 doz. Smll. Sisers at 2s., 8s.;

4 doz. large Combes at 4s. 6d., 18s.;

16 doz. ditto at 3s. 6d., 2li. 16s.;

12 doz. ditto at 3s., 1li. 16d.;

4 doz. ditto at 2s., 8s.;

9 white haft knives at 8d., 6s.;

6 bl. haft knives at 4d., 2s.;

16 bl. woden haft case knives at 4d., 5s. 4d.;

86 hower Glases at 6d., 2li. 3s.;

7 papers manchester at 4s., 1li. 8d.;

1 pc. filiting, 2s.;

½ li. fine thred at 10s., 5s.;

128 li. Colered & browne thread at 2s. 8d., 17li. 1s. 4d.;

25 Grose & 8 doz. Gimp coat buttons at 21d., 2li. 4s. 11d.;

2 Grose brest ditto at 16d., 2s. 8d.;

1 pc. Slesy holland, 15s.;

1 pr. Gerles Gren Stockings, 1s. 2d.;

a percell of hat bands & linings, 5s.;

1 pr. bandelers, 6s.;

31 old fashioned high Crowned hats at 18d., 2li. 6s. 6d.;

1 low ditto, 1s. 6d.;

2 yd. ½ Curle at 2s. 5d., 6s. ½d.;

28 wooden blocks at 4d., 9s. 4d.;

1 Ruge, 18s.;

2 Red Cushian, 5s.;

1 Red Ruge, 10s.;

old Curtaines, &c. in a Chist, 10s.;

1 Silke cradle ruge, 12s.;

1 Canvis Sute, 2s. 6d.;

1 large wainscot chist, 18d.;

1 old Chist & two old Trunks, 8s.;

1 Chaire & 1 Table, 6s.;

1 pr. weo. black shouse, 3s. 6d.;

4 tin pans, 3s.;

1 watch Glase, 1s.;

3 Sase pans, 2 tunells & 2 peper boxes, 1s. 6d.;

1 bed, bolster & pillow, 2li. 15s.;

1 bedsted & matt, 10s.;

1 pr. Grene Curtains & valients, 1li.;

2 Red Fethers, 5s.;

1 cod line, 1s. 3d.;

1 Cloake bage, 3s.;

oatmell, 6s.

IN THE LOWER WAREHOUSE.

120 hh. or thereabouts of salt at 8s., 48li.;

17 m. shingle at 5s. [per], 4li. 5s.;

[276]

2 ct. ½ Clabords at 4s., 10s.;

20 barells Tarr at 4s. 6d., 4li, 10s.;

5 barells Oyle at 25s., 6li. 5s.;

3 old hogsheads, 7s. 6d.;

1 Cask Nayles, qt. 0: 2: 25, ditto, qt. 1: 1: 24, 1 ditto, qt. 2: 0: 01, 1 ditto, qt. O: 3: 00, 1 ditto, qt. 1: 0: 09, 1 ditto, qt. 1: 0: 05, 1 ditto, qt. 1: 3: 15, total, 8: 3: 23, deduct Tare, 0: 3: 23, Rest, 8: 0: 00 at 46s. 8d., 18li. 13s. 4d.;

1 Caske hobs, 6li.;

1 Cable, qt. 3ct: 3: 2li. at 25s., 4li. 14s. 2d.;

48ct: 0: 13li. Spa Iron at 20s., 48li. 2s. 4½d.;

26: 0: 00 Lead at 2Os., 26li.;

2 doz. 3 Rubstones at 18d. [per] doz., 3s. 4½d.;

35 doz. Erthen ware, 3li.;

1 barll. yelow Oaker, qt. neat 2ct: 0: 17li. at 10s., 1li. 1s. 6d.;

a percell of old Junke, 10li.;

1 Great beame Scales & 1 halfe hundrd., 1li. 15s.;

1 Smll. beame & 2 morters, 10s.;

2 netts damaged, 10s.;

old rey in ye Garret, 3s.;

5 m. Red Oak hogshead staves at 25s., 6li. 5s.;

1 pr. old hand screws, 10s.;

2 pr. Stilliards, 1li. 5s.;

a percell of Rozin, 10s.;

1 longe Oare, 5s.;

shod shoule, 1s. 6d.;

old cask, 10s.;

1 Suger drawer, 1s. 6d.;

a percell Limestones on the wharfe, 8li.

IN THE UPER WAREHOUSE.

3 Ketles 95li.½, 15 potts 550li. at 25s. [per] ct., 7li. 4s.;

9ct: 2: 2li. lead at 20s. [per] 9li. 10s. 4d.;

4: 1: 9 Stelle att 50s. [per], 10li. 16s. 6d.;

1: 2: 8 of Old Iron at 12s. [per], 19s.;

1 hogshed Suger, qt. 6ct: 1: 16li. neat 20s., 6li. 8s.;

1 Cask Starch, qt. 150li. neate at 3d., 1li. 17s. 6d.;

7 doz. ⅔ Glase botles at 2s. 9d., 1li. 1s. 1d.;

2 barll. mattasows at 30s., 3li.;

1 pr. Great hand screws, 3li.;

12 whip Sawes at 9s., 5li. 8s.;

beanes, 3s.;

1 Chist drawers, 1li. 10s.;

wheate, 6s.;

1 pr. Great Stilliards, li. 5s.;

1 pr. Smll. Stilliards defective, 5s.;

219 fot Bords, 3s. [per], 2 harpn. Irons 12d. [per], 8s. 7d.;

old caske, 10s.;

Graine, the Sweeping of the Chamber, 3s.;

part of an old Clock, 10s.

IN THE OLD HALL.

9 turkey worke chaires wthout. backs, 5s. [per], 2li. 5s.;

4 ditto wth. Backs at 8s. [per], 1li. 12s.;

6 low Turky worke ditto wth. Backs, 8s. [per], 2li. 8s.;

2 Tables, 20s. [per], 1 ditto, 5s., 2li. 5s.;

1 Carpet, 15s.;

1 pr. large brase Andirons, 1li. 10s.;

1 large looking Glase & brases, 2li. 5s.;

3 Curtaine rods & Curtains for windows, 15s.;

2 Candlesticks, 5s.;

1 Glase Globe, 1s.

IN THE RED CHAMBER.

8 Red branched chaires wth. Covers, 16s. [per], 6li. 8s.;

[277]

1 Smll. table, 1 Red carpet, 10s.;

2 Curtaine rods & window Curtaines, 7s.;

1 Scritore & frame, 1li. 10s.;

2 Trunks, 15s.;

1 old Cuberd & Red cloth, 6s.;

1 pr. brase Andirons, 1 back, 1 pr. Tongs, 13s.;

1 looking glase, 6s.;

1 large white Quilt, 2li.;

1 ditto, 1li. 10s.;

1 ditto, 1li.;

1 pr. Shetts, 1li.;

1 pr. ditto, 1li.;

1 pr. ditto, 1li. 2s.;

1 pr. ditto, 18s.;

1 pr. ditto, 1li. 2s.;

1 pr. ditto, 1li. 2s.;

1 pr. ditto, 1li. 5s.;

1 pr. ditto, 1li. 2s.;

1 pr. ditto, 1li. 2s.;

1 pr. ditto, 1li. 2s.;

1 pr. ditto, 1li.;

1 pr. ditto, 1li.;

1 pr. ditto, 18s.;

1 pr. ditto, 12s.;

1 pr. ditto, 18s.;

1 pr. ditto, 18s.;

1 pr. ditto, 1li. 4s.;

1 pr. ditto, 16s.;

½ pr. ditto, 8s.;

½ pr. ditto, 18s.;

17 Napkins, 1 large table cloth & a Towell all of Damaske, 4li.;

9 diaper Napkins & 1 Table Cloth, 15s.;

1 doz. ditto & 1 Table Cloth, 1li. 2s.;

1 doz. ditto & 1 Table Cloth, 1li. 2s.;

1 doz. ditto & 1 Table Cloth, 18s.;

1 doz. diaper Napkins & a Table Cloth, 17s.;

1 Table Cloth, 8s.;

2 pillowbers at 2s. 6d. [per], 5s.;

1 Table Cloth, 5s.;

1 diaper Table Cloth, 8s.;

1 ditto, 8s.;

1 Cuberd Cloth, 5s.;

1 ditto, 3s.;

1 Calico Counter pain, 8s.;

18 pilobers & Napkins, 15s.;

4 towells & a Cuberd Cloth, 10s.;

1 Child's Bed, 1s.;

1 Red Cushion, 1s.

IN THE TWO CLOSETS ADJOYNING.

10 doz. Erth. ware, 15 large, 33 Small tins pans for Suger Cakes, 16 qt. botles, 3 Erthen pots, 3 long mum Glases, 2li. 10s.

IN THE GLASE CHAMBER.

1 bed sted & apurtenances, 1li.;

1 fether bed, bolster & 2 pillows, 4li. 10s.;

1 pr. Curtains & Valients, 2li. 10s.;

1 Red Ruge, 8s.;

1 large white blanket, 8s.;

1 Stript blanket, 3s.;

1 Silke blanket, 12s.;

1 large Striped blanket, 8s.;

1 Smll. blanket, 4s.;

1 pr. shettes, 14s.;

2 pillowbers, 2s.;

6 parogon Chaires at 10s. [per], 3li.;

2 longe Stooles, at 10s., [per], 1li.;

2 Stands at 4s., 8s.;

1 Table, 1 linsy carpet, 10s.;

1 Calico Carpet, 3s.;

1 looking Glase, 7s.;

1 pomader basket, 10s.;

1 Ouall fine wicker basket, 3s.;

1 painted Couberd Cloth, 3s.;

1 Glase frame for Glase worke, 1li.;

3 Curtain rods & window Curtains, 10s.;

1 pr. Andirons wth. brases, 12s.;

1 pr. brasse fire pan & Tongs, 8s.

[278]

IN THE CORNER CHAMBER.

1 bedsted, 10s.;

2 Ruges, 1li. 12s.;

1 pr. Curtains & Valients & Rods, 2li.;

1 Grene Counter paine, 5s.;

1 pr. Sheets, 12s.;

1 bolster & pillow, 1li.;

1 wainscot Chist, 10s.;

1 Table & 1 Grene Carpet, 12s.;

8 yd. bengall at 9d., 6s.;

7 yd. doulas at 20d., 11s. 8d.;

4 yd. ½ Stript linon at 16d., 6s.;

1 yd. ½ Serge at 3s., 4s. 6d.;

7 yd. Narr. brene at 15d., 8s. 9d.;

1 yd. ⅜ Grene Say at 3s. 6d., 4s. 9¾d.;

8 pcs. Tape at 9d., 6s.;

3 yd. Lockrom at 12d., 2s.;

1 yd. ¾ ticking at 20d., 2s. 11d.;

a Remnant of holland, 1s.;

19 yd. high brene at 2s., 1li. 18s.;

1 yd. Red Cotten, 1s. 9d.;

3 yd. course holland at 18d., 4s. 6d.;

3 yd. ½ narr Cloth at 8d., 2s. 4d.;

⅞ yd. Linon at 18d., 1s. 3¾d.;

2 yd. ¾ fustian at 12d., 2s. 9d.;

a Remt. fine Canvis, 7d.;

1 yd. ½ Linon at 18d. [per], 2s. 3d.;

1 yd. wte. Calico, 1s.;

1 yd. ½ linon at 18d., 2s. 3d.;

1 yd. ½ Slesy at 12d., 1s. 6d.;

1 yd. colerd Fustian, 1s.;

1 pr. Red. weo. stockings, 1s. 6d.;

2 old Chaires at 2s., 4s.;

1 bundle of Remnants, 1s.

IN THE COUNTEING HOUSE & ENTERY.

1 dozn. pins, 9s.;

1 dozn. ditto, 10s.;

2 li. Colerd thread at 2s. 8d., 5s. 4d.;

3 li. ½ wormesed at 4s. 6d. [per], 15s. 9d.;

¼ Grose Girt web at 22s. [per] Grose, 5s. 6d.;

12 books Carell upon Jobe, 1 Grt. bible & 1 Psalme Booke, 3li.;

1 booke Markham's Gramer, 2s.;

3 pls. Turtle Shell, 1s. 6d.;

1 Snafle bitt, 1 pr. Spures, 1s.;

2 pr. Stirop Irons, 2s.;

1 Inkhorne, 6d.;

1 Caine, 3s.;

1 Turned Stick, 2s., 5s.;

1 Rapier Tipt wth. Silver, 15s., 1 ditto, 5s. 1li.;

4 musketts, 2li.;

1 pr. pistolls & holsters, 1 plush Sadle layed wth. Silver lace & Sadle Cloth, 5li.;

1 Caduco box, 2s.;

1 buff belt wth. Silver buckles, 1li.;

2 old bells, 2s.

IN THE HALL CHAMBER.

1 bed Sted, 5s.;

1 pr. Red Curtaines & Valients, 2li. 10s.;

2 Ruges, 16s.;

1 pr. Shetts, 10s., 1 pillow, 5s., 15s.;

1 flock bed & 1 fether bolster, 16s.;

2 Ruges, 12s.;

1 Trundle bedsted & Curtaine rods, 7s.;

4 Trunks, 1li.;

1 Chist drawers & 1 Carpet, 10s.;

1 Table & 1 Carpet, 8s.;

1 looking Glase, 5s.;

1 Curtain Rod & window Curtaine, 3s.;

2 pr. white Calico Curtaines, Valients, tester Clothes & 6 Covers for Chaires, 2li. 5s.;

14 old Napkins at 9d., 10s. 6d.;

19 new diaper small ditto at 9d. 14s. 3d.;

2 Calico Side bord Clothes, 6s.;

[279]

3 Calico ditto, 6s.;

12 towells at 6d., 6s.;

more 35 diaper & other Napkins at 9d., 1li. 6s. 3d.;

7 Table Clothes at 5s., 1li. 15s.;

8 ditto at 2s. 6d., 1li.;

15 ditto, 18s.

WAREING CLOTHES.

1 Tropeing Scarfe & hat band, 1li. 10s.;

1 Cloake, 2li.;

1 Cloth Coat wth. Silver lace, 2li.;

1 Camlet Coate, 15s.;

1 old bla. farendin Sute, 1li.;

1 black Cloake, 2li.;

1 velvet Coate, 2li. 10s.;

1 old Tabey dublet, 5s.;

1 old fashioned duch Sattin dublet, 15s.;

1 black Grogrin Cloake, 1li. 10s.;

3 Quilts, 3s.;

1 hatt, 15s.;

1 pr. Golden Topt. Gloues, 10s.;

1 pr. Imbroidred ditto, 8s.;

1 pr. bl. fringed Gloues, 3s.;

1 pr. bl. & Gold fringed ditto, 3s.;

1 pr. new Gloves, 2s.;

2 pr. Gloves, 2s.;

3 pr. old Silke Stockings, 8s.;

2 belts and 1 Girdle, 2li.;

1 Sattin Imbroadred wascot wth. Gold, &c., 3li.;

1 yd. ¾ persian Silke at 5s. 6d., 9s. 7½d.

IN THE COUNTING HOUSE & ENTRY MORE.

1 Table, 5s.;

1 Carpet, 10s.;

1 Chaire, 4s.;

1 desk & Cuberd, 5s.;

1 pr. bandelers, 3s.;

seling wax, 3s.;

1 Cushian, 6d.;

3 flasketts & 2 basketts, 5s.;

1 Iron bound Chist, 5s.

IN THE HALL.

1 Lookeing Glase, 7s.;

3 tables, 1li. 2s.;

1 Turky worke Carpet, 1li. 5s.;

8 leather Chaires at 5s., 2li.;

5 Stra bottomed Chaires, 5s.;

1 old wicker Chaire, 2s.;

1 Napkin presse, 1li. 10s.;

1 Glase Case, 6s.;

1 Clocke, 2li.;

1 Scritore or Spice box, 6s.;

1 Screne wth. 5 leaves & Covering, 15s.;

1 old Smll. Turky worke Carpet, 3s.;

1 Armed Chaire, 2s.;

1 Stand, 1s. 6d.;

1 Great Candlestick, 1li.;

1 pr. Grt. Dogs & 1 Iron Back, 2li. 5s.;

5 Cushians at 4s. pr, 1li.;

1 window Curtaine & rod, 6s.;

1 pr. Tongs, Shoule fire & Smll. Tongs & Toster, 7s.;

Glases in the Glase case, 5s.

IN THE MAIDES CHAMBER.

1 bed & bolster, 3li.;

1 bedsted, 2s.;

1 new Bed & Case, 5li.;

1 Cushian & 2 Stoole Covers, 3s.;

1 pillion & Cloth, 1li.;

1 pr. old Shetts, 4s.;

3 pr. Shetts at 16s. 2li. 8s.;

1 pr. new Shetts, 1li. 2s.;

5 Shetts at 8s., 2li.;

3 Shetts at 4s., 12s.;

1 Table Cloth, 3s.;

1 old Sheet, 2s.;

1 wainscot chist, 5s.;

[280]

2 Cotten Ironning Clothes, 3s.;

1 Calico Cuberd Cloth, 1s. 6d.;

Starch & a bage, 2s.;

2 boxes, 2s.;

1 Rat eaten Carpet, 5s.;

1 old Bed Tick, 7s.;

1 pr. old Stript Curtaines & Carpets, 8s.;

1 Chist, 4s.;

1 Smll. brase Ketle tined, 6s.;

1 lanthorne, 5s.;

1 Calender & 1 plate, 2s.;

1 Wooden Voider, 1s. 6d.;

1 bird Cage, 2s.

IN THE GARRETTS.

12 Reame ½ paper at 4s., 2li. 10s.;

1 bolt Noyles, qt. 89 @ ¼ is 130 yd. ¾ at 16d. [per], 8li. 14s. 4d.;

1 Sadle, bridle & brest plate, 1li. 5s.;

2 pc. pole daine & a Remnt, qt. 80 yds., 4li.;

150li. Fr. lines at 10d. [per], 6li. 5s.;

1 pr. large brase Andirons, 1li.;

1 Candlebox, &c., 2s.;

1 pillion & cloth, 5s.;

1 old port mantle, 1s.;

2 Childr. blankets, 10s.;

1 Carpet, 8s.;

1 wainscot chist, 5s.;

1 pin Chest, 2s. 6d., 7s. 6d.;

gloves & Some Lumber, 5s.;

2 old Ruge, 3s.;

1 hamaker, 5s., 8s.;

1 Auger weges, & chisles, 5s.;

5 Shetts at 5s., 1li. 5s.;

1 fine Shett, 7s.;

19 napkins & towells, 12s.;

about 100li. hogs & beffe Suet at 2d., 16s. 8d.;

meale Troues, &c., 6s.;

old Bed steds, 10s.;

old cask, 5s.

IN THE ENTRY BELOW.

1 Round table & 1 Gren Carpet, 15s.;

2 Great Chaires & 4 high Chaires, 15s.;

1 Cuberd & cuberd Cloth, 8s.

IN THE CLOSET.

Erthen ware & a Glase botle, 5s.;

a parcell of honey, 5s.

IN THE PEUTER ROME.

4 boles, 1 Tray & Erth. Ware. 10s.;

1 limeback & 1 Iron pott, 2li.;

a percell of old Iron, 5s.;

1 large defective driping pan, 2s. 6d.;

4 trayes, 1 platter, 2s., Erthen ware, 18d., 3s. 6d.;

1 leather Jack.

IN THE KITCHIN.

7 Spitts, 1li. 5s.;

2 Racks, 1li.;

1 Jack & waite, 12s.;

2 Iron potts & 2 pr. pot hooks, 1li.;

4 tramells & 1 Iron barr, 15s.;

1 pr. Iron doges, 10s.;

2 fenders, 4s.;

1 pr. la. Tonges, 4s.;

1 Iron driping pan, 3s.;

1 Iron back, 1li.;

1 Iron Ketle, 6s.;

4 box Irons, 8s.;

5 old Iron potts, 1li. 4s.;

1 pr. Fetters, 3s.;

2 Fring pans, 5s.;

3 Grid Irons, 1 pr. pot hookes & treuet, 7s.;

1 Slut or larance, 1s.;

1 Cleuer & a shreding knife, 4s.;

a hooke & Iron Squers, 2s.;

1 Chafeing Dish, 1s. 6d.;

1 pr. bellows, 1s. 6d.;

1 warmeing pan, 2s.;

[281]

38 pls. Tin Ware, 1s. 4d.;

2 Iron Candlesticks & a toster, 5s.;

2 tables, 5s. 4 old Chaires, 6d., 7s.;

Erthen ware, 6s.;

453li. peuter of all Sorts at 12d., 22li. 13s.;

24li. brase in Small ware at 20d., 2li.;

1 Coper Ketle, qt. 30li. at 2s., 3li.;

2 brase Ketles, qt. 57li. at 12d., 2li. 17s.;

1 brase Stew pan, 6s.;

3 bell mettle Skilets, qt. 25l., 1li. 5s.;

1 payle, 1 bole & other wood. lumber, 5s.; 2 Cases & 7 knives, 12s.;

1 Slick Stone, 1s. 6d.

IN THE WASH HOUSE.

1 Peuter Still, 10s.;

1 Coper, 4li.;

tubes, a Table & lumber, 5s.;

1 pr. Andirons & Iron rake, &c., 5s.

IN THE STABLE.

1 horse, 4li.;

1 Cow, 3li., wth. the hay, 7li.;

2 forks, 1 Tray, 2 Grain payles, 6s.;

1 axe, 3s.;

1 Cow at 1s. Williams, 2li. 10s.

IN THE SELLER UNDER THE HOUSE.

Old Caske, 1li.;

24 qt. Jugs, 4s.;

24 Glase botles, 5s. 6d.;

4 Jares, 4s.;

1 Erth. pot, 1s.;

44li. Castle Sope at 6d., 1li. 2s.

IN THE CLOSET OF KITCHIN CHAMBER.

43 pls. Erthen ware at 2s. [per] doz., 7s., 2d.;

19 Glase cups & Smll. botles, 2s.;

1 pr. Shouse, 4s.;

5 qt. botles, 15d.;

1 Stone Juge, 2s., 3s. 3d.;

3 woden boxes, 1s.;

1 Tin Candlestick, 1s.;

1 Cap for a Clock of belmetle, 2s.

In the Kitchin Chamber.

1 large Scritore, 5li.;

1 bedsted & Teaster, 1li.;

1 fether bed & bolster cased & 2 pillows, 6li. 10s.;

1 pr. Sad Colerd Curtaines & valients & counter paine & rods, 3li.;

1 worsted Stript Ruge, 3li.;

2 pillobers, 2s.;

1 pr. blanketts, 1li.;

1 pr. Shetts, 1li.;

1 bedsted & Teaster & head peice, 1li.;

1 fether bed & bolster cased & 2 pillows, 4li.;

1 pr. Red Serge Curtains valients & Rods, 3li. 10s.;

1 Quilt of Calico Colerd & flowred, 1li. 10s.;

1 Red Ruge, 10s.;

3 blanketts, 1li.;

1 Pallet bedsted, Teaster & hed peice, 1li.;

1 fether bed & bolster, 1 pillow, 3li. 10s;

2 Curtaines & Smll. Valients, 15s.;

2 Coverleds, 1li. 12s.;

1 pr. blanketts, 1li.;

1 Shett, 5s.;

1 Stoole, 1s.;

7 Chaires Sad Colerd & 1 Grt. Chaire, 4s., 1li. 12s.;

1 Table wth. a drawer, 8s.;

2 Stands, 4s.;

1 Close Stoole, 6s.;

8 window Curtains & 4 Rods, 16s.;

1 looking Glases & brases, 1li. 5s.;

[282]

1 Chist Drawers, 25s. & Cloth, 4s., 1li. 9s.;

2 pr. bla., 1 pr. Speckled Stockings, 12s.;

4 pr. old Stockings, 4s.;

1 pr. andirons wth. brases, 10s.;

1 pr. tongs & fire pan, 4s.;

1 back, 12s.;

1 Round fender, 5s.;

1 pr. bellows, 1s. 6d.;

1 Japan Trunke. 8d.;

5 neckclothes at 9d., 3s.;

4 night caps at 15d., 5s.;

17 bands at 6d., 8s. 6d.;

2 pocket hanchesters, 1s.;

1 pr. Gloves, 1s.;

3 fustian wescoats, 6s.;

3 pr. dito drawers, 8s.;

4 pr. holland drawers at 2s. 6d., 10s.;

6 Shirts, 1li. 12s.

GOODS THAT CAME FROM ENGLAND FROM MR. JOHN IUES.

Pr. Capt. Gener. 6 pls. peniston amo. to wth. charges, 18li. 17s. 7d., wth. advance, 50li. [per] Ct., 28li. 6s. 4d.

Pr. Capt. Edwards. 20 pls. blue linon & a percell of Spice amounting to wth. Charges, 48li. 17s. 6d., wth. adva. at 50li. [per] Ct., 73li. 6s. 3d.

IN THE CLOSET IN KITCHIN CHAMBER.

18 Glass botles, 4s., 6d.;

10 pls. Erthen ware, 2s. 6d.;

2 haire bromes, 2s. 6d.;

1 knife tipt wth. Silver, 1s. 3d.;

1 woden Screne, 3s.;

3 yd. bla. broadcloth at 10s., 1li. 10s.;

35 Qn.[98] mercht. Fish at 9s., 15li. 15s.;

½ Qn. pollock at 5s., 2s. 6d.;

22 barlls. Porke at 43s., 47li. 6s.;

2 laced bands, 19s.;

2 pich potts, 8s.;

1 warehouse at Winter Island, 6li.;

1 Great beame Scales & ½ct. waites, 1li. 10s.;

112li. lead & 98li. Spa Iron, 1li. 17s. 6d.;

137li. hide, damages at 2d., 1li. 2s. 10d.;

1780 fot Bords at 2s. 6d. [per] ct. 2li. 4s. 5d.;

1 heffer, 1 Stere & 1 Cow aprized by Edward & Jno. Richards, 5li. 5s.

The house & land yt was Jno. Gatchells wth. the apurtenances, 115li.;

the house & land yt was Jno. Gatchells now Wm. Furners, 60li.;

the dwelling house & land nere Micall Coas, 40li.;

2 oxe Yoakes wth. bowes, 4s.;

2 hows, 1 peak ax & forks, 5s.;

1 barr Iron, 5s.;

1 load hay, 20s., 1li. 5s.;

1 old house & land formerly Hudsons acording to Towne Grant, aprized by Jno. Lege & Ambrose Gayle, 3li.;

total, 219li. 14s.

At Boston: The warhouse & Ground, 200li.;

1056 ounces ½ pcs. of eight, 6s. 8d., 352li. 3s. 4d.;

2 Cloakes, 2li.;

an old Trunke, a hat & wax, &c., 6s. 8d.;

aprized by Eliak. Hucheson & Jer. Dumer, 554li. 10s.;

3 pipes Madara Wine at 11li., not being filled up, 33li.;

[283]

in mony of Petter Millers freight, 2li. 16s.

Brought home in Katch Jno. & William: 130 bushells Indian corne, at 18d., 9li. 15s.;

33 bushells Rey at 3s., 4li. 19s.;

25 bushells ½ wheate at 4s., 5li. 2s.;

1 barll. Porke, 2li.;

3 barells Beffe at 25s., 3li. 15s.;

1 plaine Ruge, 10s.;

15 hower Glases, bad, 5s.;

4 pr. Stirop Irons & lethers, 7s.;

3 locks at 25d., 6s. 4½d.;

6 ditto at 11d.¼, 5s. 1½d.;

4 ditto at 8d.¼, 2s. 9d.;

6 hand sawes at 18d., 9s.;

11 trunk locks at 10d., 9s. 2d.;

6 box outsid locks, 6d., 3s.;

4 Cuberd locks at 6d., 2s.;

1 doz. combs at 2s., 2s.;

1 doz. ditto at 3s., 3s.;

1 doz. ditto at 3s. 6d., 3s. 6d.;

3 pr. parogon bodys at 8s., 1li. 4s.;

2 doz. Reap hooks at 9s., 18s.;

12 duble Girts, 9s.;

1 pr. Shetts at 16s., 16s.;

1 pr. Shetts at 10s., 10s.;

1 pr. ditto at 36s. 2 bredths ½, 1li. 16s.;

1 pr. ditto at 30s., 3 bredths, 1li. 10s.;

1 pr. ditto at 30s., 3 bredths, 1li. 10s.;

The land whereon the house comonly called Capt. Jno. Corwins stands, 35li.

The Katch John & William wth. her apurtenances, 80li.;

1 old Mainsayle of Katch Penelopy, 1li. 10s.

This Inventory amounting to five thousand nine hundred Sixty foure pounds nineten shillgs. & one peny ¾d. aprized as mony by us.

Barthl. Gedney
Benja. Browne
John Higginson, Junr.
Timo. Lindall.

—*Essex County Quarterly Court Files*, Vol. XLIV, leaf 95.

[284]

INDEX

FOOTNOTES:

[1] Rev. Francis Higginson, *New-Englands Plantation*, London, 1630.

[2] *Transactions of the American Antiquarian Society*, Vol. III, p. 12.

[3] *Transactions of the American Antiquarian Society*, Vol. III, p. 6.

[4] Between 1630 and 1643,198 ships brought over 21,200 passengers.—Edward Johnson, *Wonder Working Providence*, London, 1654.

John Josselyn, coming to New England in 1638, mentions in his journal of the voyage sighting or speaking thirteen vessels between the Scilly Isles and the New England coast.

[5] Anti-scorbutics were very necessary for the long voyage. John Josselyn during his first voyage (1638) writes that a young man, a servant to one of the passengers, "was whipt naked at the Cap-stern, with a Cat with Nine tails, for filching 9 great Lemmons out of the Chirurgeons Cabbin, which he eat rinds and all in less than an hours time."

[6] William Wood, *New-Englands Prospect*, London, 1634.

[7] William Bradford, *History of Plymouth Plantation*, Boston, 1856.

[8] John Josselyn, *Two Voyages to New England*, London, 1675.

[9] Wood, *New-Englands Prospect*, London, 1634.

[10] *Memoirs of the Long Island Historical Society*, Vol. I.

[11] *Memoirs of the Long Island Historical Society*, Vol. I.

[12] *Mourt's Relation*, Boston, 1841.

[13] *Documentary History of New York* (*1850*), Vol. I.

[14] *Essex Co. (Mass.) Quarterly Court Records*, Vol. VI, p. 363.

[15] *Essex County Deeds*, Book V, leaf 107.

[16] *Force's Tracts*, Washington, 1838.

[17] *Mass. Historical Society Colls.* (5th ser.), Vol. 7, p. 10.

[18] *Boston News-Letter*, Jan. 23, 1766.

[19] *Boston News-Letter*, Sept. 13, 1753.

[20] *Mass. Historical Society Colls.* (5th ser.), Vols. 5-7.

[21] *Mass. Historical Society Colls.* (5th ser.), Vols. 5-7.

[22] This large salt is now owned by Harvard College.

[23] *Old-Time New England*, July, 1934.

[24] *Essex County Quarterly Court Records*, Vol. IV, pp. 56-57.

[25] Beer in the making.

[26] *Probate Records of Essex County, Mass.*, Vol. I, p. 47.

[27] *Probate Records of Essex County, Mass.*, Vol. II, p. 348.

[28] Dankers, *Journal of a Voyage to New York*, Brooklyn, 1867.

[29] Watkins, "Early Use of Paper Hangings in Boston" (*Old-Time New England*, Jan., 1922).

[30] Waters, *Ipswich in the Massachusetts Bay Colony*, Ipswich, 1905.

[31] *Records of the Mass. Bay Colony*, Vol. I, p. 126.

[32] Ward, *The Simple Cobler of Aggawam*, London, 1647.

[33] *Sewall's Diary*, Vol. II, p. 231.

[34] In the inventory of the estate of Henry Landis of Boston, Shopkeeper, deceased, taken, Dec. 17, 1651, appears his clothing, viz.:

1 suite of fine broad cloth	£1.10.0
1 French serge suite,	18.0
1 Stuffe Cassoke & 1 pr breeches,	16.0
1 French serge Cassocke	£1. 0.0
1 pr red drawers,	5.0
1 wascoate	5.0

1 pr cotton breeches	2.0
5 pr stockings & a hoode	12.0
1 hatte	2.6

—*Suffolk Co. Probate Rds.*, Vol. II, p. 127.

[35] *Records of the Massachusetts Bay Colony*, Boston, 1853, Vol. I, p. 27.

[36] Felt, *The Customs of New England*, Boston, 1853.

[37] Felt, *The Customs of New England*, Boston, 1853.

[38] Edward Johnson, *Wonder Working Providence*, London, 1654.

[39] *Essex County Quarterly Court Records*, Vol. II, p. 28.

[40] *Laws and Liberties of the Massachusetts Colony*, Cambridge, 1672.

[41] Bradford, *History of Plymouth Plantation*, Boston, 1853.

[42] R. P. Baker, "The Poetry of Jacob Bailey" (*The New England Quarterly*, Jan., 1929).

[43] Wood, *New Englands Prospect*, London, 1634.

[44] William Bradford, *History of Plymouth Plantation*, Boston, 1912.

[45] *Transactions of the American Antiquarian Society*, Vol. III, p. 90.

[46] *Winthrop's Journal*, New York, 1908.

[47] *Massachusetts Bay Records*, Boston, 1853.

[48] *Ibid.*

[49] *Winthrop's Journal*, New York, 1908.

[50] *Calendar of State Papers, Am. and W. I.* (1661-1668), 347.

[51] *Massachusetts Archives*, XXXV, folio 61.

[52] *Cal. State Papers, Am. and W. I.* (1696-1697), 84.

[53] Viscount Bury, *Exodus of the Western Nations*, London, 1865.

[54] Dow and Edmonds, *Pirates of the New England Coast*, Salem, 1923.

[55] *Cal. State Papers, Am. and W. I.* (1675-1676), 408.

[56] *Cal. State Papers, Am. and W. I.* (1675-1676), 466.

[57] *Ibid.*, 221-222.

[58] *3 Collections* (*Mass. Hist. Society*), Vol. VIII, pp. 336-339.

[59] *Probate Records Essex Co., Mass.*, Salem, 1917.

[60] Hull, *Letter Book* (American Antiquarian Society).

[61] Corwin MSS. (Essex Institute, Salem, Mass.).

[62] John Caxy v. Joseph Mallenson, *Mass. Archives*.

[63] Public Record Office, C.O. 5: 848-851 (copies at Essex Institute).

[64] Rev. W. A. Bartlett, *The Frontier Missionary*, Boston, 1853.

[65] *Journal of a Lady of Quality*, New Haven, 1921.

[66] Malcolm Storer, "Pine Tree Shillings and other Colonial Money," in *Old-Time New England*, October, 1929.

[67] *Bradford's Letter Book* (1 Mass. Hist. Colls., Vol. III).

[68] 4 Mass. Hist. Colls., II, 164.

[69] *Prince Society Publications*, IV, Boston, 1867.

[70] Sprague, "Some Aspects of Medicine in Boston" (*Old-Time New England*, Vol. XIII, p. 14.)

[71] *Ibid.*

[72] "Fox Lungs for the mending of human lungs hardly able to respire, and Bone of a Stag's Heart" are mentioned in the English Dispensatory (Quincy), London, 1742.

[73] *Quinsey.* First bleed, and purge with *Dincassia*, after vomit with *Vinum Antimonii*; rub the tongue with the juyce of Crabfish and Housleek, taking a little inwardly; ... ashes of burnt Crabs, of Swallows, and Tincture of Corals, are excellent in the bastard Quinsey; the ashes of an owl (feathers and all) blown into the throat, opens and breaks the Imposthume wonderfully.—*Compendium of Physick* (*Salmon*), London, 1671.

[74] *Deafness and Slow Hearing.* The juyce of Radishes, fat of a mole, eele, or Serpent, juyce of an Onyon soaked in Sperrit of Wine and roasted, essences of a mans or Bullocks gall, are all very excellent. In difficulty of hearing, distilled Boyes Urine is good; but better is the Oyl of Carawayes.—*Compendium of Physick* (*Salmon*), London, 1671.

[75] *Cup Moss.* This with some other Mosses of like kind, have been mightily in vogue amongst the good Women for their Children's Coughs; but they have not obtained in official nor extemporaneous Prescriptions. They are said to be infallible in that which is commonly called the *Chin-Cough.*—*English Dispensatory* (*Quincy*), London, 1742.

[76] Burning "Spunck," an excrescence growing out of black birch, in two or three places on the thigh of a patient, helps sciatica.—*New England's Rarities* (*Josselyn*), London, 1672.

[77] *Falling-Sickness.* In Children. Ashes of the dung of black Cow [dram]i. given to a new born Infant, doth not only preserve from the Epilepsia, but also cure it. In those of ripe Age. The livers of 40 water-Frogs brought into a powder, and given at five times (in Spirit of Rosemary or Lavender) morning and evening, will cure, the sick not eating nor drinking two hours before nor after it.—*Compendium of Physick* (*Salmon*), London, 1671.

Peacock's Dung is reckoned a specific in *Epilepsias*, and its use is commended in *Vertigo.*—*English Dispensatory* (*Quincy*), London, 1742.

[78] *Salt of Mans Skull.* The skull of a dead man, calcine it, and extract the Salts as that of Tartar. It is a real cure for the Falling-Sickness, Vertigo, Lethargy, Numbness, and all capital diseases, in which it is a wonderful prevalent.—*Compendium of Physick* (*Salmon*), London, 1671.

It is to be feared that this has obtained a place in medicine, more from a whimsical Philosophy, than any other account.... *A dead Man's Hand.* This is supposed, from some superstitious Conceits amongst Common People, to be of great Efficacy in dispersing *scrophulous Tumours.* The part, forsooth, is to be rubbed with the dead Hand for some time. And Report furnishes us with many Instances of Cures done hereby; some of which may not improbably be true, both as the Imagination in the Patient contributes much to such Efficacies, and because the Sensation which stroaking in that manner gives, is somewhat surprizing, and occasions a shuddering Chilness upon the Part touched; which may in many cases put the Fibres in such Contractions, as to loosen, shake off, and dislodge the obstructed matter; in which consists the Cure.—*English Dispensatory* (*Quincy*), London, 1742.

Mummy. This is the Flesh of Carcases which have been embalm'd. But altho it yet retains a place in medicinal catalogues, it is quite out of vse in Prescription.—*English Dispensatory* (*Quincy*), London, 1742.

[79] *Goose-Dung.* The Excrements of most Birds are accounted hot, nitrous, and penetrating; for this reason they pass for inciders and Detergents, and are particularly reckon'd good in Distempers of the Head; but they are now almost quite laid aside in Practice. *Elk's Hoof* is also esteemed of mighty Efficacy in Distempers of the Head. Naturalists tell us that the Creature itself first gave to Mankind a Hint of its Medicinal Virtues; for they say, whenever it ails anything in the Head, it lies in such a Posture as to keep one of the tips of a Hoof in its Ear; which after some time effects a Cure. But this I leave to be credited by those of more faith than myself.—*English Dispensatory* (*Quincy*), London, 1742.

An Hysteric Emulsion. Take Assafoetida 2 drams, dissolve cold in a mortar with a pound and half of Black-Cherry-water, and strain for Vse. This is tolerable, for its stinking Scent, but to few; yet where it can be got down, it is very prevalent in checking the inordinate Orgasm of the Spirits, and preventing those Convulsions and Frenzies of Mind which arise therefrom; it may be drank in the quantity of 2 ounces, according to the Urgency of the Symptoms.—*English Dispensatory* (*Quincy*), London, 1742.

[80] *Hog-Lice Wine. Take Hog-Lice* (i.e. Wood lice or Sow bugs), half a pound, put them alive into two pound of White Port Wine, and after some Days Infusion strain and press out very hard, then put in Saffron, 2 drams, Salt of Steel, a dram, and Salt of Amber, 2 scruples, and ater 3 or 4 Days strain and filter for Use. This is an admirable Medecine against the Jaundice, Dropsy, or any cachectic Habit.—*English Dispensatory* (*Quincy*), London, 1742.

[81] *Plaister of Spinders.* Venice Turpentine [dram]iii, melt it; then adde live Spiders No. XXX mix them with a Pestle till the Turpentine be of an Ash colour, and the Spiders appear not; then heat it, and adde of small Spiders No. XL. Stir them again, adding powder of Asphaltum, and white Sal Armoniack, [dram]iii. grinde them till the matter be cold and very black; keep it 14 dayes, then soften it at the fire, and with your hands dipt

in oyl, make it up. Make Plaisters thereof, and cover them with leaf-silver or gold, and lay them to the pulses of both wrists an hour before the fit of a Feaver or Ague comes, leave them on nine days, then at the same hour cast them into running water; by this means the Pliaster cures all Feavers or Agues.—*Compendium of Physick* (*Salmon*), London, 1671.

Herring in Pickle is often prescribed in a Cataplasm to the Feet in Feavers; because it is reckoned to draw the Humours downward and thereby relieve the Head.—*English Dispensatory* (*Quincy*), London, 1742.

[82] *Flux of the Belly. Burnt Harts' Horn* is reckoned a Sweetner and is much used in Decoction against Diarrhoeas; and Fluxes of the Belly. *Shavings of Hartshorn* is much more in esteem amongst *Family Doctresses*, than in the shops; but what most gives it a Title to this Place, is that *Jelly* which it is easily boiled into in common water, and is accounted very nourishing and strengthening. *Shavings of Ivory* is much of the same nature as the former, and boils in the same manner into a *Jelly*.

Goat's Blood. This is in a few Compositions under the same Intention as the former; but it is not at all known in common Prescription; and is deservedly almost forgot.—*English Dispensatory* (*Quincy*), London, 1742.

[83] Beaver's cods are much used for wind in the stomach and belly, particularly of pregnant women.—*New England's Rarities* (*Josselyn*), London, 1672.

[84] *Bleeding at Nose.* If the flux be violent, open a vein on the same side, and cause the sick to smell to a dried Toad, or Spiders tyed up in a ragg; ... the fumes of Horns and Hair is very good, and the powder of Toads to be blowed up the Nose; ... in extremity, put teats made of Swines-dung up the nostrils.—*Compendium of Physick* (*Salmon*), London, 1671.

Cow's Dung. This seems to be of a hot penetrating Nature; and is experienc'd to do good in Erysipelous Swellings. This Cataplasm is also highly commended by some in the *Gout. Pigeon's Dung* is sometimes ordered in Cataplasms, to be applied to the soles of the Feet in malignant Fevers and Deliriums. *Hog's Dung.* Is also used by the Country People to stop Bleeding at the Nose; by being externally applied cold to the Nostrils.—*English Dispensatory* (*Quincy*), London, 1742.

[85] *Pleurisy. Stone-Horse Dung*, seems to owe its present Credit in medicine to the modern Practice. It is certainly of great Efficacy in

Pleurisies, Inflammations, and *Obstructions* of the *Breast.* In all these Intentions it is now very much prescribed.—*English Dispensatory* (*Quincy*), London, 1742.

[86] *Goat's Blood* is mentioned in the English Dispensatory of 1742 as "deservedly almost forgot."

[87] *Quintessence of Vipers.* Fat Snakes, Adders or Vipers in June, cast away their heads, bowels and gall, cut them into bits, and dry them in a warm Balneo; then put them into a bolt head with Alcohol of Wine, so much as may overtop them eight fingers breadth; seal the glass Hermetically, and digest for twenty days in Balneo, then decant, etc., etc.

This quintessence is of wonderfull virtue for purifying the blood, flesh and skin, and taking away all diseases therein; it cures the falling-sickness, strengthens the brain, sight and hearing, preserveth from gray hairs, and renovates the whole body, making it become youthful and pleasant; it hindereth miscarriage, provokes sweat, is good against the Plague, and all malign Feavers; it cureth the Gout, Consumption, and French Pox, and ought to be esteemed of the Sons of Men as a Jewel. Dose [dram]i. morning and night.—*Compendium of Physick* (*Salmon*), London, 1671.

Take any number of Vipers, open and cleanse them from all Worms and Excrements, and the Females from their Eggs: Take out their Hearts and Livers; dry them in the shade separately from their Bodies, etc., etc.— *English Dispensatory* (*Quincy*), London, 1742.

[88] *Paracelsus His Perfume.* Cow-dung, and distill it in Balneo, and the water thereof will have the smell of Ambergrease. It is a most excellent Perfume, abates the Heat of Feavers, and cures all inward inflammations. Dose [dram]i.—*Compendium of Physick* (*Salmon*), London, 1671.

[89] *Sympathetick Oyntment.* Boars grease, brains of a Boar, powder of washed Earth worms, red Sanders, Mummy, Bloodstone, a. [oz]i, moss of a dead mans Skul not buried [dram]i, make an Oyntment, S.A.

All wounds are cured by this Oyntment, (provided the nerves and arteries be not hurt) thus: Anoint the weapon that made the wound daily once, if there be need, and the wounds be great; otherwise it will be sufficient to annoint it every other day. Where note. 1. that the weapon be kept in clean linnen, and in a temperate heat, lest the Patient be hurt; for if the dust fall, or it be cold, the sick will be much tormented. 2. that if it be a stab, the weapon be anointed towards the point descending. 3. if you want the weapon, take blood from the wound upon a stick, and use as if it were the weapon; thus the Tooth ach is cured by pricking the Gums, and anointing the instrument.—*Compendium of Physick* (*Salmon*), London, 1671.

Earth Worms. These are often used in Compositions for cooling and Cleansing the Viscera. They are good in *Inflammations* and *Tubercles* of the Lungs and in Affections of the *Reins* and Urinary Passages. *Syrup of Snails.* Take Garden-snails early in the morning, while the dew is upon them, a pound; take off their shells, slit them, and with half a pound of fine Sugar put into a Bag hang them in a Cellar, and the Syrup will melt, and drop through, which Keep for Use. This is not kept in the shop, but is worth making for young Children inclining to Hectics and Consumptions. A Syrup of Earth-worms may be made in the same manner for the like Intentions. *Frog's Spawn.* This another Cooler, but it is an insipid Phlegm, and good for nothing more than common Rainwater; and will not Keep long without mothering and stinking.—*English Dispensatory* (*Quincy*), London, 1742.

[90] *Tooth Ache.* Picking the gums with the bill of an osprey is good for the tooth-ache. Scarifying the gums with a thorn from a dog-fish's back is also a cure.—*New Englands Rarities* (*Josselyn*), London, 1672.

[91] Robert Hunt, a lime seller of Boston, differing with a man, drew a sword and made two or three passes at him, upon which the man seized the sword and broke it and went for a warrant to apprehend Hunt who at once shut himself up in his house with a loaded gun and two pistols beside him. When the officers appeared he fired out of the window several times and wounded two boys but at last was taken and committed to prison where three days later he committed suicide by hanging "with an old single Garter." The same afternoon his body "was carried thro' the Town in a Cart, and buried near the Gallows, having a stake first drove thro' it."—*Boston Gazette*, Apr. 18, 1749.

[92] Thursday last, in the Afternoon, *Mark*, a Negro Man, and *Phillis*, a Negro Woman, both Servants of the late Capt. *John Codman*, were executed at *Cambridge*, for poisoning their said Master, as mentioned in this Paper some Weeks ago. The Fellow was hanged, and the Woman burned at a Stake about Ten Yards distant from the Gallows. They both confessed themselves guilty of the Crime for which they suffered, acknowledged the Justice of their Sentence, and died very penitent. After Execution, the Body of *Mark* was brought down to *Charlestown* Common,

and hanged in Chains, on a Gibbet erected there for that Purpose.—*Boston Evening-Post*, Sept. 22, 1755.

[93] At the Court of Assize, at Springfield, the 2d Tuesday of September last, Daniel Bailey and Mary Rainer, of a Place adjoining to Sheffield in that county, were convicted of Adultery, and were sentenced to suffer the Penalty of the Law therefor, viz. to sit on the Gallows with a Rope about their Necks, for the Space of an Hour; to be whipt forty Stripes each, and to wear for ever after a Capital A, two Inches long, and proportionable in bigness, cut out in Cloth of a contrary Colour to their Cloaths, and sewed upon their upper Garments, either upon the outside of the arm, or on the back.—*Boston Evening-Post*, Oct. 9, 1752.

A case of incest in Deerfield: "the man was set upon the Gallows with a Rope about his Neck for the space of one Hour, to be whipped in his Way from thence to the Goal 30 stripes, and to wear a Capital I of two Inches long, and proportionable Bigness on his upper Garment for ever. Sentence against the Woman, for special Reasons, we hear, is respited for the present."—*Boston Evening-Post*, Oct. 7, 1754.

At the Superior Court held in Cambridge last week, one Hannah Dudley of Lincoln was convicted of repeatedly commiting Adultery and Fornication with her own Mother's husband, an old Man of 76 years of age. She was sentenced to be set upon the Gallows for the space of one Hour, with a Rope about her Neck, and the other end cast over the Gallows, and in the way from thence to the Common Goal, that she be severely whipped 30 stripes, and that she for ever after wear a Capital I of two inches long and proportionable bigness cut out in Cloth of a different Colour to her Cloaths, and sewed upon her upper Garment on the outside of her arm, or on her Back, in Open View. [No further mention is made of the step-father.]—*Boston News-Letter*, Aug. 16, 1759.

[94] On Tuesday the 12th Instant, about 3 p.m. were executed for Piracy, Murder, etc., three of the Condemned Persons mentioned in our Last viz. *William Fly*, Capt., *Samuel Cole*, Quarter-Master, and *Henry Greenville*.... *Fly* behaved himself very unbecoming even to the last; ... Their Bodies were carried in a Boat to a small Island call'd Nicks's-Mate, about 2 Leagues from the Town, where the above said *Fly* was hung up in Irons, as a spectacle for the warning of others, especially sea-faring men; the other Two were buried there.—*Boston News-Letter*, July 7-14, 1726.

[95] *Suffolk County Court Files*, Vol. I.

[96] The list here printed, is in abstracted form in the order as printed and does not include the rates imposed, deemed immaterial for the present purpose. For complete data consult *The Statutes of the Realm*, London, 1819, Vol. V, pp. 184-202.

[97] Quantity.

[98] Quintal.

CPSIA information can be obtained
at www.ICGtesting.com
Printed in the USA
BVHW041812280719
554526BV00018B/391/P